Reflections

By

Johnnie Ann Burgess Gaskill

Blessings,
Johnnie Ann Gaskill

© 2002 by Johnnie Ann Burgess Gaskill.
All rights reserved.

No part of this book may be reproduced, stored in a retrieval system, or transmitted by any means, electronic, mechanical, photocopying, recording, or otherwise, without written permission from the author.

ISBN: 0-7596-8558-4

This book is printed on acid free paper.

Cover photo by James F. Gaskill, © 2001

1stBooks - rev. 4/3/02

Unless otherwise indicated, all Scripture quotations are taken from the *Holy Bible*, New Living Translation, copyright © 1996. Used by permission of Tyndale House Publishers, Inc., Wheaton, Illinois 60189. All rights reserved.

This book is dedicated to each person (especially my daughters, Jennifer and Jena) who provided inspiration for its content, encouragement, and/or assistance in the writing and publishing of it. God knows who they are—even those whose names are not mentioned! I humbly thank Him and them.

TABLE OF CONTENTS

Reflections About My Childhood 1
   Disciplined by Daddy 3
   Come, My Little Ones! 5
   Aunt Delia's Plant 7
   The Influencers 9

Reflections About My Children 11
   How 'Bout We Talk 'Bout Panda Bears 13
   A Simple Act of Giving? 14
   Make A Wise Decision…Today! 15
   The Rat I Am 16
   Who's the Patient? 17
   Sand Spur 18
   Dealing with the Puzzle Pieces 19
   Time for a Tizzy? 20
   Little Girl, Big Dog 21
   Marco Polo! 22
   When Mama Is Near 24
   Cries in the Night 25
   Glary Eyes 27
   All Grown Up 29
   Without or Without a Medal 30
   Understanding the Message 32
   Burying the Bird 33
   The Scissors 34
   Fussin' and Fightin' 35
   Forgeticus 36
   To Change or Not to Change? 37
   What to Wear? 38
   Something for Thee 39
   Drives a Body Crazy! 41
   An Occasional Twinkie? 43
   Just How Do We Sound? 44
   Look for Unseen Barriers 45
   Messiah Complex 47
   Catering to Cowards 49
   Oh, No! I Sound Like Mama! 50
   Waving Goodbye 52

Mama's Memory Book 54
Loving Care 56
A Special Purpose 58
How Are You? 60
Shake the Sock! 62
The Meringue Mishap 64

Reflections about the Words and Actions of Others 67
Unspoken Communication 69
But…But…I Thought I Had More Time! 70
Too Busy? 71
Get Rid of the Buts! 72
Father, Forgive Them 73
Turtles in the Fast Lane 74
I Had to Help Her! 75
What Do You Do For Fun? 76
No Sacrifice Is Too Great 78
Expert Help 79
Make Deposits and Enjoy the Dividends 80
I Has a Good Fwiend 82
Know the Value 83
Releasing a Loved One 85
A Comforting, Constant Companion 87
Mirror of the Soul 89
Uninvited 90
Amazing Grace 92
Are You Listening, God? 93
Hurt In the Heart of a Parent 95
Jewels or Zirconias? 96
Waiting for Clearance 98
Quit Looking Where You've Already Been 100
Conversations of Substance 101
A Verse to Remember 102
The Right Source of Power 103
Well-worn Bibles 104
"Planting" a Loved One 106
A Time to Begin Again 108
Something Special About Him 110
Prepared for Life and for Death 112
When Weeping Won't Stop 114
He's Just Remembering Me 116
The Side Effects of Self-Neglect 118

A Remarkable Decision 120
Doubly Good! 122
The Highest Compliment 124
Resting Like a Child 126
Settling In 127
Here I Am! 129

Reflections About Pets and Nature 131
A Childlike Faith 133
Monuments to Foolishness 134
The Snake in the Apple Tree.. 135
C. C.'s Lesson 136
Reacting to Everything 137
Boo Boo and the Bacon 139
Leaving the Nest Too Early 141
Just Who Does He Think He Is? 143
Laying Up Treasures 144
No Longer a Captive 145
Hidden Till Now 147

Reflections About Scripture... 149
The Painful Truth About Martha 151
What One Thing…? 152
Arise! 153
A Simple Question?.. 154
Spiritual "Smarts"... 156
Never Alone!... 158
When God Is Nearby 160
Know the Author! 162

Reflections About This 'n That 165
"Miss Blue" 167
A Distressed Sheep.. 169
A Lesson from the Trees 170
My God Has Died 171
Don't Fall Off the Runway! 173
Are We On the Right Road?... 174
Choosing the Best 175
Carl... 176
The Golden Rule 177
A Tranquil Heart 179
Where Jesus Wants to Go 181

Exteriors and Interiors 183

Reflections About Myself 185
Two Vital "C"s 187
Speak, Lord; I'm Listening! 188
What a Week! 190
Sleeping Soundly 191
Keeping Everything Clean 192
A Friend Like Linda 193
Regaining Control of a Runaway Horse 195
Moving Beyond the Comfort Zone 197
Running on Empty 199
Warm Fuzzies 201
All the Difference 203
Focus on the Center 205
Life Will Trash Your Treasures 207
Due and Payable Upon Receipt 209
The Debtor 211
More Religious Than Righteous? 213
His Will or Mine? 215
I Will Help You 217
Can't Earn Life 219
Rest? Yes! 220
What Hinders Me? 222
Revealing the Wounds 224
Just As I Am 226
Returning Ownership to the Owner 228
A Meeting with Myself? 230
Physical Bankruptcy 232
Narrowing the Gap 234

Reflections About Various Places 237
Lest We Forget 239
A Prepared Place 241
A Safe Harbor 242
The Way Out 243
The Former Days 245
Only *One* Point? 246
A House with a View 248
Shining Lights 249
Ebb and Flow 250
A Hiding Place 251

Climb On! Stay On! 253
When Morning Gilds the Sky 255
A Time to Build Sand Castles? 257
No Shuttle Bus for Me! 259
Please Remain in Your Seats 261
A Short Delay 263

Reflections About Holidays 265
As Unto the Lord 267
A Grateful Heart—Always 268
The Things We Have and Have Not 270
The Stable Must Go 272
He's More Than a Babe In Bethlehem! 273
Good News for Lonely, Fragmented People 274
Room for Him? 276
Rest Beside the Weary Road 278
The Best Gift of All 280
Let There Be Peace 281
Christmas Will Come! 283
The Struggle to Understand 285
Because He Loved Us First 287
Big Goals 289
The Cross-stitched Prayer 291
Facing the Future Fearlessly 292
Their Contribution to Freedom 294
Freedom Isn't Free! 295
A Mother's Love 297
Honors Day Program 299
Graduation 301
The Father Who Waits 302

Preface

After a friend read a newspaper column that I had written about a little squirrel, she called to say how much she enjoyed it. Then she said, "Johnnie, I have squirrels that play in my yard, too, but I never see anything unusual in their behavior. Why is that you watch them and learn so much more than I do?"

"I don't know!" I replied. "I just do!"

Her question started me to thinking about what did make the difference. I realized that I began being more perceptive along about the time I sensed God wanted me to be a writer. That awareness came to me on February 24, 1984. Early that morning, I took my Bible, along with a pen and sheets of paper, and settled myself on the sofa in the living room. I sat quietly for a few minutes, and then I asked God to reveal to me what He wanted me to do with my life. I felt I had several options available, but I earnestly desired to know what **He** wanted me to do.

I waited for several more minutes and tried to keep my mind as free as possible from any distracting thoughts. Suddenly, an idea popped into my head. Immediately, I wrote it down. As I looked at the words on that sheet of notebook paper, I began to laugh. "Write a book. Who? Me? Surely not!"

Even though I resisted the idea, I started to realize that I had not misunderstood God's directive. So, that very morning, I began to write about the little lessons God taught me as I went about my regular activities. The more I wrote, the more He gave me to write about! The more I opened my mind and heart to receive, the more He revealed to me.

In August of that year (1984), my first column appeared in our local newspaper, and I've been a newspaper columnist from then till now. As the months passed, I began to understand that "the book" was to be a compilation of the columns that I was writing week by week.

Now, after seventeen years, the first book is ready for publication. I wrote some of the columns eagerly and joyfully. Certain others were written with what I call "gut-level" obedience to the assignment He gave me on February 24, 1984. Regardless of my motivation, regardless of the ease or difficulty with which I wrote, God remained faithful to me. He revealed truths to me I would have otherwise missed. He provided time and ability to write when I thought I had neither. He sent encouragement to me via strangers, as well as friends and family. He allowed me to learn from other writers. He waited patiently year after year as I struggled to complete the book.

Now, at long last, I have completed it. Although the re-typing and final editing of nine years of columns (written between 1984 and 1992) has exhausted me, I feel indescribably elated about having completed my "assignment." At this climactic moment, three verses of Scripture are uppermost in my mind:

- Psalm 40:8: "I take joy in doing your will, my God…"
- Zechariah 4:6: "It is not by force nor by strength, but by my Spirit, says the LORD Almighty."
- Romans 11:36: "For everything [including the ability to write this book] comes from him; everything exists by his power and is intended for his glory. To him be glory evermore. Amen."

Johnnie Ann Gaskill
October 27, 2001
Thomaston, GA

Reflections About My Childhood

Johnnie Ann Burgess Gaskill

Reflections

Disciplined by Daddy

Many years have passed since I was a preschool child, but time has not erased all the memories of my childhood. In fact, one experience that happened when I was around five or six remains particularly vivid.

The sun was shining that early Summer day as my sister and I played near Mother and Daddy while they hoed the garden. When I saw one of our neighbors walking down the unpaved road that ran within an arms' length of our front porch, I ran to meet him, thrilled at the rare pleasure of seeing anybody in that rural setting.

Even though Truman was on his way somewhere else, he stopped to chat for a moment with us. When he started to go on his way, I begged to be allowed to accompany him just a bit farther. "You can go to the top of the hill," Daddy said, "but then you come straight back home."

I nodded in happy agreement.

Truman and I walked along the narrow dirt road that twisted and turned between the barn and the pasture where our cows were grazing. We walked slowly past the sugar apple tree and climbed to the top of the next hill—my stopping place.

I said goodbye to him—reluctantly—and started home. On the way, I noticed a large sandy spot on the side of the road, a place that was wide enough for one car to pull over so that an on-coming car could pass. I decided to stop there—"just for a minute"—to play.

Soon I had forgotten Daddy's instructions to come straight home. I was oblivious to everything except the warm sunshine on my back and the feel of the fine, silky sand that poured through my pudgy fingers as I repeatedly filled and emptied an old envelope I'd found beside the road.

I played much longer than I realized. I came to my senses when I heard Daddy calling my name and saw him walking resolutely toward me. When he was close enough to tell that I was okay, he broke off a weed with which to "switch" my legs. I'm sure he didn't physically hurt me—since he loved me dearly and was using only a wimpy weed—but I cried all the way home.

Having my daddy, whom I adored, be upset with me enough to punish me was more than my child's heart could bear. At that time, I did not appreciate the concern that my daddy had for me, a concern that prompted him to put aside his work in order to make sure I was okay. Neither did I realize that Daddy was trying to teach me the importance of obedience, even when what I wanted to do seemed infinitely more delightful. I considered his treatment of me harsh and unfair.

Johnnie Ann Burgess Gaskill

But now that I'm much older and a little wiser, I see his actions in a very different light. I concur with the writer of the letter to the Hebrews. "Since we respect our earthly fathers who disciplined us, should we not all the more cheerfully submit to the discipline of our heavenly Father and live forever? For our earthly fathers disciplined us for a few years, doing the best they knew how. But God's discipline is always right and good for us because it means we will share in his holiness. No discipline is enjoyable while it is happening—it is painful! But afterward there will be a quiet harvest of right living for those who are trained in this way" (Hebrews 12:9-11).

Yes!

Reflections

Come, My Little Ones!

Growing up in the country afforded me many opportunities to observe animals with their offspring. I recall always being impressed with the tenderness with which each mother cared for her young.

I especially enjoyed seeing the mother cat wash her kittens. I liked hearing her purr softly as she allowed them to nurse. Though my sister and I loved to hold the tiny kittens, the mother cat didn't appreciate having such good "kitten sitters." Therefore, she often picked up her young ones by the back of the neck and moved them to a place that provided greater safety for her babies. Frustrated as Kathie and I were over being deprived of access to the kittens, we respected the cat for doing whatever was necessary to protect her helpless babies.

During my growing up years, I also liked to watch a mother hen and her chicks. Although her behavior differed from that of the cat, the hen also exhibited tenderness as she protected her little ones. The hen constantly scratched the ground till she found something for her chicks. Then she clucked repeatedly to invite them to eat. The little biddies, looking much like yellow cotton balls toddling around on legs made of painted toothpicks, responded immediately to the hen's clucking.

At first, the hen and chicks stayed close together. As the chicks grew, they gradually put more and more distance between themselves and the hen, and they learned to scratch for their own food. However, when the hen sensed danger of any kind, she clucked loudly and insistently. As she sounded the warning, her biddies came running to hide under her widespread wings. Once they were safely underneath, the hen settled herself on top of her babies so that no one could get them without first dealing with her. She, in effect, put her life on the line for her little ones.

At the close of each day, the mother hen clucked again to the biddies. They came to her. She spread her wings, and, after considerable shuffling and rearranging, she settled down over the chicks. Warmed by her body and secure in her ability to protect them, they slept soundly through the night.

The memory of the hen and chicks comes to mind every time I read these words spoken by Jesus: "O Jerusalem, Jerusalem, the city that kills the prophets and stones God's messengers! How often I have wanted to gather your children together as a hen protects her chicks beneath her wings, but you wouldn't let me" (Matthew 23:37).

I see how foolish I am when I am unwilling to turn to Jesus, especially when the alternative is certain destruction, as it was for the inhabitants of Jerusalem: "And now look, your house is left to you, empty and desolate…" (Matthew 23:38). Like the folks in Jerusalem, I am free to go my own way, but my outcome will also be needlessly tragic! Like a rebellious biddy, I can refuse to come when bidden or I can let Jesus gather me unto Himself. The choice is mine.

Reflections

Aunt Delia's Plant

When I was a young girl, Aunt Delia and Uncle Howard lived the road from us, almost in sight of our house, but not quite. Aunt Delia loved plants. She always had a big garden and she spent many hours tending it and canning the vegetables it produced. In addition, she grew flowers everywhere—inside her little white frame house, all around the edge of her yard, on her front porch, and all along the long graveled driveway that led from the dirt road to her house at the top of the hill.

Her pride and joy (and the plant I remember most vividly) was the one she called "Christ in the Manger." The plant's bloom was a large white pod that reminded me of a giant egg. As soon as the tightly closed pod appeared, Aunt Delia began watching the plant carefully for signs that it would be opening soon. During the years of observing her special plant, Aunt Delia had developed a keen knowledge of its stages. Consequently, she could accurately predict the night the pod would open fully and reveal its amazing contents.

When she saw the tell-a-tale signs, Aunt Delia told everyone, "Come over to my house tonight so you can see Christ in the Manager." Though we didn't have telephones, the news of the pending event spread rapidly throughout our small rural community. Around dusk folks began to gather in Aunt Delia's yard.

While the grownups sat in wooden chairs and talked, the children played games and had a perfectly grand time. Every now and then we'd take time out to run over to see how the plant was progressing. Just before midnight, when the pod began to open wide, we joined the adults to watch and wait in reverential silence for the first glimpse of Christ in the Manger.

We were never disappointed. The pod always opened on schedule to reveal what did indeed look like the Christ Child lying in a manger. I remember the awe I felt whenever I looked upon such a representation of the blessed event. I recall thinking, *How can something so beautiful be contained in such an ugly pod?*

Years later, I still do not know the answer to that question; it remains a great mystery to me. Thinking about Aunt Delia's plant reminds me of yet another wonder, an infinitely more significant one. The Apostle Paul says we have within our frail and sinful human bodies the glorious Gospel of Jesus Christ. How can it be that "this precious treasure—this light and power that now shine within us—is held in perishable containers, that is, in our weak bodies" (2 Corinthians 4:7)? Although it is certainly beyond my ability to explain, I am awed that God would place such a wonderful treasure within you and me and then give us the on-going privilege of revealing Him to those who are longing for a glimpse of the Christ.

May we never disappoint those who watch our lives for such a revelation.

The Influencers

Several years ago I was asked to write a collection of childhood memories to share at an upcoming family reunion. Of course, I had no idea where to begin. So, before I ever started writing anything on paper, I spent many hours recalling episodes from my past. The more I remembered, the more difficult the selection became.

As the possibilities raced through my mind, I felt overwhelmed by how many people had contributed to my becoming the person I am today. Each of them, in their unique way, influenced the views and principles that continue to impact the choices I make each day.

One key thing I learned from observing Daddy's life: the greatest joys are derived from our relationships. Loving the Lord and being loved by Him is the primary joy. Second to that is the network of warm relationships we build with one another.

Mother showed me that it is possible for a woman to be strong. Though she didn't possess abundant physical strength or material goods, she used what she did have to meet the needs of our family. During most of my childhood, I did not realize how strong Mother was because her behind-the-scenes role often hid her true strength. After I established a home of my own, however, I began to see Mother's true strength and to be inspired by it.

From my sister I learned that it is possible to survive sibling rivalry. (Just kidding, Kathie!) Now that we are adults and have families of our own, I cherish the close relationship we have, and I strive to follow the fine example she sets for me, her *older* sister.

From Aunt Berta I learned that a positive attitude and a cheerful voice make any situation more pleasant—for all concerned.

Aunt Delia taught me that one can cope with being surrounded by about a half dozen grandchildren and nieces—all under age fourteen. I remember how she calmly and efficiently prepared bountiful meals with homegrown vegetables, then settled down to work on one of her beautiful quilts while all of us young'uns played happily together.

As I reflected on the past, I thought of many others who had influenced my life. As I thought of each of them—family members, teachers, neighbors, and friends at school and at church—I realized what a debt of gratitude I owed to them and especially to God since He allowed me to fall within their sphere of influence. How different my life surely would be had it not been for each of these special persons who shaped my life.

Johnnie Ann Burgess Gaskill

    As I sorted through my accumulation of memories, I wondered, *What significant insights and values am I passing on to those who come within my sphere of influence? When those who know **me** are called upon to share their memories of the past, what will they say about how I influenced their lives?*

Reflections About My Children

Johnnie Ann Burgess Gaskill

Reflections

How 'Bout We Talk 'Bout Panda Bears

When I was hospitalized due to premature labor with our second child, our three-year-old spent one night with Bob and Shirley, our next-door-neighbors.

After making all the necessary bedtime preparations, Shirley and Jennifer went to bed. Once there, Jennifer snuggled up next to Shirley and said, "Let's talk."

"About what?" Shirley inquired.

"How 'bout we talk 'bout panda bears," Jennifer suggested.

Well, that remark delighted and surprised our neighbor, since she expected copious tears accompanied with loud wailing of "I want to go home!" from a three-year-old on her first night away from Mama and Daddy.

Certainly, Jennifer could have chosen to focus on the negatives of the situation. She *was* in an unfamiliar environment; she *was* away from her parents who lovingly tucked her in each night. However, she knew she was with trusted friends who would take care of her, so she put the scary thoughts aside and viewed that new experience as a wonderful adventure, one to be enjoyed to the max—hence, her request to "talk 'bout panda bears."

Every time I recall that story, I think about how wonderful it would be if everyone possessed such child-like qualities: complete trust, freedom from worry, a positive outlook, the ability to enjoy each moment, honesty, openness, enthusiasm, the ability to focus on something other than the cares of life, the ability to transform troublesome times into fun adventures…

Whenever I think about children, I always remember how Jesus loved them and welcomed them into His presence. Surely He felt they were a refreshing change from the adults who constantly surrounded Him, especially the adults whose motive was to entrap Him and those who demanded Jesus send the children away so that He could handle the more "pressing" problems the adults brought to Him.

But Jesus refused to turn the children away. He did, however, rebuke the straight-laced, somber, negative-thinking, mean-spirited adults. "Let the children come to me. Don't stop them! For the Kingdom of Heaven belongs to such as these" (Matthew 19:14).

Because He loves and enjoys all those with a childlike spirit, I believe that He, like my neighbor, would have laughed with pure delight had one of the children snuggled up to Him and said, "How 'bout we talk 'bout panda bears."

Johnnie Ann Burgess Gaskill

A Simple Act of Giving?

"Mama, I want to use my money to buy a gift for a little girl at the children's home," Jennifer said.

Her desire pleased me and shamed me, since my six-year-old had to remind me to reach out to others. In order to ease my own guilt, I said, "Honey, you save your money for something else. I'll buy the gift for you to take."

Jennifer refused my offer. She insisted on using the five-dollar bill someone had given her as a gift. When I took her to the store, she spent a long time making her decision. Then, one rainy Sunday afternoon just before Christmas, while I drove the twenty miles to the children's home, Jennifer sat in the back seat and held on tightly to the package she had carefully wrapped.

Upon arrival, we located the lady in charge. After Jennifer explained to her the reason for our visit, the lady stepped into the hall and called for one of the girls. As the child came forward, the lady said, "This pretty little girl and her mama have a present for you. Would you like to accept it?"

The child nodded and her eyes sparkled with anticipation. Jennifer smiled and handed the gift to her. She immediately tore off the paper and squealed with delight as the gift came into view.

"Thank you!" she yelled as she raced down the hallway to show the gift to her friends.

We said little on the way home, each of us thinking about the significance of what had happened. I wondered, *Was it a simple act of giving or was it more?*

The answer came as I recalled the words of Jesus. "...when you [ministered] to one of the least of these my brothers and sisters, you were doing it to me!" (Matthew 25:40).

Jennifer is an adult now, but the memory of that day lives on in our hearts. From time to time, she asks, "Mama, do you remember the day we went to the children's home?"

"Yes, Honey. How could I forget?"

Make A Wise Decision...Today!

Our daughters looked forward to receiving their weekly allowance on Fridays. They were particularly excited one "payday" when I suggested we go shopping. They ran to retrieve their savings, which they had stashed in several unlikely places. As they began to discuss what they hoped to buy, I heard eight-year-old Jena say, "I'm gonna buy a Barbie doll!"

"Honey, that's the last thing you need!" I said. "Why don't you choose something else?" She looked so disappointed, especially after I added, "Saving your money is also a good idea. You don't have to spend *all* your money today, you know."

After pausing to consider what I said, *she began to suggest ways she could make wise use of the few dollars she had accumulated. Wow,* I thought, *convincing her to change her mind about buying the Barbie doll was easier than I thought. I do believe she has heard me this time!*

However, as we prepared to leave the house, Jena turned her innocent eyes up to me and said sweetly, "I'll spend my money wisely next time. Today, I want to buy a Barbie doll. Okay, Mama?"

So much for the profitable discussion! I thought.

Although Jena knew the logic of what we had talked about and had even given verbal assent to it, the desire of her heart held more power over her than her reason. Therefore, she decided to yield to that desire rather than to wait for something that would bring her greater and longer-lasting pleasure.

Don't many adults make that same kind of choice regarding their salvation? When confronted with the good news that they can receive eternal life by believing in and accepting Jesus as their Savior and Lord, some choose to remain in their sinful, doomed condition. Certainly, a percentage of them *intend* to accept Christ some day...but not today. Today they choose to yield to their desire to sin, to indulge the flesh. Yet, God's Word says, "...choose **today** whom you will serve..." (Joshua 24:15) because "**Today** is the day of salvation" (2 Corinthians 6:2, emphasis added).

Jena could safely delay choosing to save money; however, the consequences for delaying to accept Christ **today** may be tragic.

Johnnie Ann Burgess Gaskill

The Rat I Am

Three days before my birthday, I found a note underneath my pillow. "Dear Mommy," our seven-year-old had written, "I'm writing this letter with a lot of care. I'm very, very sorry that I don't have enough money to buy you a birthday present. You should know what a rat your child is. Love, Jena."

Why does she feel sorry about not having a gift? I wondered. I knew she could not have forgotten the beautiful ring our family had given me for my birthday. Why, only a few weeks earlier, the girls and their dad and I had shopped for the perfect stone and a beautiful setting for it. Once the one-of-a-kind ring was in place on my finger, I'd hugged them individually and thanked them profusely, saying, "No more birthday presents! This ring is more than enough!"

So…why has she written this note? I wondered. *Does she feel as if the ring isn't a gift from her, although we told her it was? Is she longing to give me something on her own?*

If so, then I could understand that feeling. For example, I enjoy being a part of a church family. I like knowing that when we work together and give collectively we are able to accomplish tasks that would be impossible for individuals to do. Yet, when I feel that I have not contributed personally to a project or ministry, I don't derive nearly as much joy and satisfaction from our combined efforts. In fact, when I know that I've used my time and talents carelessly, I grieve over my inability to present my Lord with those things that please Him and express my love for Him.

Even so, Jesus keeps right on loving me. And He graciously forgives me the very moment I tell Him what "a rat" I am, for He knows my remorse is genuine.

Who's the Patient?

Late one afternoon when Jennifer was about eleven years old, she and I tried to remove a sliver of glass from her heel. Being unsuccessful, I asked her dad to serve as the chief surgeon, since he had proven his skill in handling such major catastrophes. I held the flashlight and provided advice while he used a sterile needle and tweezers to remove the glass.

Jena, our younger daughter who was eight, positioned herself near Jennifer's face in order to offer encouragement and comfort as the painful probing of her heel got underway. Only moments into the surgery, Jennifer began to scream, as we expected she would. However, my husband I became confused when we heard *two* voices screaming and shrieking—in unison! We immediately stopped the surgery in order to figure out what on earth was going on. To our surprise, Jennifer and Jena had tears streaming down their faces and both were screaming, "Stop!" although we already had.

As the four of us looked at each other, we started laughing. "Who's the patient?" I asked.

Later, as I reflected on that experience, I realized that we had witnessed a true display of empathy. Jena, having no physical pain herself, had become so immersed in her sister's suffering that she reacted as if she were the one undergoing the removal of the glass fragment. She forgot about all previous fusses and fights she'd had with her sister. That little sweetheart became more than a casual observer with a "Gee-I'm-so-sorry-for-you" attitude. Instead, she had entered fully into her sister's pain, illustrating so beautifully the empathy Romans 12:15 urges us to express. When people rejoice, we should rejoice with them. Likewise, when they weep, we are to weep with them.

Every time I remember Jena's weeping with Jennifer, I pause to thank God for the two precious children who constantly teach me so much about Biblical truth, and I ask Him to give me a sensitive heart like theirs.

Johnnie Ann Burgess Gaskill

Sand Spur

A quick glance revealed the reason for Jena's screams. A rather large sand spur hung tenaciously to her small foot. But she refused to let us remove it, fearing doing so would cause more pain than leaving it attached. So, our nine-year-old daughter hobbled across the sand to our car.

"Jena, you can pull that spur out yourself," we told her, but she still lacked the courage to do so. She remained quiet on the short ride from the beach to the condominium we had rented for our vacation. When we arrived there, I stayed with her at the car. "Jena, the spur has to come out. You can't walk across this hot pavement and I cannot carry you. Just give it a quick yank and that pesky little thing will come right out."

She made several attempts to remove it. She'd place her fingers as close to the spur as possible—without actually touching it. Then she's count to three. But, time and again she'd wail, "Mama, I just can't do it!" If I started to do the job for her, she screamed loud enough to make someone think I was inflicting mortal wounds on her.

After trying so hard to be brave, she finally blurted out, "I need Jesus!"

"He'll give you courage, if you ask Him to," I assured her.

"I've been asking Him all the way from the beach!" she said.

"Well, Honey, let's ask Him one more time," I suggested.

We bowed our heads and humbly asked for divine assistance. Within moments after our simple prayer, we quickly and painlessly removed the sand spur, and Jena ran inside to share the good news with her dad and her sister.

Reflecting on that experience always brings to mind Philippians 4:6-7, "Don't worry about anything; instead, pray about everything. Tell God what you need, and thank him for all he has done. If you do this, you will experience God's peace, which is far more wonderful than the human mind can understand. His peace will guard your hearts and minds as you live in Christ Jesus."

Indeed, we can and should ask for help with any difficulty we face, even the removal of a tiny sand spur.

Reflections

Dealing with the Puzzle Pieces

"Oh no!" I moaned as I looked at the puzzle pieces and frames scattered across the floor of the church nursery. "How will I ever make any sense out of this mess?"

My two-year-old daughter seemed surprised by my reaction, since she didn't realize what a tremendous problem she and her little friends had created for me. No, she thought they had behaved well as they played with the puzzles while their mothers and I worked in the kitchen directly across the hall. "It's okay, Honey," I said to her. "We'll just take these home with us."

Jennifer and I dumped all the pieces and frames into a large paper bag. While Jennifer took her afternoon nap, I reassembled the puzzles. The ones that contained only three or four large wooden pieces were easy to do; however, those having several pieces required more time and skill. (My having no idea what the finished puzzles were supposed to look like compounded the problem!)

As I looked at the jumbled mess, I said, "Okay, there's got to be a way to get this job done before suppertime!" I began working, as methodically as possible. First I grouped the pieces I thought might go together. Next, I filled in the edges of each puzzle. As soon as I finally finished the task, I decided to make the job easier for the next person (hopefully not me!) who had to go through the ordeal. I assigned each puzzle a number, and then wrote that number on the back of each of the frames, as well as on the back of each piece that belonged with it.

Many years have passed since that afternoon when I struggled to make the pieces of the puzzle fit together. I've reflected on that experience many times, particularly as I've struggled to more fully understand who God is, to know what is His perfect will, and to differentiate between truth and heresy. The Scriptures contain clues; however, putting them together is often like assembling pieces of a puzzle. But, I've come to realize that **all** understanding comes "a line at a time, in very simple words" (Isaiah 28:10). And I get so excited when the Holy Spirit enables me to piece simple words together in order to reveal more of the truth.

Johnnie Ann Burgess Gaskill

Time for a Tizzy?

During a regularly scheduled parent-teacher conference some years ago, the teacher winked at me. "Is it true, Mrs. Gaskill, that you sometimes have a tizzy?"

I started laughing. "What are you talking about?"

With eyes twinkling, she said, "Recently I asked the students to write about a typical morning at their house. Jennifer made it clear that you have a *tizzy* whenever you all are running late."

When I learned what my eleven-year-old daughter had written about me, I was embarrassed. But, since the teacher and I were good friends and had been co-workers at one time, I laughed as I admitted the truth. At the time I wasn't really sure, and neither was Jennifer, exactly what a *tizzy* was, but we knew it meant something similar to pushing the panic button. When I got home, I grabbed the dictionary and discovered that Webster defined *tizzy* as "a highly excited and distracted state of mind." So, Jennifer was right! I did indeed have an occasional tizzy or what a friend calls a *stir-doodle*.

Those tizzies aren't as frequent now, since I've learned to plan ahead and to allow ample time to get things done. However, even careful planning doesn't eliminate all factors that might trigger a tizzy. When it seems that all that *can* go wrong *is*, it helps if I say to myself, "Be silent, and know that [God] is God" (Psalm 46:10). Another verse that calms me is Psalm 138:8: "The LORD will work out his plans for my life."

Time for a tizzy? Not if I do my best, then depend on God to accomplish His purpose(s) in every situation, even stressful or chaotic ones.

Reflections

Little Girl, Big Dog

One of my favorite photos of Jena was taken at Six Flags Over Georgia one month before her second birthday. It shows Jena carrying a heavy, four-foot tall stuffed dog given to her by a man who had won more prizes than he could carry. The dog was much taller than Jena and so large that she could not reach around it. Yet, she insisted on carrying it herself.

When I look at the photo, I see Jena struggling to carry the heavy load. I see her toddling along, unable to see where she is going, determination written all over her sweet little face. I see myself only a step or two behind her, my arms outstretched to catch her if she stumbles or decides to surrender her load.

I also see something about myself in that photo. Like Jena, I have an "I do it!" attitude. Consequently, I often assume responsibilities and carry burdens that are too big or too numerous for me to carry alone, loads no one expects me to carry. Yet, like Jena, I stubbornly struggle and stumble along—at least for a time. But, when my strength fails, I gratefully accept the tender invitation Jesus extends to me: "Come to me...you who are weary and carry heavy burdens, and I will give you rest. Take my yoke upon you. Let me teach you, because I am humble and gentle, and you will find rest for your [soul]. For my yoke fits perfectly, and the burden I give you is light" (Matthew 11:28-29).

Johnnie Ann Burgess Gaskill

Marco Polo!

I reclined in a chair beside our aboveground pool and listened to the happy sounds the children were making. Nine-year-old Jena said, "Let's play 'Marco Polo!' I'll be *it*." Then, she closed her eyes and yelled, "Marco!"

When Jennifer answered, "Polo!" Jena moved in the direction of her twelve-year-old sister's voice. As Jena attempted to find her sister, Jena yelled "Marco!" again and again, each time eliciting the "Polo!" response from Jennifer. To avoid detection, Jennifer moved through the water as quietly as a tadpole, though she did reveal her whereabouts each time she responded, "Polo!" Meanwhile, Jena continued to grope blindly for her sister.

As they continued their game, I thought about how Jena's searching for Jennifer reminded me of these words written centuries ago by the Apostle Paul. "From one man [God] created all the nations throughout the whole earth. He decided beforehand which should rise and fall, and he determined their boundaries. His purpose in all this was that the nations should seek after God and perhaps feel their way toward him and find him—though he is not far from any one of us. In him we live and move and exist" (Acts 17:26-28).

I also thought about how we are all seekers, from the moment of birth. Even as babies we seek nourishment, comfort, and love long before we are able to verbalize our needs. We kick and scream in order to let it be known that we have a need, although we depend on the adults in our environment to figure out just what that need is. Even after developing an extensive vocabulary, we find it hard to identify our own needs and to express them. Sometimes, we only know that "something" is wrong or that "something" we urgently need is missing from our lives. That craving creates frustration and initiates searching that can last for years.

In an attempt to fulfill this mysterious inner longing, we try a little bit of everything—all to no avail. We look; we seek—in all the wrong places. No matter how hard we try, we can't satisfy the hunger within the soul. It is only when we, like Saint Augustine, realize that God made us for Himself and that our hearts are restless until they find rest in Him, that we begin to call out to God and to reach toward Him.

Hebrews 11:6 tells us how we can find God. "Anyone who wants to come to him must believe that there is a God and that he rewards those who sincerely seek him." Thus, when we cry out, "God, where are You?" God answers, "Here I am." And His tender voice guides those who grope in the darkness for Him. Unlike those who hope to avoid detection in the game of "Marco Polo," God *wants* us to find Him.

Johnnie Ann Burgess Gaskill

When Mama Is Near

Once when nine-year-old Jena wasn't feeling well, I stayed home from work to give her some extra TLC (tender loving care). As I cared for her, I realized how much alike we are, especially when we aren't feeling up to par. During such times, Jena and I like a bit of extra attention, while my husband and Jennifer prefer to be left alone.

During Jena's bout with the bug, I remembered an incident that happened years ago. I don't recall just how old she was at the time, but I do remember her sitting at my typewriter in order to compose a message for me. Using the one-finger, hunt-and-peck method, she typed the note that became one of my most treasured memento. "Jena and mommy are in the beddie because I am sick and I am sad but as long as mommy is there I am safe and I never be ufrade the end."

Though she knew little about the rules of punctuation, she expressed her feelings quite well, feelings that are universal. As I read her note, I recalled the times when, as a child, I wanted my mother. Back in those days, we didn't have a telephone or a second car. Consequently, if my sister or I became ill at school we just had to tough it out until we could get home. Many times I remember longing for Mother as I kept my head down on my desk for hours at school or pressed my feverish face against the cool window of the school bus during the long trip home.

When I finally made it home, Mother began caring for me immediately. She turned back the covers of the bed and I gratefully slid between the sheets. I thought her cool hand on my hot brow felt so silky and so soothing. Like Jena, I felt better just knowing that Mother was there and that she was taking care of me as best she could with our limited resources.

I don't think we ever outgrow our need for someone to love us and care for us. It is one of our most basic needs. But as we mature and life becomes more complicated, we see even more clearly that we need someone who will never leave us or forsake us, someone who will be with us at all times. Although mothers are willing, they cannot be with us in *every* situation. However, there is One who is always near. We, like the Psalmist, can experience great comfort in any situation as long as we can honestly say, "But as for me, how good it is to be near God! I have made the Sovereign LORD my shelter" (Psalm 73:28).

Reflections

Cries in the Night

Jena's screams woke me from a sound sleep. I jumped out of bed and ran toward the direction of her voice as she continued to yell, "Mama! Mama!"

In those days, we did a lot of hollering in our home, mainly because we didn't have an intercom system in our split-level house. To get each other's attention, we shouted out the name of the person we wanted to talk to and/or we banged on the wall at the foot of the stairs that led to the bedrooms. I often thought that we sounded a lot like the Waltons as they called out their goodnights.

Anyway, I realized that Jena's screams in the wee hours of that morning differed from our normal calls to one another. In her desperation, she made "Mama!" sound like two distinct words. She needed help—immediate help!

Having no idea why she needed me, I raced toward her, my heart pounding with fear. I found her in the bathroom. Then I knew. She had come down with the stomach virus that had been going around.

My children had learned to handle routine emergencies with a fair amount of calmness, but vomiting was an exception. Maybe they believed that upchucking was something one cannot go through alone because I had always been there for them, as my mother was for me. In fact, I grew up thinking that when I experienced stomach upheavals, it was absolutely necessary to have Mother standing behind me with her arms wrapping me in a kind of bear hug—one hand over my churning stomach, the other one on my clammy forehead.

As I matured, I realized that there were many situations other than stomach distress that caused people to cry out for help. For example, financial problems, sickness, grief, failure, broken relationships, and the like, prompt us to seek comfort and assistance from someone who cares. Whenever we make our plea(s) for help, we need and expect someone to come to our rescue.

If our cries are ignored, we wonder, *Why doesn't **someone** come to help me? Doesn't **anybody** care? Is there no one to help? Do I have to face this alone?*

Yet, we must reach that low point before we turn to our *real* source of help. Unable to find the human assistance we need, we cry out to God. When we convey to Him our desperation and frustration, He hears and responds.

David the Psalmist had learned just where to go for real help. "O God, listen to my cry! Hear my prayer! From the ends of the earth, I will cry to you for help, for my heart is overwhelmed. Lead me to the towering rock of safety, for you are my safe refuge, a fortress where my enemies cannot reach me. Let me live forever in your sanctuary, safe beneath the shelter of your wings!" (Psalm 61:1-4).

By using figurative language, David lets us know that he considered God's presence a place of refuge and safety, a place where he found comfort and shelter from whatever threatened his well-being. When you and I call upon God for help, He responds to us even more speedily than I did to Jena's cries in the night. In another psalm, David assures us that the Lord has not and will not forsake those who seek Him, nor does He forget those who cry to him for help. (See Psalm 9:10,12).

Reflections

Glary Eyes

A trivial matter sparked the controversy between Jennifer and Jena. During their heated discussion, charges and counter charges flew back and forth so rapidly that I became dizzy as I tried to maintain eye contact with the speaker.

The girls, ages twelve and nine, soon abandoned the original issue and began dredging up seemingly forgotten hostilities, injustices, acts of unkindness, and the like. They saturated their conversation with remarks such as, "Yeah! And I remember when you…" and "I'll never forget what you said…"

After they vented their pent-up feelings, a strange quietness filled the den where the three of us sat. However, the air was still so emotionally charged that no one dared speak lest we set off another verbal explosion.

When I felt it safe to speak, I looked each child in the eye before asking, "Do you have anything else to say? Any denials? Any other accusations?"

Jena, the nine-year-old, said softly, "How about confessions?"

Surprised by her response, I said gently, "Confessions are always in order."

Having received the green light of parental approval, Jena began. "Well…God did give me a big mouth, but…" she hesitated while angrily studying her sister, "He gave you glary eyes!"

When I heard that, I exploded with laughter. Soon the three of us were laughing uncontrollably. *Surely,* I thought, *Jena doesn't consider that a confession.* Though she had admitted to having a big mouth, she had made it plain that having one wasn't her fault. God had given it to her! And, unwilling to be the only person with a flaw, she quickly pointed out an imperfection in her sister.

Whenever the three of us look back on that incident, we still laugh about it, though hopefully we've learned that confession is a serious matter. It is a difficult one because it involves admitting our faults and mistakes. No excuses. No blaming others for their role in the situation. No comparing ourselves to others. Just total honesty. "Yes, I am ____" or "Yes, I did ____."

When such confession is followed by a sincere apology and an attempt to remedy the situation, then relationships can be mended. Like the Psalmist David, we must learn to say, "For I recognize *my* shameful deeds…Purify *me* from *my* sins, and I will be clean; wash *me*, and I will be whiter than snow…Remove the stain of *my* guilt…Create in *me* a clean heart, O God. Renew a right spirit within *me*" (Psalm 51:3-10, emphasis added). Or, to paraphrase an old song, it's not my brother or my sister, but it's **me**, O Lord, who needs to confess and to be cleansed.

Each of us can and should come to God for that, for if we "cover over [our] sins, [we] will not prosper. But if [we] confess and forsake them, [we] will receive mercy" (Proverbs 28:13).

Reflections

All Grown Up

Our babies grew up so quickly, as verified by the following words I wrote as Jennifer approached her thirteenth birthday and Jena her tenth.

Personal grooming items have replaced the Rubber Ducky and other bathtub toys. A swimming pool occupies the place where the sand box once was. Grass grows along the fence where the hot cycles once made a well-worn path as our girls raced with the children next door.

My husband and I no longer get up for 2 a.m. feedings. Now we are up before sunrise to say "Goodbye" to Jennifer as she participates in youth trips sponsored by our church or her school. Once we endured the times of hearing the girls cry when we left them in the church nursery. Now we listen to them sing solos and duets during worship services.

Dinner table conversation no longer revolves around the adventures of Big Bird or Bert and Ernie. Real friends and real happenings provide plenty to talk about. No more diaper bags for us! Instead I lug cupcakes, cookies, and soft drinks to group activities. We don't visit the pediatrician as frequently as we once did, Now, we keep weekly appointments with piano teachers and dance instructors.

My husband and I have enjoyed our girls immensely during all of their ages and stages. Whether nestling in our arms or dashing off to another activity, they have brought joy to our heart. As I think of our girls, I keep remembering something Dr. Keith Parks said in his prayer during a commissioning service for foreign missionaries. 'All that they are, all that they have been, and all that they are yet to be is all in Thy keeping.'

My heart echoes the truth of those words. As a parent I cannot thank God enough for the two precious ones He entrusted to our care. I pray that we will be able to guide their lives in a way that will be pleasing to Him. Although I realize God expects us to do our part, their lives are in His keeping. He knows what is best for each of them. He loves them more than we ever could. His ability to care for them far surpasses anything we could ever do for them.

Therefore, as I reflect on those truths, I confidently place my children in God's keeping, for I, like the Apostle Paul, can say, "I know the one in whom I trust, and I am sure that he is able to guard what I have entrusted to him until the day of his return" (2 Timothy 1:12).

Johnnie Ann Burgess Gaskill

Without or Without a Medal

For days and days, ten-year-old Jena and her best friend practiced a dance they planned to do during the Spring Olympics that were to be held at their elementary school. As they worked up their routine, they decided to incorporate some of the basic steps they were learning during their weekly dance lessons. That wasn't too hard, but when they had to figure out what arm motions they'd use and how to stay "in sync" with each other…well, that proved to be very difficult.

With shoes tap, tap, tapping on the concrete floor of the garage, the two girls did flaps, ball changes, and shuffles. To help maintain their rhythm, they counted out loud till they were hoarse. In order to maintain synchronization, they watched each other's every move. They constantly changed their routine until they created one they felt they could carry out perfectly.

On the day of the competition, the two tired but excited little girls lugged their cassette tape and recorder, leotards, tights, and tap shoes to school. In the afternoon, they brought all that stuff home again—and with "gold medals," as well.

The next morning I wrote a short note and clipped it inside Jena's notebook, as I frequently did. "Congratulations! I'm so proud of you, not just for winning the gold medal, but for being the kind of person you are. Love, Mama."

I wanted Jena to understand that my pride in her did not—and would not—depend on an accumulation of accolades. Although I shared her excitement over having earned a gold medal, my real joy had come prior to the competition as I observed the creativity, determination, and cooperation that she and her friend exhibited during their long hours of preparation.

As I reflected on the value of character, I remembered the Old Testament account of God sending Samuel to anoint the one whom He had already selected to be the new king of Israel. God directed Samuel to go to Bethlehem, to the house of Jesse. Upon seeing Jesse's son Eliab, Samuel thought, **Surely he is the chosen one**.

But the Lord corrected Samuel. "Don't judge by his appearance or his height, for I have rejected him. The LORD doesn't make decisions the way you do! *People* judge by outward appearance, but *the LORD* looks at a person's thoughts and intentions" (1 Samuel 16:7, emphasis added).

After seven of Jesse's sons had passed before Samuel, he said, "The LORD has not chosen these. Is there another?"

"Yes," Jesse said, and sent for his youngest son, David, who was out tending sheep. When David entered, God said to Samuel, "This is the one; anoint him" (1 Samuel 16:12).

Throughout his reign, King David experienced failures as well as victories; yet, God spoke highly of David, describing him as one who "obeyed my commands and followed me with all his heart and always did whatever I wanted him to do" (1 Kings 14:8). Receiving such divine commendation is worth more than a houseful of gold medals.

Understanding the Message

Once when I needed to take Jena to an appointment at the beauty shop before Jennifer came home from school, I taped this one-word note on the front door in order to remind my older daughter of where we were: "Cherrie's."

As we got into the car, Jena remarked, "Mama, if anybody comes to our door they won't know what the note means, will they?"

"That's right! That message isn't intended for anyone except Jennifer. She'll know exactly what it means, and she can get in touch with us at Cherrie's if she needs anything."

Since the girls and I had been going to Cherrie's for over ten years, I knew I did not need to write Jennifer a lengthy note. No, just that one word told her what she needed to know. Likewise, when God speaks to us in the midst of seemingly ordinary events, we hear His voice and understand what He means.

For example, one day as Moses was tending sheep in the wilderness near Mount Horeb, he noticed that a bush was on fire. There was nothing too unusual about that, so Bible scholars say. However, Moses said, "Amazing!...Why isn't that bush burning up? I must go over to see this.' [And] when the LORD saw that he had caught Moses' attention, God called to him from the bush, 'Moses! Moses!' [So] 'Here I am!' Moses replied" (Exodus 3:3-4).

When Moses approached the bush and removed his sandals, as per God's instructions, God introduced Himself to Moses and explained to Moses what He wanted him to do. Now, I do not know whether or not God spoke to Moses in an audible voice. Perhaps He did; perhaps He didn't. Nevertheless, Moses "got the message" and, like Jennifer, he knew what it meant and what he was to do with it.

Burying the Bird

That Saturday, the weather was dreary and cold, as well. Because the girls and I were tired when we arrived home late that afternoon, we planned to head straight for our favorite resting places. Our plans changed, however, when Jena, our ten-year-old, discovered the lifeless form of a small gray bird on our front porch. Apparently he had crashed into our glass storm door and broken his neck, as many other birds had done over the years.

Jena, who has such a tender heart, insisted on a proper burial for the tiny bird. She located a shovel that was almost as tall as she was and brought it to the front porch. Using a paper towel, she picked up the bird, laid him gently on the shovel, and carried him to the far edge of the back yard. Braving the cold, she dug a shallow hole, lay the bird in it, and replaced the dirt. When finished, she stood for a few moments beside the grave. Then, in a flash of inspiration, she located a piece of bark and stood it up like a tombstone near the grave.

As I watched her care so lovingly and gently for the dead bird, I remembered the words of Jesus in Matthew 10:29: "Not even a sparrow, worth only half a penny, can fall to the ground without your Father knowing it." *How wonderful*, I thought, *to have a heavenly Father who is so intimately involved with His creation that not even a tiny bird dies without His awareness*. That thought comforted me; but even more so did these words of Jesus: "So don't be afraid; you are more valuable to him than a whole flock of sparrows" (Matthew 10:31).

God knows. God cares. Even when we aren't consciously aware of His presence, He is watching over us, protecting us, providing for us, and loving us in every situation.

Johnnie Ann Burgess Gaskill

The Scissors

When Jena was in the fourth grade, she said, "Mama, the teacher took up my scissors today."

"Why?" I asked.

"Well, I let [a friend] borrow them and she left them on the back table, so the teacher took them up."

"Does the teacher know they're *your* scissors and that *you* didn't leave them in the wrong place?" Jena nodded, her eyes filling with tears.

Well, the more I thought about that situation, the angrier I became. My child had been treated unfairly, and I didn't like it—not one little bit! So, like a mother bear protecting her cub, I decided to defend my child.

The next morning I wrote a note to Jena's teacher. In a sentence or two I explained what had happened, according to Jena. Mentally, I gave the teacher a bit of leeway, since as a parent and as a former teacher, I knew that there can be more than one version of the same episode. I intended to conclude the note with this question: "Should I buy Jena another pair of scissors or will you return hers soon?" But I was so upset over the unfairness of the situation that I continued, "Jena and I have discussed the need for classroom rules. She understands that when rules are broken, the offender must suffer the consequences. She knows that leaving scissors where they do not belong results in their being taken up by the teacher. However, I feel that this situation will cause Jena to be hesitant to share her supplies with others, lest someone else's irresponsibility deprive her of that which is rightfully hers."

The teacher returned Jena's scissors that day, but that didn't settle the issue—at least not for me. I continued to do a slow burn each time I thought about sweet Jena being punished because of her generosity while the real offender suffered no loss whatsoever.

However, God began to deal with me about my anger and my unwillingness to forgive such a trivial injustice. I remembered the agony Jesus endured for my sins. Jesus took the punishment I deserved so that I, like Jena's classmate, escaped the penalty of my sins. Not only did He do that for me, but He also "lives forever to plead with God" (Hebrews 7:25) on my behalf (and that of everyone who has come to God through Jesus.) Having received such undeserved forgiveness, could I refuse to forgive such a minor offense? Absolutely not!

Fussin' and Fightin'

Our daughters, who are three years apart, did their fair share of fussin' and fightin'. However, by establishing a few guidelines, we managed to eliminate some of it. For example, when they no longer needed a car seat, they fussed about who would get to sit in the front seat. We solved that problem rather easily. Since Jennifer was born on October 7th, she rode in the front seat on odd-numbered days, while Jena (who was born on December 16th) rode beside the driver on even-numbered days.

Using such carefully-devised plans did not eliminate all the fussin' and fightin'. There were situations when rules were inadequate. They simply had to learn to "Love each other with genuine affection, and to take delight in honoring one another" (Romans 12:10), or, as one person said, "Take a step backward in order to let someone else take a step forward."

That was hard for the children to do. It is also hard for adults. Real hard. All our instincts are geared toward self-gratification and self-preservation. Voices inside us say, "Do what's good for you. Get ahead. Don't worry about anybody else. You have rights; claim them. Don't let anybody stand in your way."

With that kind of reasoning going on inside, we resist the command to give another the place of privilege or the seat of honor. Having put self first for so long, we can hardly manage to consider putting others first. So, we respond, "That's crazy. It will never work. I'll never get ahead if I do that."

But it *will* work. Christ is the proof of that. He came to earth in the form of a man and gave His life in order that others might live. The result? "God raised him up to the heights of heaven and gave him a name that is above every other name, so that at the name of Jesus every knee will bow, in heaven and on earth and under the earth, and every tongue will confess that Jesus Christ is Lord, to the glory of God the Father" (Philippians 2:9-11).

Should we be willing to "Take a step backward in order to let someone else take a step forward?" Definitely, if we're motivated by a love like that of Christ.

Forgeticus

When the girls were in elementary school, they enjoyed memorizing the names of the books of the Bible. Part of the nightly bedtime ritual included a recitation of the list.

One night I sat in the rocking chair beside Jennifer's bed and waited as she prepared to recite the names of all sixty-six books. She settled herself "Indian-style" in the middle of her bed, leaned forward slightly, took a deep breath, and began. "Genesis. Exodus. Leviticus. Numbers…"

She said the names slowly, deliberately, and accurately. When she saw my proud smile, the nine-year-old asked, "Mama, can I say them another time. I'll bet I can go even faster this time!"

Though the hour was late, I did not deny her request. She was so excited. I loved the look of anticipation on her sweet face as she mentally prepared herself for the challenge.

"Genesis. Exodus. Leviticus. Numbers…" she said with more speed than before. Again and again she begged to go through the entire list "just one more time." Each time she increased her speed. Soon she was rushing through the lists so fast that her words ran together. But she did not sacrifice accuracy for speed. I thought, *This child has a fantastic memory!*

For a long time everything went well—up until she renamed a book of the Old Testament! "Genesis. Exodus. Forgeticus." Then we exploded with laughter as we realized how her unintentional substitution of "Forgeticus" for Leviticus indicated how intensely she was trying to avoid forgetting.

Jennifer and I still laugh over her slip of the tongue, but I continue to be much impressed with my daughter. Though I'm glad she learned to recite the names of all the books of the Bible at an early age, I'm even more delighted to see her reading the content of those books and obeying the truths found therein. I pray that Jennifer will always say, "I will study your commandments and reflect on your ways. I will delight in your principles and forget not your word" (Psalm 119:15-16).

Reflections

To Change or Not to Change?

The evening before the mock presidential election that was to be held at her school, Jena put the finishing touches on her campaign speech. She and the other girl who had been chosen to represent their fifth grade class had carefully researched the political platforms of the candidates (Bush and Dukakis) and had located biographical data relevant to the candidate they were to represent. Using the information they had gleaned, the two candidates had written the campaign speeches they were to give to the student body prior to the time to vote.

After listening to Jena practice her speech, I said, "I'm impressed! You've really done a great job, Honey. I like your opening remarks. You've organized your material well. Your speech sounds very professional. But, I'm thinking you may want to rephrase parts of it since the younger students may not understand some of the big words you've used."

Jena thought about my suggestion. "You're right," she agreed. Then she erased and erased and erased. She'd just about finished making all the changes I'd suggested whenever I saw one more that needed to be made. When I pointed it out, I knew she agreed with me, yet she said, "I'll tell you what I'll do. If my pencil lands on the eraser, I'll make the change. If it lands on the point, I'll leave the word just like it is."

I wondered, *What's she talking about*?

I watched as she closed her eyes tightly and began twirling her pencil like a baton. After a few seconds, she lowered her pencil onto the paper. Sure enough, it landed lead-first. Jena looked smiled at me, obviously relieved that she wouldn't have to erase anymore.

I said, "You really lucked out that time, didn't you, you little stinker?" We laughed together, realizing full well she should have made the change even though she no longer felt compelled to do so.

As I reflected on that episode, I realized that one question is constantly before every one of us. "To change or not to change?" Even when God says, "My child, this habit needs to go" or when He says, "This attitude is not becoming to you as a child of Mine," we, like Jena, search for a way to avoid making the change. Often we're tempted to resort to tossing a coin or getting a second opinion! Yet, how much better it would be if—instead of looking for a reason *not* to do as He asks, we would simply say, "You're right, my Father. I'll begin right now to make the necessary changes and I will not stop until I'm done, even if I get weary in the process!"

Johnnie Ann Burgess Gaskill

What to Wear?

The girls and I hadn't done any serious shopping in a long time. Oh, we'd made frequent trips to local stores, but we usually ran in just long enough to purchase the essential items. Though we definitely weren't members of the "shop-till-you-drop" club, we did enjoy occasional trips to the mall. Even if we didn't buy much, we liked walking around and seeing what was "in" and munching on some cookies in the food court. So, we became quite excited when an unexpected turn of events enabled us to clear our calendars and schedule a Saturday shopping trip.

A couple of nights before our trip to the mall, I sat down to rest a few minutes and to list some things I wanted to be sure and look for. I thought, *A medium-weight coat—one that's neither too dressy or too sporty—will be perfect for Jennifer. Jena has a nice coat, but she needs a lightweight cardigan. If I had a white pullover, I could wear it with several of my skirts and slacks; and, by swapping out scarves and belts, that one new item will allow me to create several different looks.*

I added other items to the list, knowing that I certainly couldn't afford to buy all of them, even if I were to find them. Having completed my shopping list, I picked up my Bible and began to read. Since the words in Colossians 3:12-14 seemed larger than any other words on the page, I realized immediately that I was to pay particular attention to them. "Since God chose you to be the holy people whom he loves, you must clothe yourselves with tenderhearted mercy, kindness, humility, gentleness, and patience. You must make allowances for each other's faults, and forgive the person who offends you. Remember the Lord forgave you, so you must forgive others. And the most important piece of clothing you must wear is love. Love is what binds us all together in perfect harmony."

As I read those words that were written centuries before, I knew God's message to me was quite clear: "Johnnie, it's okay to go shopping for new clothes and accessories; but, as you go, remember you'll never find anything in the stores as becoming on you as compassion, kindness, humility, gentleness, patience, helpfulness, and forgiveness. These things are appropriate for you and your girls to wear year around, and they will never go out of style. And, Johnnie, remember love is the one perfect accessory. It matches and enhances everything else I've asked you to wear."

Reflections

Something for Thee

Jena pounded the keys on the piano. Then she tried once again to play the song. Finally, after many wrong notes and long pauses, she folded her arms, placed them on the keyboard, and used them as a pillow for her head.

As I looked at my twelve-year-old daughter, I identified with her. I knew what it was like to want to do something well, yet to despair during the struggle to do it. Many times while trying to meet a writing deadline, I'd felt like putting my head on the keyboard and saying, "God, I can't do this!"

As I looked at my daughter who despaired of ever learning to play that song correctly, I prayed, "Lord, give me the wisdom to help her."

He answered that prayer so quickly that even I felt astonished when I heard myself say, "Jena, look at the words to the hymn you are trying to learn."

She read the words to "Something for Thee" which was written by Sylvanus D. Phelps in 1864. "Savior, thy dying love Thou gavest me,/Nor should I aught withhold, dear Lord, from thee:/In love my soul would bow,/My heart fulfill its vow,/Some offering bring thee now,/ Something for thee."

I took the advice I'd given to Jena. As I thought about those words, I sensed anew the importance of offering whatever we have to Jesus as an expression of our love for Him. Being convinced that whatever we give to Him, He accepts and then transforms, I suggested to Jena that she play her song for Him—as an offering. "But I can't play it right!" she protested.

"That's okay, Honey. Just do the best you can—for Him. Don't try to master the song just to impress your teacher at the music workshop next weekend. Don't feel that you have to play it right to please me. Just play your song for Jesus. See what He will do with it."

I could tell Jena wasn't really convinced that my suggestion would have any effect on her piano playing; and, I confess, I had a few doubts of my own when I heard only a slight improvement in her playing. However, the next day when she sat down at the piano, she played beautifully. She ran upstairs, shouting, "Mama! Did you hear it? Did you hear how good it sounded?"

Of course, I had. In celebration of the miracle, we laughed and hugged each other tightly before she went back downstairs to play the song again and again.

As I busied myself with household tasks, I remembered the story of the feeding of the four thousand people (Matthew 15:32-38). I recalled how the disciples had no idea how they could get enough food in that desolate place to feed the multitudes who had been listening to Jesus as He taught them.

When the disciples explained the problem to Jesus, He said to them, "How many loaves do you have?"

"Only seven loaves and a few small fish," they answered. "Not nearly enough to feed all these thousands of people."

Jesus paid no attention to their doubts. Instead, He accepted the small amount of food they had, gave thanks for it, and handed it back to the disciples so that they could distribute it to the hungry crowd. After everyone had eaten all they wanted, the disciples gathered seven large baskets of leftovers.

Whatever our "something" for Him might be—a simple meal, a song, a newspaper column—it will be enough if we offer it to Jesus and ask Him to bless it. He only asks, "How much do you have?" and "Are you willing to give it to Me?"

Reflections

Drives a Body Crazy!

Jena wore a frown as she entered the kitchen that morning. As our twelve-year-old daughter made her way to the table, I asked, "Are you upset about all the alarms going off?"

With eyelids at half-mast, Jena nodded mutely. I laughed. "It's enough to drive a body crazy, isn't it?"

She rolled her eyes in agreement.

We did have a problem with our alarm clocks. Because the four of us were on different school and work schedules and also had different waking patterns, we each set our clock for the time of our choice. Thus, the four *loud* alarms that sounded intermittently between 6:30 and 7:30 a.m.—made enough noise to give all of us, especially Jena, a severe case of the "grouchies." But when all those alarms sounded multiple times, it was indeed enough to "drive a body crazy!"

After an extended period of hearing alarms going off every five minutes, all of us were awake, whether we needed to be or not. Finally, we were all out of bed—except Jena. I suspected that she snuggled deeper and deeper under her covers each time an alarm sounded. Then, after enduring an hour of frequent, nerve-jangling buzzings and beepings, she would reluctantly crawl from between the sheets to begin her new day.

There was a simple solution to making mornings more pleasant. Each of us could have set our clocks for the time we needed to get up, not twenty minutes before so that we could repeatedly hit the snooze bar. If we had done that, only four alarms would have sent shock waves through our bodies. What an improvement that would have been! However, even though the solution seemed simple, we never got around to implementing it since all of us (with the exception of Jennifer) had programmed ourselves to keep one sleepy eye on the clock and to hit the snooze bar until our "last call" sounded.

Hitting the snooze bar was a form of procrastination. And, the habit of procrastinating about getting out of bed caused us to procrastinate in other areas of life as well. I should know, since I've had many years to develop my procrastination skills. As a highly qualified procrastinator, I should write a book on that subject, and I just might—if I can ever get around to it.

Seriously, the more frequently we delay our response to a call for action, the more firmly ingrained procrastination becomes, even in spiritual matters. For example, whenever I read Bible passages that remind me to confess my sins and to turn away from them, I understand that I need to; I want to; I intend to; but then I delay. In effect, I "hit the snooze bar" in order to give myself additional time before doing something that I think will be difficult. Meanwhile, all sorts of negative emotions build up within me—guilt, shame, remorse, self-contempt, frustration, and the like.

In addition to having an adverse effect on me, my procrastination affects others. I sometimes drive people crazy whenever the call to action sounds and I am slow to respond. That need not happen. By learning to respond promptly, I can change stressful situations into peaceful ones.

Reflections

An Occasional Twinkie?

When Jena was twelve-years-old, she wanted desperately to be a cheerleader and to win the Miss American Preteen title. Later on, she did become a cheerleader, but the Miss American Preteen title eluded her. Although she did receive other honors that made us extremely proud, Jena never felt that those awards made up for the disappointment she felt over not being able to achieve two of the things she desired the most that year. Seeing her so sad and dejected made me feel terrible.

I talked with our pastor about the situation. "I am afraid that Jena is going to become fearful that the Lord will keep her on a diet of meat and potatoes all her life."

Our pastor, a close friend of ours, grinned. "Well, I guess she *would* like for the Lord to give her a…"

As he searched for the name of some delectable dessert he thought Jena would really like, I interrupted him. "She'd like the Lord to give her an occasional Twinkie!" (Now, if we'd been talking about my preferences, I'd have mentioned coconut cake, strawberry pie, apple pie a la mode, or cheesecake! But we weren't talking about me. We were talking about Jena, and she loved Twinkies!)

The thought of asking the Lord for something comparable to a Twinkie seemed ludicrous to us, so the pastor and I enjoyed a good laugh. After enjoying that little bit of humor, however, I began to think seriously about how we often ask God for things that we want, even if those things aren't necessarily good for us.

Even though the Lord blesses us with all the things we need to sustain life and to live godly, we aren't satisfied with having such basics supplied to us. Though a "meat and potatoes" diet is a strengthening one, we crave other things which, though appealing, may not be the things that will nourish us and help us to grow into mature persons, "full grown in the Lord, measuring up to the full stature of Christ" (Ephesians 4:13b).

When we ask for things that do not contribute to our well-being, our all-wise and all-loving Heavenly Father says no to the requests we ask of Him. To avoid being upset with God when He doesn't immediately give us everything we ask of Him, we must first learn to "Take delight in the LORD" (Psalm 37:4). When we delight in Him, we will not constantly ask for Twinkies. Rather, our humble prayer will be: "Father, provide for me those things which will cause me to grow more and more like Christ."

When our hearts are thus in line with the will of God, we will experience complete satisfaction at the Father's table, even if He provides no Twinkies for us.

Johnnie Ann Burgess Gaskill

Just How Do We Sound?

Before we purchased an electronic keyboard, Jena and I frequently locked horns whenever she practiced playing the piano. Since I did not know how to play, she resented my pointing out her mistakes. (I could see her point. I probably would have felt the same way had our positions been reversed.) However, as her mother, I felt obligated to help her correct her mistakes.

Our conflict ceased whenever we bought a keyboard with a memory. To activate that option, Jena pressed two buttons before she played her song and another two when she finished. Then, as she sat back and listened to herself play, she heard her own mistakes, especially those dealing with rhythm. Previously, she refused to believe that she hesitated during complicated passages, but she could no longer deny that she did so. Neither could she argue with the electronic keyboard for it recorded her playing, errors and all. As Jena became her own critic, I gratefully stepped down from that role!

Several weeks later, the Sunday School lesson that I was teaching contained this verse: "Those who love to talk will experience the consequences, for the tongue can kill or nourish life" (Proverbs 18:21). That verse, along with several others, helped my class members and me see the importance of choosing our words carefully. We discussed how our choice of words and the way we speak them produce a profound effect on others. "Yet," I asked, "do we really hear ourselves? Do we know how we sound?"

Then, remembering how the keyboard had been a real eye-opener for Jena, I said, "What we need is a bugging device for ourselves."

The ladies laughed, but I'm quite sure none of them rushed out the next day to purchase one. I assume they were like me. The more I thought about it the less certain I was that I could stand to listen to a recording of my words. I feared that many of them would indict me, even though I try to speak constructively and kindly at all times.

Since my eleven-year-old daughter had enough courage to use an electronic keyboard with a memory, I should have summoned the courage to wear a recording device, shouldn't I? Had I done so, we would have enjoyed harmony in our home and lots of golden silence as well, for this Mom would have been saying less!

Reflections

Look for Unseen Barriers

Jena and I quickly removed her electronic keyboard from the cardboard box. We put the batteries in, we flipped the "on" switch, and Jena sat down to play. Nothing happened, nothing at all.

"Jena, we must have made a mistake when we put the batteries in," I said. We reinserted the batteries, being careful to follow the diagram. Even so, she still couldn't coax a sound from the keyboard. By that time we were more than a little frustrated. Although we read and re-read the directions and repeatedly replaced the batteries, the keyboard remained silent.

The next afternoon we returned it to the store. The salesclerk cheerfully exchanged the malfunctioning keyboard for one that we felt sure would work. Again, we hurried home and assembled it, only to discover that the new one worked no better than the previous one.

"Jena, we're doing something wrong. We can't have gotten *two* keyboards that won't work!"

I called the store and explained our problem. "Hold on, Mrs. Gaskill," the clerk said. "I'll check the keyboard you returned."

Within minutes he was back on the line with the solution. "Mrs. Gaskill, you forgot to remove the clear plastic cover on the positive end of each battery. Therefore, the current wasn't able to pass through."

"Well," I exclaimed, "that's a new one on me!" And it was. I could not recall ever having to remove plastic shields from batteries. Armed with that bit of new information, I returned to the keyboard in order to take a closer look. Sure enough, those little plastic shields *were* there. Once I removed them and reinserted the batteries, Jena played for hours and enjoyed herself immensely.

I still feel embarrassed about my foolish mistake; I still wish the sales clerk had been a stranger rather than the teenage son of a friend of mine! I know that by failing to remove those unseen barriers I turned a simple task into a frustrating one. Because of that *one* oversight, all my other careful efforts were wasted.

In like manner, whenever I fail to remove the barriers between myself and God, I experience failure no matter how hard I work or how carefully I try to follow God's instructions. The reason for my failure is that the divine power I need to live a godly life cannot flow through me as it should. It is available, yes; but the barrier my sins have created hinders it.

Even when my sins are not glaringly evident, their presence still blocks the flow of divine power. Therefore, they must be removed. The Bible says that if I "confess my sins to him, he is faithful and just to forgive

[me] and to cleanse [me] from every wrong" (1 John 1:9). When God removes the barriers, He removes them "as far away from [me] as the east is from the west" (Psalm 103:12). Then the divine power flows in and through me, and I function as I should.

Although I'm still embarrassed about my foolish mistake, I am grateful for the valuable lesson it taught me. Now, whenever my life isn't working as it should, I'm learning to ask, "God, what barriers are between You and me? What prevents me from receiving and using the power You've made available?"

Reflections

Messiah Complex

One morning as Jennifer prepared to leave for high school, we had a few minutes to talk. Recalling a situation we'd discussed the night before, I said, "I really feel sorry for them, don't you?"

Jennifer merely shrugged her shoulders. My facial expression must have let my daughter know that I expected her to react more strongly to such a sad situation.

In defense of her response, my wise fifteen-year-old said, "Mama, you have to learn that there are some situations you can't fix. There are some things you just have to learn to deal with."

"You're right, Honey. I guess my 'Messiah Complex' is bothering me again today!" We laughed, but I noticed that Jennifer looked sympathetically at me as she left.

Intellectually, I agreed with Jennifer. There are some situations I can't fix. I know that. However, I hate pain. I hate grief. I hate suffering. I hate injustice and all forms of cruelty. Whenever I see others wounded by those very things I hate, I want so very much to "fix it," to get rid of all the negatives. My heart cries out, "There has to be a way! This agony must end. Somebody has to *do* something!"

When what my head knows conflicts with what my heart feels, I tend to follow my heart. I try everything I know to bring relief to the person who is hurting. When I fail, and I usually do, I cry out to God for help. (I know that's in reverse order, but I have a hard time learning how to do it right!)

Whenever I talk to God, He gently reminds me, "Johnnie, you are not the Messiah. There is only one. I sent My Son to be the Savior of the world. I have not asked you to assume His responsibilities."

I gratefully agree with God on that point, for I am all too well aware of my human limitations. However, I hang on tenaciously to my desire for relief for those who hurt.

"But, God, isn't there something I can do for them?"

"Yes. You can help them deal with the situations they face. There are many thoughtful deeds you may (and should!) do in order to minister to those who are hurting. Be sensitive. Be aware of opportunities to help. Even though you can't remove other people's burdens, you can help carry them."

As I resolved to do that, I thanked God that He did not ask me to carry the problems of the world on my shoulders. Instead, He has graciously allowed me to work alongside the true Messiah. One day He will put an end to evil and all the problems associated with it. Until then, I'll try to do my part to alleviate human suffering. And, I'll remember to thank Him for giving me a precious daughter to remind me of the lesson I have a hard time learning.

Reflections

Catering to Cowards

Jena looked toward the receptionist's window and began to giggle. "Mama, read that sign!"

After reading "We cater to cowards!" I joined in her laughter. "Well, we can relax now. We're in the right place!"

Indeed we were. The previous visit to that dentist had confirmed that the words were true. Jena had so dreaded her first visit to that particular dentist, despite being told by several of his other patients that he was wonderful, that we had waited several weeks before making the appointment to have one of her six-year-molars extracted. (I knew removing the tooth would not be painful since it had been hanging on by one "corner" for quite some time. However, because Jena had had a painful experience with another dentist who had attempted to extract a baby tooth that was not nearly as loose as he had thought, I could not convince her how easily the six-year-molar could be removed.)

Finally, Jena agreed to let me take her to see the new dentist, one who treated only children and adolescents. And both of us were glad she had, for her first experience with him had been very pleasant. In fact, she did not even know when he removed the tooth. Consequently, as we waited for her second appointment with the pediatric dentist, she was no longer overcome with fear. Instead, we laughed about the "We cater to cowards!" sign.

Of course, I felt grateful for the sensitivity of the dentist. Had he not been aware of the fears of his young patients, he would not have gone to such great lengths to make sure each child had a positive and painless experience. Because of that commitment, even preschool children played happily in the waiting room and then trotted off calmly—without a parent—for their turn to see the dentist.

I felt truly thankful not only for the dentist and his staff but also for all those special people whom the Lord sends to cater to cowards. Many, many times such people helped me face situations that made me anxious or fearful, for God sent them at just the right time, and they provided exactly what I needed—comfort, encouragement, assistance, information, and so forth. His sending them has helped me learn to trust Him. Like the Psalmist, I now can say, "But when I am afraid, I put my trust in [God]" (Psalm 56:3), for I know He does indeed cater to cowards like me.

Johnnie Ann Burgess Gaskill

Oh, No! I Sound Like Mama!

Jennifer found the item of clothing she needed to purchase and was happy to see that it was on sale. However, when the cashier rang up the item, the total did not reflect the sale price.

"Excuse me," Jennifer said, "but I think this item is on sale."

The clerk verified the price and then charged Jennifer the correct amount.

When Jennifer told me about what had happened, she laughed and said, "As soon as those words came out of my mouth, I thought, 'Oh, no! I sound just like Mama!'"

"Well," I teased, "is that such a bad thing?"

She shook her head.

Both Jennifer and Jena always hated for me to say anything at the register. They preferred that I simply pay and leave, no matter what the problem. However, my sense of integrity never allows me to do that; I like to set the record straight whether I'm overcharged or undercharged.

I know that most parents do things that embarrass their children, particularly their teenagers. (However, if the worst thing I do is correct errors at the checkout, then I'm not doing too badly!) So, rather than becoming upset over Jennifer's "Oh, no! I sound just like Mama!"I allowed it to stimulate my thinking.

I began to think about the proverb mentioned in Ezekiel 16:44: "Like mother, like daughter." Since that is true, I decided I'd better get my act together and be the kind of woman I want my daughters to emulate. I considered making a long list of qualities I'd like to see in myself and in my two daughters, but I decided to find out what kind of woman God's Word said I should be.

After reading Proverbs 31, I concluded that I should be trustworthy, diligent, sensitive to the needs of others, etc. As the Bible says, a woman who will be praised is not necessarily one who possesses great charm, for that is deceitful, nor one who has beauty, for that is fleeting; "but a woman who fears the LORD will be greatly praised" (Proverbs 31:30).

Therefore, what is praiseworthy is my reverence for the Lord, not externals such as physical appearance, career, or home management skills—though these will be affected by the attitude I have toward the Lord. When I reverence Him, I am aware of who He is; I honor Him with my words and with my works; I look my best and do my best in order to avoid bringing any dishonor on Him; and I defer to His wishes and His plans for my life, thereby giving Him the first place He deserves.

Reflections

    I want to be a woman who reverences the Lord. God knows that and He knows my desire to be a godly role model for my daughters, even if I sometimes do or say things which, when imitated, cause my daughter to say, "Oh, no! I sound just like Mama!"

Johnnie Ann Burgess Gaskill

Waving Goodbye

Every September when the big yellow school buses rumble up and down the road, I get a lump in my throat. I remember seeing Jennifer, our firstborn, climb the big steps of the minibus that picked her up for kindergarten. She seemed so small, so young, to be going off alone into her new world.

As I waved goodbye to Jennifer, I felt alone and incredibly sad because the child with whom I had spent nearly every waking moment for the past six years had just boarded the bus that would take her to a school where she would encounter more new faces and experiences than familiar ones. No longer would I have the privilege of meeting the majority of her needs. Instead, I was relinquishing her to others. I knew full well that even the kindest and best teachers and friends would never love her as much as I did.

Letting children go into a world that may not love them or treat them kindly is one of the most difficult tasks a parent must do. As I write these words, I've had years of parenting experience, but waving goodbye hasn't gotten much easier even though the children have matured. I still get that very familiar lump in my throat as Jennifer and Jena—"my babies"—venture into the unknown.

The uncertainty of what's ahead for them in the new world causes tightness in my stomach. The sadness of being separated from them and being unable to care for them produces tears.

My feelings are not uncommon. Mothers throughout the world ask questions such as these: Will my child be safe? Will my child make friends? Will my child resist temptation to do the wrong things and to run with the wrong crowd? Will my child be happy and successful in the new situation? Will my child find someone who will genuinely care for him or her?

Releasing the child is easier if the answer to all the above is "Yes." However, if the answer is "No," letting go becomes extremely difficult.

As the child goes into a world filled with crime, drugs, prejudice, perversion, injustice, misunderstanding, and the like, the words Jesus spoke to His disciples take on a new meaning. "Look, I am sending you out as sheep among wolves. Be as wary as snakes and harmless as doves" (Matthew 10:16).

Several times in the Gospels Jesus assured those who trusted Him that He would never leave them, that He would always be with them. His promise still holds true today. Therefore, our children do not go out into the world alone, neither are we left home alone. That lessens the lump a bit, doesn't it?

Johnnie Ann Burgess Gaskill

Mama's Memory Book

When Jena was fourteen, she made a "Mama's Memory Book" and presented it to me on my birthday. Her gift, a labor of love that revealed her humor and creativity, became an instant "hit" with me.

As I looked at the photos she had included, I experienced a virtual flood of emotions. The pictures and the captions she had written caused me to alternate between laughing and getting all teary-eyed.

After her hand-written title page, the book began with a photo of a very pregnant woman (me!) resting on a couch. Underneath that snapshot, Jena had written, "Even before we were born…" The following pages included pictures of Jena and Jennifer that chronicled their development from newborns to teenagers. On each page, Jena had carefully written an appropriate caption, such as: "Through many 'Tuck me ins' and many glasses of water…" and "Through school activities and fishing trips…" In conclusion, she wrote, "Till the way we turned out the way we are today…You've always been our mama and you always will be. I hope you have a great birthday! And remember I love you!"

The memory book has become a treasured one. I've spent hours looking at the photos and reading the captions. While doing so, I learned, or rather I was reminded of, an important truth: relationships and personal interactions are more memorable than other activities that often occupy a larger portion of our time.

When Jena chose the photos for the book, she didn't select those that showed us dressed in our best and impeccably groomed. Neither did she choose photos in which the house was in ready-for-company order. Instead, she picked out pictures that portrayed us as we really were on a daily basis rather than how we were after getting ready to impress others.

The girls remember the personal interaction we enjoyed over the years much more than they remember any other things that occupied so much of my time. They remember the long conversations we had together, the "Tuck-me-ins" and the numerous glasses of wa-wa that followed bedtime stories and prayers, the baking of birthday cakes and cookies, driving lessons, crying together when family members and pets died, and so forth.

I doubt they remember too much about the endless loads of laundry I did or how often I mopped the floors, the number of committees on which I served, the number of PTA meetings I attended, the workshops I attended and/or taught, the educational degrees I earned, etc. Perhaps they do remember that Mama was gone a lot.

Reflections

I wish I had spent even more time with the girls—and on my relationship to God, as well. Like my children, God is not impressed with my list of activities and achievements, although they may be worthwhile, if they take away the time that He and I could have spent enjoying each other.

Johnnie Ann Burgess Gaskill

Loving Care

Jena had been sick for a couple of days. During that time, I'd given her a lot of tender, loving care. As I sat beside my thirteen-year-old daughter's bed, I learned that all my acts of kindness had not gone unnoticed.

"Mama, you are so good to me. You've fixed my favorite foods. You even made a special trip to get my medicine…"

Although I felt pleased that she noticed the extra attention, I did not feel that I'd made any sacrifices worthy of the gratitude she was expressing. So, I interrupted her. "Honey, I did those things because I 'lub' you."

We smiled at each other and I sat with her a little longer while we waited for the pain medicine to take effect. We talked about some fun times we'd shared. We sang some silly songs she'd learned during childhood. Several times during our conversation, Jena asked, "Mama, do you remember when…?"

I was surprised that the things she remembered weren't necessarily the ones in the top drawer of my memory bank; but as Jena mentioned episodes and sayings that were special to her, I realized I remembered them, also.

As she drifted off to sleep, I gently scratched her back and sorted through some more of those memories. What a pleasant task! In fact, I enjoyed it so much that I resented—for a moment—the flash of insight that brought me back to the present.

In that "Aha!" moment I saw how Jena's pain—unsolicited and unwelcome though it was—had given me another opportunity to express my love for her. Although Jena and I knew that the love between us was genuine and constant, we often overlooked little ways to say, "I 'lub' you."

Even though we would have preferred a more pleasant interruption in the daily routine, Jena's bout with a severe earache had provided time for me to tend her carefully. Jena had interpreted all my concern, all my assistance, and all my attention as acts of love for her, which was exactly what they were.

Likewise, God does not choose pain for us. He does, however, so tenderly and lovingly care for us during our suffering that we, like Jena, feel His love. If we remained on the go and if things kept functioning normally, we might not be as aware of His continual love for us. But when He comes to us in the midst of our pain, we feel especially grateful for His presence and for His unlimited kindness.

When we realize anew how much He loves us, our hearts overflow with gratitude, and we begin to thank Him for the many ways he expresses His love, as did the prophet who wrote the book of Lamentations. As he recalled his times of afflictions and his grief over the destruction of Jerusalem, he remembered the source of his hope and began to praise the Lord.

"The unfailing love of the LORD never ends! By his mercies we have been kept from complete destruction. Great is his faithfulness; his mercies begin afresh each day" (Lamentations 3:22-23).

God wants us to praise Him for who He is. He wants us to be aware of His presence and to thank Him for what He does for us. As we express our gratitude, He will whisper, "My child, I do it all because I love you."

Johnnie Ann Burgess Gaskill

A Special Purpose

As we ate breakfast, Jennifer told about going to the guidance counselor's office to use the computerized career assessment program. "I have a wide range of jobs available to me," our tenth grader said seriously. Grinning, she added, "The computer says I'm even suited to be a poultry and egg farmer!"

Everyone in the family laughed, not to make light of those who are involved in poultry and egg production, but because none of us could picture Jennifer doing that particular job. She doesn't like getting up early, even though she is the first one out of bed on school mornings. She dislikes dust, dirt, and unpleasant smells. She is also afraid of animals that peck and/or bit.

On the other hand, she loves to sing. She relates beautifully to children. She organizes quietly and quickly. She enjoys home-making tasks, like cooking, sewing, decorating, and cleaning, and she really has an eye for colors. Shouldn't her career choice build on her skills?

Knowing Jennifer's likes and dislikes, I asked, "Honey, what *other* careers did the computer suggest?"

She rattled off quite a list. Then she said, "I've decided to get a degree in family and children's services and minor in education."

"That's a much better choice for you," I said.

Jennifer felt relieved to have some direction for her future. She disliked being asked, "What do you want to be when you grow up?" She sensed everybody expected someone with her maturity and academic ability to have their future completely planned.

After the girls left the breakfast table that morning, I lingered a bit, savoring the excitement of seeing the direction that my daughter's life might take. During all those years of parenting as best as my husband and I knew how, during all the praying, during all the trusting God to lead our daughters in the right paths, during all the choosing between better and best…we wondered what career decisions our girls might make. At last, a profession seemed to be coming into focus.

As I reflected upon Jennifer's interests and talents, I saw how God had been sharpening her skills. God had clarified her future by using opportunities in the public schools, as well as the experiences she had had in and through the church. For example, one summer when she served as a counselor at a church-sponsored children's camp, she began to see how well she related to children, how they trusted her, how they respected her, and how much she enjoyed them.

Reflections

God does use all our experiences in order to mold and shape our lives. That is exciting. However, I find it even more thrilling to know that God has a plan for each person, even before birth. Several Scriptures teach this. For example, Jeremiah heard the Lord say, "I knew you before I formed you in your mother's womb. Before you were born I set you apart and appointed you as my spokesman to the world" (Jeremiah 1:5).

Likewise, God announced specific plans to the mother of Sampson. "You will become pregnant and give birth to a son, and his hair must never be cut. For he will be dedicated to God as a Nazirite from birth. He will rescue Israel from the Philistines" (Judges 13:5). And, according to Luke 1:11-17, Zechariah, the father of John the Baptist, received detailed information about his son's mission even before John had been conceived. And the Apostle Paul said, "For it pleased God in his kindness to choose me and call me, even before I was born! What undeserved mercy! Then he revealed his Son to me so that I could proclaim the Good News about Jesus to the Gentiles" (Galatians 1:15-16a).

Even when God's plans are not announced to the parents, God does have a special purpose for each child. That's why we get excited whenever God begins to reveal the direction He intends for our children! Then we realize that the questions regarding their life's vocation should never have been "What do I want my child to become?" or "What does my child want to be when she grows up?" Rather, two questions should have been uppermost in our minds: "What does God want my child to become?" and "How can I help prepare my child for a life of usefulness to the Master, whether she becomes a poultry and egg farmer, a home economist, a teacher, a missionary, a musician…?"

Johnnie Ann Burgess Gaskill

How Are You?

The doctor scanned the chart, then smiled at Jennifer and asked, "How are you?"

"I'm fine," she said brightly as she gave him a smile perfect enough for a toothpaste commercial.

"Jennifer," I chided, "I think the doctor really wants to know how you are!"

She grinned and began to tell him about her high fever, persistent cough, and other symptoms that proved she was not fine. Actually, she hadn't been that sick for twelve years.

As I reflected on that brief experience, I wondered, *Why is it so hard for us to be truthful about ourselves? Have we learned to conceal the truth because we believe that the folks who are asking really do not care, but are simply inquiring for the sake of conversation?"*

However, doctors want to know how we really are. That was true in Jennifer's case, but she didn't feel comfortable with an immediate description of all her ailments. Had Jennifer been at the pediatrician's office, she would have given *him* a straight answer immediately, but since this was her first visit to the family practitioner, she felt the need for polite conversation.

Jennifer was not in a social situation, however. When her doctor asked, "How are you?" he wanted specific information, not generalities. He checked to see exactly how high her fever was. He checked her blood pressure and listened carefully to what was going on inside her chest. If he hadn't gotten enough information from the examination, then he would have ordered blood work, a chest x-ray, or other tests. As Jennifer matured, she learned to "shoot straight" with the doctors, since failing to answer specifically and accurately only delays the healing process.

That principle applies to all areas of healing, but we tend to forget that. Although we learn to speak freely to a doctor who is treating our physical ailments, we often refuse to be open with God, despite the fact that He knows how sin sick we really are!

The Bible says, "For the word of God is full of living power. It is sharper than the sharpest knife, cutting deep into our innermost thoughts and desires. It exposes us for what we really are. Nothing in all creation can hide from him. Everything is naked and exposed before his eyes. This is the God to whom we must explain all that we have done" (Hebrews 4:12-13).

Thus, trying to hide ourselves from Him is utter foolishness. God wants us to "shoot straight" with Him, or as my girls used to say, "fess up!" Like the medical doctors, God doesn't deal in generalities. He wants specific information—not so He will know what's wrong but so that we will know.

What happens if we are not honest with God? David described his experience this way: "When I refused to confess my sin, I was weak and miserable, and I groaned all day long. Day and night [God's] hand of discipline was upon me. My strength evaporated like water in the summer heat. Finally, I confessed all my sins to [God] and stopped trying to hide them. And [God] forgave me! All my guilt is gone" (Psalm 32:3-5).

Both God and David knew how sin sick David was, but his healing did not begin until he was willing to quit playing games with God. Once David admitted his sins, God forgave him and removed his guilt.

God wants to do the same for you and me. Therefore, when our Great Physician asks, "How are you?" we should avoid the superficial, "I'm fine!" We should say, "Father, I have a real problem with…" and **name** the sins one-by-one as honestly and as specifically as we can. Once we've described our problem, God will direct us to the Bible, for it contains His prescriptions for total well-being.

Johnnie Ann Burgess Gaskill

Shake the Sock!

Jena found a sure way to awaken her pet squirrel. She discovered she had to shake his sock! Naturally, Ralph did not like being forcibly removed from his "nest." He protested by barking and trying to climb higher into the toe of the white tube sock. When he did that, Jena grabbed hold of the toe and slid her hand down the sock as she continued to gently shake it. Ralph tried to hold on, but Jena never abandoned her mission. When Ralph neared the opening, Jena folded the top of the sock backward, and out came Ralph.

Having been roused and routed, Ralph enjoyed his activity time. He climbed on the curtains or explored Jena's room. His favorite place was the piano. While Jena practiced, Ralph hid pencils and scraps of paper behind the rack that held Jena's sheet music. In fact, he liked his freedom so much that he protested being returned to his cage.

Although Ralph lived in a birdcage that was four feet tall and contained two branches on which Ralph could climb, he quickly became bored with his quarters and crawled back inside his comfy sock. He slept the day away, totally oblivious to the sounds and activities going on around him. Even the vacuum cleaner failed to rouse him! Therefore, when Jena returned from school, she'd shake his sock and give Ralph a chance to exercise.

I always laughed whenever Jena shook the sock while Ralph fussed and tried so hard to remain in his dark little world, ignoring Jena's positive, pleading voice urging him to, "Come on out, Ralph. Time to wake up and have some fun!"

Jena understood Ralph's reluctance to rouse himself, for she, too, had difficulty getting out of bed in the mornings, even when fun-filled days awaited her. That's why I sometimes laughed and said, "Jena, if you don't get out of that bed, I'm gonna have to shake your sock!"

Although I laughed about Ralph enjoying his tube socks and Jena her soft bed, I must admit that I, too, have comfort zones from which I do not want to be moved. Don't we all?

That may be why God sometimes shakes the sock in order to awaken us from our slumber, to cause us to be up and about the challenges that are all around us. God, who is all-wise, doesn't want our muscles to remain undeveloped or to atrophy due to lack of use, even though that's what happens if we remain in our comfort zone all the time. Unless God shakes the sock, we will never realize our full potential. We, like Ralph, will be content to stay in safe places and sleep instead of climbing to new heights, instead of exploring new areas that stimulate our curiosity and creativity. Unless we are moved from our comfort zones, life's challenges will pass us by.

While watching Jena and her pet squirrel, I learned that God permits us to rest, for a time, before He begins to gently, yet persistently, shake the sock. He allows us to fuss and to try to hang onto our beloved comfort, but He continues to shake the sock. As we resist, He speaks gently to us. He urges us to give up the struggle to hold onto the safe and the familiar and to move toward the exciting challenges that await us. God shakes the sock because He loves us and wants us to experience the joy of living fully.

Johnnie Ann Burgess Gaskill

The Meringue Mishap

"Mama, look at this!" ten-year-old Jennifer wailed.

I looked at the meringue. It was hard to tell which looked worse, the runny meringue or Jennifer's woebegone face. I felt so sorry for her. She'd insisted on baking a lemon pie—all by herself—for her daddy on Father's Day. Now, she believed all her efforts had been wasted.

"Honey, what did you do? Did you beat the egg whites long enough? Did you add the sugar and the cream of tartar? Did you follow the directions?" I asked. She nodded her head in response to the questions that tumbled rapidly from my mouth.

Unable to figure out why her egg whites weren't stiff and ready to spread over the filling, I began a new line of questioning. "Okay," I said gently, "let's go over this one more time, step by step. You did beat the egg whites *before* you added anything to them, didn't you?"

Jennifer's eyes opened wide. "No, I just put everything in the bowl and then I used the mixer. I thought that would be quicker. And," she said proudly, "I did mix for a very long time." Blinking back tears, she added, "But nothing happened. They just wouldn't mix!"

"Honey, you have to follow the directions when you're making meringue. With some recipes, you can alter the instructions just a little bit, but not when you're making meringue. You have to beat the egg whites before you add anything to them."

She headed back to the kitchen to try again. Later, she proudly served her dad a delicious lemon pie that was topped with perfect, mile-high, golden-brown meringue.

Jennifer may take some creative shortcuts when preparing other recipes; but, I daresay, she will never do so when making meringue! She learned a hard but important lesson: Doing the right things the wrong way results in failure. There are certain steps that must be followed precisely in order to achieve the desired results.

That principle extends beyond the kitchen and into all areas of life. For example, we are to speak the truth, but we must speak it in love (Ephesians 4:15), or else the results can be disastrous. Likewise, doing good deeds is not enough. We must do every good thing "in the name of the Lord Jesus." If we fail to acknowledge our dependence upon Him and to give praise to Him for whatever good He accomplishes through us, we are simply tooting our own horns; and, in the final accounting, we will learn all our hard work produced nothing worthy of His praise.

Reflections

    The writer of Proverbs 26:20 knew the value of doing the right thing the right way, for he wrote, "Those who listen to instruction will prosper." That principle applies whether we're making meringue or seeking to please our Lord.

Johnnie Ann Burgess Gaskill

Reflections about the Words and Actions of Others

Johnnie Ann Burgess Gaskill

Unspoken Communication

Fear possessed me as I sat alone in my den during the predawn hours. I wanted the time to pass quickly, yet I knew that each tick of the clock brought me closer to the time when I would undergo the EEG and Cat Scan my neurologist had ordered.

While everyone slept but me, I watched the clock and allowed memories of the past to trouble me. I recalled seeing my seventy-nine-year-old father after he had undergone his EEG seven months ago. I remembered seeing the bloody spots in the crown of his bald head, spots that indicated where the electrodes had been inserted. I also recalled his description of how painful the test had been. Those memories, along with thoughts of "What if I have a brain tumor?" filled my mind during those anxious hours when I stayed awake, as per the doctor's instructions.

With each passing hour, my fear increased. Finally, the appointed time came. The technician treated me kindly and gently. I felt only slight stings as she inserted the electrodes all over my scalp. When everything was in place, she said, "Close your eyes and just relax."

Yeah, right! I thought. *I'm a bundle of nerves*! But, surprisingly enough, I found myself relaxing. As I did so, the words to a Fanny J. Crosby hymn came to mind, "For I know whate'er befall me, Jesus doeth all things well." Those words came over and over, like a chant. Soon I was more relaxed than I would have been during peaceful slumber. The words brought such comfort and reassurance to me that I knew I'd be fine—whatever the diagnosis.

Soon the technician returned to my room. "Mrs. Gaskill," she said, "you have the nicest alpha waves. They indicate that your brain is healthy and very active."

I smiled at her, knowing she had been privileged to record unspoken communication between a loving Heavenly Father and one of His children who desperately needed to be assured of His presence and His power.

Johnnie Ann Burgess Gaskill

But...But...I Thought I Had More Time!

When the phone rang at 6:15 one Wednesday evening, we learned that a woman who had been a dear friend for seventeen years had died a short time ago. Though her doctors had said she would never come out of the coma she'd been in for nearly four months and that her death could occur at any time, the news of her passing shocked us.

Immediately, memories flashed through my mind. I recalled that whenever one of us rejoiced over a new house or a new car, the birth of a child or some other blessing, the other one rejoiced. Likewise, when one of us mourned the death of a loved one, grieved over a miscarriage, recovered from a serious car accident, or experienced any kind of distress, the other one always came to comfort and to help.

Though she was such a good friend, I failed to share with her the one thing she most needed to know—how she could have a personal relationship with Jesus Christ. Oh, she knew of my commitment to God and my desire to serve Him. She knew I believed in prayer, for just a month before she slipped into a coma she and I had bowed together in a small prayer room at Crawford Long Hospital in Atlanta, GA, and asked God to spare the life of her husband who was seriously ill. On a few occasions my friend had attended church with me, and I often shared with her how God had been so faithful to comfort and strengthen me, especially during the more difficult periods of my life.

Since neither of us had reached middle age, I **assumed** we had many years left for continued caring and that I would have the perfect opportunity to invite her to accept Christ as her personal Lord and Savior, if she hadn't already done so. I was wrong, very wrong.

Reflections

Too Busy?

"Johnnie, I've needed to talk to you," my friend said softly, "but I haven't called you because I know how busy you are."

Tears filled my eyes as her gentle words indicted me. I *was* busy, too busy for my friends to approach me, too busy to minister on a personal level. I *knew* that, and had known it for a long time. I tried to ease my guilt by convincing myself that I was using my skills to do good things, such as organizing workshops and teaching classes that equipped others to minister to people. However, doing all those good and necessary things kept me busy, busy, too busy to be personally involved in the lives of people.

After that conversation, I began to seek answers to the agonizing question asked by those who carry a heavy load of responsibilities. *How can I meet the needs of individuals and still deal effectively with all the other demands on my time? (After all, there are only 24 hours in a day!)*

As usual, I searched for answers in the Scriptures. As I read familiar accounts of the life and ministry of Christ, I saw how His actions and His teachings revealed His concern for individuals. For example, even while walking toward Jerusalem where He would spend His last days on earth, Jesus took time to stop along the way and help individuals who needed His touch.

For example, when Jesus heard a blind man in the crowd cry out to Him for mercy, Jesus stopped and restored the man's sight. Jesus also spotted Zaccheus who was sitting in a sycamore tree in order to get a better glimpse of the Christ. Jesus said, "Zaccheus, hurry and come down, for today I must stay at your house." Then, the whole procession stopped while Jesus dined with Zaccheus, whose life was forever changed as a result of that encounter with Jesus.

Although the needs around Jesus were great and although He was on an important mission, one with eternal results, Jesus remained approachable, compassionate, and sensitive to the individuals who comprised the crowd. He was never too busy to reach out to them.

Johnnie Ann Burgess Gaskill

Get Rid of the *Buts*!

After listening to me talk about my concerns, my friend Dianne looked straight into my eyes and said gently but firmly, "Johnnie, get rid of the *buts*!"

Her simple, yet profound advice shocked me into silence. Slowly I began to realize why she'd said that to me. Though I, of course, had heard the words I'd spoken aloud to my friend who was sitting across the table from me, I was not aware of how frequently I'd used the word *but*. However, my dear friend had listened as I lamented my lack of fulfillment. She noticed how sentences such as these permeated the conversation: *I know I need to [this] but…* and *I'd really like to do [that], but…* Thankfully, she heard my excuses and loved me enough to point out the truth.

I needed someone to tell me to get rid of all my excuses and uncertainties and to start moving ahead in the right direction. Her advice to me was, in essence, the same as that found in a familiar Bible passage. "…let us strip off every weight that slows us down, especially the sin that so easily hinders our progress. And let us run with endurance the race that God has set before us. We do this by keeping our eyes on Jesus, on whom our faith depends from start to finish. He was willing to die a shameful death on the cross because of the joy he knew would be his afterward. Now he is seated in the place of highest honor beside God's throne in heaven" (Hebrews 12:1-2).

Since I've become aware of how frequently I make excuses for myself, the Holy Spirit of God is helping me get rid of the *buts*. When I say, "I know I should do [thus and so], but I don't have the [money, time, equipment, knowledge, etc.]," the Spirit reminds me of the words of the Apostle Paul: "And this same God who takes care of me will supply all your needs from his glorious riches, which have been given to us in Christ Jesus" (Philippians 4:19).

Whenever I say, "I'd go ahead with [the task], but I'm not sure how to proceed," He whispers, "You will see your teacher with your own eyes, and you will hear a voice say, 'This is the way; turn around and walk here'" (Isaiah 30:21).

With His wonderful help, I'm slowly but surely getting rid of the *buts*!

Father, Forgive Them

One day when I joined my daughter for lunch at her school, a beautiful child sat directly across the table from me. *Surely this isn't Susan**, I thought, as my daughter introduced us. I saw nothing in her appearance that provided any clue that *she* was the child ridiculed and shunned by her classmates. She was clean, well-dressed, and without any obvious impairments.

My daughter and the children seated around us were bursting with things to share with me. Meanwhile Susan said nothing. She just ate her lunch quietly and listened to the chatter going on around her. As I glanced at her, my heart ached for this young one who was the object of daily sarcastic, hurtful remarks made by her classmates.

Smiling at her, I said, "Susan, you have such beautiful eyes." For a brief moment her eyes sparkled and her face started to light up in response to my sincere compliment. Then, before either of us could say anything further, one of the other girls began to give me a word for word account of how other students described Susan.

As the "informer" continued her little speech, I was at a loss for words. I simply could not believe she was repeating such cruel, untrue remarks at all, especially in Susan's presence! A quick glance at Susan revealed the damage the insensitive gossipmonger had done. Susan sat with her head slightly bowed and her eyes lowered, as if too ashamed to look at any of us.

Intense anger welled up inside me, along with tender compassion for Susan. I wanted to get up from the table and "get'em good!" How dare they be so cruel to one so young and vulnerable!

Instead, I spoke softly to Susan. "People treated Jesus badly, too, even though He was absolutely perfect. He never did anything wrong, yet they still did not like Him." She nodded as I whispered, "And, Susan, *He* loves you and He understands exactly how you feel right now."

I couldn't say anything more for everyone stood up when the teacher motioned for the students to turn in their trays. But, I prayed that my words encouraged Susan to seek to know the fullness of the love of Jesus and to make His prayer hers: "Father, forgive these people, because they don't know what they are doing" (Luke 23:34).

*Name changed.

Johnnie Ann Burgess Gaskill

Turtles in the Fast Lane

The rain tapped a steady rhythm on the car windows as a friend and I talked. The dreariness of the day matched our mood.

As Joann and I discussed what Dr. James Dobson refers to as "fatigue and time pressure," we realized we how much we had in common. Each of us had been born and reared in small towns where the pace was slow and where people had time for one another. Each of us had had close friends and time to cultivate and enjoy those friendships. Although we had lived in the metro Atlanta area for more than a decade, we still found ourselves longing for the slower pace and the relationships we'd thrived on as children and teenagers.

That's what we wanted, but not what we had! Our lives were filled with stress as we juggled family responsibilities, job demands, church and community activities, etc. We lamented the fact that our busy schedules allowed little time for relaxation or for being with those dearest to us. We talked on and on, oblivious to the downpour of rain. Suddenly, Joann started to giggle. "Johnnie, we're just two old turtles being forced to live in the fast lane!"

We exploded with laughter at her "homey" illustration; and, while I didn't particularly feel flattered at being compared to a turtle, the truth of her words began to dawn on me. God did not equip turtles to travel safely on interstate highways. Neither did He design people to live in the fast lane. Quite the contrary!

"The Sovereign LORD...says, 'Only in returning to me and waiting for me will you be saved. In quietness and confidence is your strength'" (Isaiah 30:15). Yet, if we stubbornly insist on living in the fast lane, we—not God—will be responsible for the carnage on the highways of life.

I Had to Help Her!

As Mother and I entered the nursing home, we saw two residents slowly making their way down the hall. We paused to allow them to pass. As the ladies neared us, the one on the left said, "I couldn't let her come alone. I had to help her!"

In her left hand she held her cane; with the other hand she supported the arm of her friend. Seeing them together and hearing her explanation caused a lump to form in my throat, especially when I recognized that the lady who was being helped back to her room was my daddy's cousin whom I'd always called Aunt Pearl.

Apparently Aunt Pearl and her friend had been to the dining room for the noon meal. And now that dear, compassionate lady was doing all she could to make sure Aunt Pearl got back safely to her room. She asked, "Is this your room?"

"No," Aunt Pearl answered cheerily, "mine's the second one."

As Mother and I walked behind them, I noticed that Aunt Pearl's steps were so tiny that she shuffled rather than walked. I also observed how she needed both the handrail and her friend's gentle assistance in order to maintain her balance.

While Aunt Pearl's friend helped her get settled in a chair by the window, Mother and I waited outside the door. On her way out, the friend smiled at us once more and repeated her previous explanation. "I couldn't let her come alone. I had to help her!" She smiled again and hobbled down the hall toward her own room. That touched me, especially when I saw that she was scarcely able to get about herself, yet she was aware of and responsive to the needs of others.

Days later I was still thinking about the lady's words and her example. I believe God used her to help not only Aunt Pearl, but also to help me, although in a different sort of way. I began to understand that God does strengthen, help, and uphold, as He promises to do in Isaiah 41:10: "Don't be afraid, for I am with you. Do not be dismayed, for I am your God. I will strengthen you. I will help you. I will uphold you with my victorious right hand."

In order to provide the needed strength and support, God often uses people. People like the woman at the nursing home. People who have enough of His love and compassion to say, "I couldn't let her come alone. I had to help her!" People like you? People like me?

Johnnie Ann Burgess Gaskill

What Do You Do For Fun?

Daddy's breathing became increasingly labored. Baffled by the change in his condition, the doctors in Ellijay, Georgia, decided to transfer him to a much larger hospital in Atlanta.

Soon after Daddy arrived there, a doctor entered his room and began to ask question after question.

"Does he smoke?"

"No," Mother answered.

"Does he drink?"

Again Mother replied, "No."

With a twinkle in his eye, the doctor looked at Daddy and said, "Well, Pops, what do you do for fun?"

Before Daddy could answer, my husband responded, "He goes to church!" All of us, even Daddy, laughed at the unexpected remark, and the doctor resumed his questioning.

I don't know why I remember that scene so vividly. Perhaps because it took place only a few hours before Daddy died. Anyway, since then I've often thought about what Daddy did for fun.

He enjoyed hard work. He really did. He especially liked to cut grass. Even when he was seventy-eight years old, he pushed a lawnmower for six hours a day for he loved the sight and the smell of freshly-mowed grass.

Talking on the phone was another activity on his fun list. He called certain people every day—some before breakfast! And he greeted each one with a booming, pleasant voice. As he and his friends joked with each other, his laughter could be heard throughout the house.

Daddy loved for his family to come for a visit and, as long as he was physically able, he'd always come outside to greet us, walking toward us with open arms to enfold us in a big bear hug. To the grandchildren, he always said, "And how are my babies?" even when they were almost school age.

But as much as he enjoyed working and socializing, he put both aside whenever it was time to go to church. Oh, we knew Daddy loved us. We never doubted that—not for a moment. But we also knew that he loved being in God's house with God's people. He went there not because he had to, but because he wanted to.

Consequently, when our family gathered to make Daddy's funeral arrangements, we never considered holding the memorial service in the chapel of the funeral home. Instead, Daddy's body was taken to the little country church he loved, and his body was planted in the church's grassy cemetery, the one he and my brother regularly mowed.

How thankful I am for having had a father who so obviously enjoyed being in God's house. Whenever I read Psalm 27:4-5, I think of Daddy, and, although he didn't write the words, he agreed wholeheartedly with them: "The one thing I ask of the LORD—the one thing I seek most—is to live in the house of the LORD all the days of my life, delighting in the LORD's perfections and meditating in his Temple. For he will conceal me there when troubles come; he will hide me in his sanctuary. He will place me out of reach on a high rock."

Johnnie Ann Burgess Gaskill

No Sacrifice Is Too Great

Because the beach was so crowded that day, I scarcely noticed the lady and her four children when they staked out a claim near where I had spread our towels. However, after they returned to eat lunch on their quilt and the woman had put her little boy down for his afternoon nap, I turned toward her and said, "He's so cute!"

And he was. His blond curly hair contrasted beautifully with his evenly tanned skin. The darling little cherub looked like the picture of health, but he wasn't. His mother began to tell me about his medical problems. "He was born with only half a heart and with only one lung. The day after he was born, the doctor told us that he would not live."

Instead of allowing the life support system to be removed, the parents chartered a plane and flew their son to a Boston hospital where surgeons operated on him immediately. "Since he was fed intravenously for the first six weeks of his life, he never learned to suck. And he has never learned to chew. That's why I have to feed him through a tube in his stomach."

As I listened to her talk so matter-of-factly about his condition and as I saw how calmly and expertly she took care of her son, I realized she was not singing "Poor Little Ol' Me." Neither was she grumbling or complaining about the constant care he needed or the financial burden his care placed on her and her husband. Rather, her words and actions conveyed this message: "There's no sacrifice too great for this child."

Because she refused to play the role of martyr, God spoke to me through her. "My child," He said, "having seen this outpouring of a parent's sacrificial love on a helpless child, can you better understand how tenderly and lovingly I care for you? Do you now understand that you don't have to earn my love or feel worthy of my attention?"

My heart whispered, "Yes, Father. Oh, yes!"

Expert Help

Whenever the equipment in our office broke down, we needed help fast. Fortunately, we knew someone we could call who understood our situation and would immediately come to make the repairs.

One particular day when it was especially crucial for us to be operational, I called for help. As the smiling young technician entered my office where the equipment was, I said, "Chris, seeing you is like having a doctor enter the emergency room and begin to take charge."

We laughed at my remark, both of us knowing full well what a relief it is to have a skilled person come to our rescue during an emergency. As usual, Chris identified the problem, fixed it, and had us back in business in a very short time.

Sometimes the repairs took only a few minutes, as they did that day. At other times, they required days or weeks. Nevertheless, we always trusted Chris to help us. He knew our equipment. He knew our need. Consequently, we stopped worrying as soon as he arrived on the scene because we knew were in capable, skillful hands.

In like manner, I've learned through previous experiences that I can trust God. He created me and daily watches over me; therefore He knows me. (See Psalm 139.) He knows my needs. He has total power, both in heaven and in earth. In addition, he loves me more than I can possibly imagine. What reason do I have to worry? In all situations I'm certainly in good hands, the very best of hands.

Therefore, these words of the Psalmist thrill me. "But as for me, how good it is to be near God! I have made the Sovereign LORD my shelter, and I will tell everyone about the wonderful things [He] does" (Psalm 73:28).

May each of us come to the point where we can say, "God knows what He is doing with me. Though I do not understand all He does nor do I understand why He sometimes takes so long, I do trust Him. He is the One I call upon whenever things in my life are going wrong."

Johnnie Ann Burgess Gaskill

Make Deposits and Enjoy the Dividends

Near the end of the vocal concert, the director of the seventy-voice choir stepped to the microphone. "I'd like to introduce Chance Scoggins, who has served as the student conductor this year. He will be leaving [this school] soon. He will now conduct our final selection for the evening."

With those words, Ms. Charlsa Taul, the director and teacher of the choral group, took a place among her students and waited expectantly for the music to begin. Her face glowed with pride as she looked at the high school senior as he prepared to lead his fellow students.

As the choir sang a beautiful arrangement of "The Battle Hymn of the Republic," I became aware of the goose bumps spreading over my skin. I think a combination of several factors caused them. Of course, the words and the melody stirred my heart, as usual. But on that particular evening, I believed what moved me so was something akin to the changing of the guard or to the passing of a baton.

There is, I believe, a moment of significance when one who has invested time, talents, and skills in the teaching of another chooses to step aside and let the student perform. For the teacher, it is a moment of receiving the dividends earned from the deposits made in the life of the student. For the pupil, it is a moment of honor, one that recognizes the achievements he made as a result of applying himself during years of study and struggles.

In such a moment there is great joy. I saw it on the teacher's face. I saw it on the student's face when, after leading his teacher and his peers so professionally, he turned to face the audience. The big grin he was wearing then remained on his face, even as the curtain closed on a moment that would never be forgotten.

The Apostle Paul knew the importance and the rewards of investing in the lives of young people. Shortly before his death, Paul wrote a letter to Timothy, a young man whom Paul had led to faith in Christ and then discipled him in that faith. Paul, who was being held in a Roman prison at the time, wrote to Timothy, the young evangelist, in order to encourage him to remain true to the faith despite the hardships that were sure to come his way.

"Hold on to the pattern of right teaching that you learned from me. And remember to live in the faith and love that you have in Christ Jesus. With the help of the Holy Spirit who lives within us, carefully guard what has been entrusted to you" (2 Timothy 1:13-14).

Paul also said, "Timothy, my dear son, be strong with the special favor God gives you in Christ Jesus. You have heard me teach many things that have been confirmed by many reliable witnesses. Teach these great truths to trustworthy people who are able to pass them on to others" (2 Timothy 2:1-2).

Young people, you must protect the good deposit entrusted to you. Use it wisely and well. Then pass it on to faithful persons who will, in turn, pass it on to others.

Adults, the question is: "What significant values and instructions are you depositing into the lives of young people?" Without a deposit, there is no return, no joyous moment of receiving dividends of incalculable worth such as the one shared by the vocal director/teacher and her student.

Johnnie Ann Burgess Gaskill

I Has a Good Fwiend

A friend of mine who worked with preschool children at her church told me a story about a two-year-old child. The little girl had attended Vacation Bible School on Monday. Then on Tuesday, she brought a guest with her. As the two children arrived, hand-in-hand, the little girl approached the teacher and sang a verse to one of the songs the class had learned the day before. Beaming proudly, she sang, "I has a good fwiend; David is his name."

That story about the little girl and her cousin made my eyes misty, even though I did not personally know either of the children. However, I visualized the radiant expression on her face as she proudly brought David to a warm, loving church where he could hear such truths as: God loves me; I am special; there is no one exactly like me.

In addition to picturing her sweet face, I could almost hear the child's voice as she sang, "I has a good fwiend. David is his name." I recalled the days when my own daughters weren't able to determine when to use *has* and when to use *have*. I also remembered the times when Jennifer and Jena found it hard to pronounce words containing "r" and certain other letters. And I remembered the sweetness with which my little girls spoke. Despite their errors in grammar and speech, their words sounded like music to my ears!

Jesus loves the children, too. He esteems them highly, according to His statements that have been recorded in the Holy Bible. For example, He said, "Let the children come to me. Don't stop them! For the Kingdom of God belongs to such as these. I assure you, anyone who doesn't have their kind of faith will never get into the Kingdom of God" (Mark 10:14-15).

He wants adults to come to Him as humbly and as trustingly as the little children do. Doing so indicates our willingness to allow Him to love us and bless us. Once we've experienced the sweetness of the love of Jesus, we'll be as excited as the two-year-old child, and we will want to bring our friends to Jesus so He can bless them, too.

Reflections

Know the Value

When my sister-in-law gave me one of her original oil paintings, I assured her I would treasure it not only for its beauty but also because it was one she had painted. She seemed pleased that I liked her gift. As I left her house, she said, "If you ever decide to sell it, it's worth ____."

I wondered why she had said that. Why would she think I might sell it? Couldn't she tell that I liked it? Did she think it wasn't good enough to hang in my house? Although she had learned to paint after she retired, she'd surprised everyone (especially herself!) with her creativity and skill. In fact, she'd sold several pieces of her work.

After reflecting on her words, I realized she'd told me the market value of her painting not to impress me with the value of her gift but in order to keep me from being shortchanged in the event I decided to sell it. She simply wanted me to have full value of the gift whether I kept the painting or sold it.

I appreciated her thoughtfulness and her wisdom. She knew that people often make the mistake of letting things go without stopping to contemplate their value.

The Bible tells many stories about people who exchanged a precious possession for one of much lesser value. For example, Adam and Eve gave up the "good life" for one filled with frustration. Once they lived in the ideal environment and enjoyed an unmarred relationship with God. However, all that changed when they sold out to the deceiver who promised them the opportunity to better themselves, to become like God. Only after the sale of their souls did Adam and Eve realize the extent of their loss.

Solomon, who was the richest and wisest man who ever lived, gave up his God-given blessings in order to enjoy having many wives. These women so influenced Solomon that in his old age, "they turned his heart to worship their gods instead of trusting only in the LORD his God, as his father, David, had done" (1 Kings 11:4). The result? God became angry with Solomon, removed his kingdom from him, and gave it to someone else.

But we need not think that only the people mentioned in the Bible made unwise exchanges. You and I, and people we know, often easily let go of valuable assets that have been given to us. The tempter persuades some to exchange a marriage for an illicit affair. Many people sell their families to employers in exchange for a few extra dollars each week. People willingly give up their health and well-being in order to enjoy eating junk food and lying around on the couch. Yes, the "going price" of precious possessions in today's market is very cheap.

Oh that we had more people, like my sister-in-law, who point out the value of the gifts we now possess. We need people who will remind us to think long and hard before we release something of great value at a price far below its true worth.

Reflections

Releasing a Loved One

Wiping his tears, a pastor told me about his recent visit with the family of a dying child.

"When I entered the hospital room," he said, "I saw the mother holding one of the child's hands. A sister clasped the other one. The grandmother, wanting to have some precious, final contact with the child, was holding onto his foot. It was obvious the child was dying, and I knew they had to release the child."

Whenever he got to that point in the story, the pastor was so overcome with emotion that he had to pause before finishing the story.

"Releasing a loved one is so hard, but it must be done. I know that from personal experience. My sister and I had to do that when Mama died."

I knew exactly what he meant, though I had not realized until that moment that my experience was what he called "releasing a loved one."

I only knew what happened on March 6, 1982. The evening before, doctors at an Atlanta hospital had assured us that they expected Daddy to be well enough to go home in a few days. Even so, I remained quite concerned about his condition, especially when I talked with Daddy and Mother by phone the next morning and realized his breathing was quite labored.

As soon as I hung up the phone, I felt such a need to pray. First, I thanked God for the long life (eighty years) that He had given to Daddy. I also thanked Him for the love Daddy had given and received, for the friendships he had enjoyed, and for the lives he had touched.

Then I did something I'd never done before. Instead of pleading with the Lord to make Daddy well, I said, "Lord, Daddy belongs to You. You do what is best for him." Those words were simple, but sincere. And, coming from the heart of a "Daddy's girl," they were strange words. Yet, having said them, I felt a peace I could not explain.

Daddy died a couple of hours later. As our family wept together and made the funeral arrangements, the unexplained peace never left me. In fact, it remains with me even to this very day. Certainly, I have shed many tears. I have experienced intense longing to see him again. But in the midst of all the sorrow and the loneliness, the peculiar peace has been there.

Not until the day I talked with the pastor did I realize it was my act of releasing Daddy that contributed so much to that peace. Had I not surrendered my will and my wishes to the Lord and given Him permission to do what was best, I would not have known such wonderful peace for I would have remained in conflict with the Lord.

    When we release a loved one, we give God the freedom to be the Sovereign Lord. Then He blesses us with a sustaining, never-ending peace. Once felt, that indescribable peace can never be forgotten.

Reflections

A Comforting, Constant Companion

All during my first plane flight on June 7, 1989, I felt like a child on the first day of school. Everything in the strange environment intrigued me. I listened intently to all the instructions given by the flight crew. I watched the other passengers and took my cues from them.

As we flew from Atlanta, Georgia, to Houston, Texas, Jena, our eleven-year-old daughter, occupied the seat nearest the window. I sat beside her. To my left sat a man who, obviously, was an experienced passenger, for he appeared quite relaxed. He thumbed through a magazine. Then he rested his head of the back of his seat and closed his eyes.

The time passed quickly. We enjoyed a smooth flight. Suddenly, the plane began descending rapidly, much too rapidly for me. I didn't say anything, but I pressed my spine tightly against the back of my seat, as if that bit of resistance would cause the plane to slow down. As we lost altitude, my ears began to hurt—not just a little, but a lot. Soon the pain was almost unbearable.

By that time, even the napping passengers were awake. When the man beside me opened his eyes, I whispered, "Are we going to be okay?"

"Sure," he said. "We're getting ready to land."

Whew! What a relief to know the plane wasn't crashing!

Surmising that I was an inexperienced passenger, the man explained that not all descents were swift. "Sometimes you hardly know you're landing until you feel the plane touch down." That made me feel better, for I was already dreading having to board our connecting flight from Houston to Denver, Colorado.

As we talked, I began to relax. However, the pain in my ears intensified, making me shudder. The man told me some things I could do to alleviate the discomfort. As we exited the plane, I thanked him for helping me and wished him a pleasant evening.

As a result of that experience, I began to understand more fully the inexpressible comfort of having a caring, experienced, knowledgeable person nearby. The passenger's presence and his words transformed the situation for me by relieving my panic as well as my pain.

I believe God sends such persons into our lives. More importantly, He also sends the Holy Spirit whom Jesus referred to as the Counselor and the Spirit of truth. "When [He] comes, he will guide you into all truth. He will not be presenting his own ideas; he will be telling you what he has heard. He will tell you about the future. He will bring me glory by revealing to you whatever he receives from me. All that the Father has is mine; this is what I mean when I say that the Spirit will reveal to you whatever he receives from me" (John 16:13-15).

Imagine that! No matter where we are or what we are facing, we have a constant companion who whispers God's instructions to us. And that Counselor, that Spirit of Truth, that Helper knows exactly how to deal with *all* the issues of life, not just panic and pain during first flights.

Mirror of the Soul

When I answered the doorbell, I saw an elderly man standing on my porch. Since neither of us knew the other one, we immediately sized each other up. I noted his small frame and his bright eyes peering at me through his oversized glasses. I saw the Bible that he was holding under his arm. I realized he was staring intently at my face.

He broke the silence first. "You're a Christian, aren't you?"

"Yes, I am," I replied, wondering how he knew.

He smiled and said, "I could see it in your face."

Then he told me he was out in the neighborhood talking with people about the Lord and inviting them to church. Suddenly, he changed the conversation. "You know, today's my birthday. I'm 82!" he said proudly.

I congratulated him, and we talked for a few more minutes. Then he left to visit other people on my street.

Long after he had gone, I thought about his willingness to go door-to-door to tell others about Jesus. The rain didn't stop him; neither did his age. And, I figured, he must have visited a whole lot of folks, since he could size up strangers so quickly. Why, in a matter of seconds he had concluded I was a Christian, having nothing more to go on than the expression on my face, for I wasn't carrying a Bible or wearing "cross" jewelry.

Puzzled though I was about his correct assessment of me, I understood that faces, particularly the eyes, express more about a person than they realize, especially during unguarded moments when expressions mirror the soul.

While reflecting on that truth, I prayed, "Lord, thank You for the reminder You sent to me about how transparent we are to others even when we don't know that we are! And I'm glad the man easily detected the presence of Jesus in my heart. May that evidence always be there!"

Johnnie Ann Burgess Gaskill

Uninvited

Our church choir enjoyed a delicious meal at a local restaurant. As the waitress cleared the table where I was sitting, our Minister of Music said to her, "Have we been nice to you?"

"Yes, you have."

"Well," I said, "if you were to come to our church you'd find out how nice a whole lot of people can be."

"As a matter of fact," she said eagerly, "my husband and I have been looking for a church. We've only lived in the area for a month and haven't decided just where to go."

"Have we got a great church for you!" I said as I searched my purse for a business card to give her. "Here. This shows the times of the services. And," I added, "there's a map on the back."

She accepted the card, then said, "You know, we serve a lot of preachers and church folks, especially on Sunday, but no one has ever invited me to their church."

What an indictment! What a message of unconcern had been sent to that precious woman who wanted to find a church she could call home. I couldn't point any accusing fingers at anyone else without realizing that I, too, was guilty of the same sin of unconcerned silence. Though I had not been in that particular restaurant for more than a year, I had eaten at other establishments and had failed to ask those who served me there about their church affiliation.

I may not feel comfortable sharing the plan of salvation with everyone, but I can invite them to worship with my congregation. If they already have a church home, fine. If not, then I can at least let them know about one local church where they can go and find a group of people who love the Lord and who will love and care for them as well.

Thinking about the waitress' words caused me to ask, "Lord, are there others I have neglected?"

He immediately brought to my mind neighbors, as well as people whom I see regularly but do not know personally: the inactive members of our church, parents of my children's friends, and many folks who need an invitation to attend Bible study and worship services where they can hear the Word of God explained to them and where they will have an opportunity to respond to God's invitation to salvation and/or service.

As the Lord brought so many people to my mind, I asked Him to forgive for my sin of unconcern and silence. I asked Him to make me sensitive to the people around me, to help me see them as persons rather than as faces in the crowd, for each individual carries special burdens; each needs to be loved.

Although I can't "save the world," I can make a difference in the lives of those God places in my path.

Johnnie Ann Burgess Gaskill

Amazing Grace

The woman blinked back tears as she told me about her mother's illness and death. I could hear the pain in her voice as she spoke of the times when her mother neither recognized her nor was able to speak.

"As her brain tumor spread, Mother slept more and more each day. But, Johnnie, one day when Mother had been unable to say one word, she suddenly started singing 'Amazing Grace.' Her voice was perfectly clear as she sang those beautiful words." Wiping tears, she whispered, "I won't ever forget that moment."

I sensed how grateful she was for that unexpected blessing. In the midst of one of the darkest times in her life, God gave my friend's precious mother the ability to testify to His amazing grace and to comfort her heart-broken daughter as well.

I'm sure my friend will never sing the words to "Amazing Grace" again without remembering how her mother used some of her last breaths to testify to the truth contained within them.

And His grace truly is amazing! Only by His grace are we able to reverence Him. Only by His grace are we even permitted to hear and to believe that Jesus died for our sins. Only by His grace are we brought through difficulties rather destroyed by them. Only by His grace are we assured of His presence with us all the days of this life and in the life to come. Only by His grace can we rejoice, even in the darkest hours of our lives.

As we sing and speak about God's goodness to us, we honor Him and encourage others whose strength may be failing or whose faith may be giving away to doubt. The words of praise we offer become like ripples in the water. Like the dropping of a stone, our words are heard only for a moment but their effect goes on and on.

Nancy's mother's words of praise caused ripples not only in Nancy's life but also in mine, as well as those with whom I share them. May the ripples of praise continue on and on as we joyfully speak and sing about God's amazing grace.

Reflections

Are You Listening, God?

Clutching the phone in his hand, the six-year-old boy seemed oblivious to the tears streaming down his face. As I entered the church office, the friend who was waiting for him came up to me and said matter-of-factly, "He's gotta call his mother. She's supposed to pick him up after Sunday School and she ain't here."

"That's fine," I replied and stepped into the adjoining closet-size room to use the copier. Naturally, I couldn't help overhearing what the child was saying.

"Mama! This is Larry (name changed). If you are home, please come and get me."

Larry sobbed again, then said, "Mama! This is Larry. If you are home, please pick up the phone."

My heart broke as I heard the increasing desperation in his voice. "Mama!" he said even more loudly. "If you can hear me, please pick up. Please! Please!"

He sobbed quietly as he waited for his mother to respond. When she didn't, he hung up.

I left the copier and went to see what I could do for the little fellow. I noticed that the friend remained calm even though Larry was almost hysterical. The friend told me how they had searched the parking lot for Larry's mom. "We even ran almost all the way back to the road to look for her, but we didn't see her *anywhere*."

I acknowledged his comments with a smile and an understanding nod. Then I bent down and talked to Larry. Once I was eye level with him, I offered him a tissue and said, "You go check the parking lot one more time. I'll wait right here in case your mom calls back."

Larry managed a weak smile.

"Now if your mother isn't out there," I said, "you come right back here and we'll decide what to do. Okay?"

Larry nodded. He and his friend left the office.

I waited by the phone for several minutes before going out to the parking lot to check on them. When I did not see the two boys anywhere, I felt confident Larry's mom had picked them up. *She must have been on her way here when Larry called her*, I thought. I pictured Larry's happy face as he climbed into the car.

Feeling relieved that the "crisis" was over, I entered the sanctuary for the morning worship service. However, I had difficulty concentrating on the music because I kept seeing Larry's tear-stained face and hearing his desperate pleadings.

Larry had been so fearful, so uncertain about his mother's whereabouts and what would happen to him if she didn't come for him. Suddenly, I realized that his behavior was typical of adults when we face a crisis. Fear comes upon us, and we cry out, "God, where are You? Are You there? Please help me!"

If God doesn't immediately do what we ask of Him, then we turn our tear-stained faces heavenward and with desperate voices beg God to respond. We say, "God, if You can hear me, please answer. Please! Please!"

Even when help is on the way, we sometimes think that God is silent, that He isn't responding to us. We plead with God, as David the Psalmist did: "O LORD, you are my rock of safety. Please help me; don't refuse to answer me. For if you are silent, I might as well give up and die. Listen to my prayer for mercy as I cry out to you for help, as I lift my hands toward your holy sanctuary" (Psalm 28:1-2).

After pleading with God in much the same way as Larry had with his mother, David realized that his cries had not fallen on deaf ears. David said, "Praise the LORD! For he has heard my cry for mercy. The LORD is my strength, my shield from every danger. I trust in him with all my heart. He helps me, and my heart is filled with joy. I burst out in songs of thanksgiving" (Psalm 28:6-7).

Though David, like Larry, may have felt that his message wasn't getting through, help was on the way. God never ignores the cries of His children. Neither does He forget to take care of us. Be assured of that.

Hurt In the Heart of a Parent

One day as I stood beside Jena, a friend of mine walked up and said, "Johnnie, what are you going to do with two grown girls?"

I looked at my fourteen-year-old and, with a twinkle in my eye, said, "Guess I'll have to marry them off!"

The three of us laughed. Then my friend said, "Well, at least you have girls and will get to see them after they get married." She hesitated then added, "We seldom see our son. His wife keeps him busy with other things."

We looked at each other and I saw the tears in her eyes. "That hurts a mother's heart, doesn't it?" I said gently.

She nodded and walked away.

I thought about her for many days thereafter. She came to my mind again the day I read one of God's messages to His people. Remembering my friend's emotional pain helped me understand God's heartache as He described His parenting of the nation of Israel.

"When Israel was a child, I loved him as a son, and I called my son out of Egypt. But the more I called to him, the more he rebelled, offering sacrifices to the images of Baal and burning incense to idols. It was I who taught Israel how to walk, leading him along by the hand. But he doesn't know or even care that it was I who took care of him. I led Israel along with my ropes of kindness and love. I lifted the yoke from his neck, and I myself stooped to feed him…[even so,] my people are determined to desert me. They call me the Most High, but they don't truly honor me. Oh, how can I give you up, Israel. How can I let you go?" (Hosea 11:1-8a).

God's children broke His heart, and they missed out on the blessings that could have been theirs if they had not abandoned the One who loved them. How grateful we ought to be that He is also our Father who loves us and wants us to love Him. Why deprive Him, and ourselves as well, of a parent-child relationship that will bring inexpressible joy and blessing? Why bring tears to the eyes of our loving Father?

Johnnie Ann Burgess Gaskill

Jewels or Zirconias?

A few years ago, a new Sunday School class needed a name. As the teacher, I encouraged each of the ladies in the class to think about an appropriate name and to be ready to make suggestions on a given date.

As we assembled that Sunday morning, I asked the class members to share their ideas. Though several appropriate names were suggested, the group did not respond enthusiastically to any of them. After several minutes, we ran out of names. Silence prevailed. I suggested, "Why don't we consider using alliteration? Names with repeated initial consonants sound creative and are fun to say."

They liked that idea. Several serious-sounding names were offered, but when none seemed right for our class, we began to get silly. Someone asked, "How about 'Wonderful Women' or 'Lovely Ladies'?"

I laughed. "Since we aren't wonderful and lovely all the time, a name like that would be hard to live up to, wouldn't it?" The class agreed.

"I know! I know! I've got the perfect name for us!" said one lady who always kept us laughing. "Let's call ourselves 'Jesus' Jewels.'"

When the laughter died down, I said, "If we choose that name, we'll have to make sure we are jewels rather than cubic zirconias!"

After those lighthearted moments, we settled down and selected an appropriate name for ourselves, one that was neither boastful nor pious.

Long after we had the selection of a name behind us, I continued to think about "Jesus' Jewels." I recalled an Old Testament passage that mentioned jewels (in the King James Version). I located the verse in a modern translation and read it carefully. "Then those who feared the LORD spoke with each other, and the LORD listened to what they said. In his presence, a scroll of remembrance was written to record the names of those who feared him and loved to think about him. 'They will be my people,' says the LORD Almighty. 'On the day when I act, they will be my own special treasure [*jewels*, in the KJV]. I will spare them as a father spares an obedient and dutiful child. Then you will again see the difference between the righteous and the wicked, between those who serve God and those who do not" (Malachi 3:16,18).

Though I usually feel more like a cubic zirconia, the desire of my heart is to be a genuine jewel, and I will be if I am the kind of person who reverences the Lord and speaks often to others about Him.

However, before I tell others how wonderful He is, I must personally know and worship the Lord. Reading the Bible, meditating on its truths, and obeying its commands helps me put the Lord first and foremost in my thoughts. Once I've done those things, speaking often and spontaneously about Him comes easily and naturally because I've saturated my mind with thoughts of Him.

Perhaps one day I (and you, too, dear reader!) will be one of the jewels Jesus claims for His own.

Johnnie Ann Burgess Gaskill

Waiting for Clearance

Speaking in a well-modulated voice, the pilot said, "We are waiting for clearance. We expect to be cleared for takeoff within the next three or four minutes."

As we waited, I noticed that other planes were arriving and departing, so I did not question the pilot's decision to wait for clearance. Only a foolish pilot would have taken off whenever he wanted to rather than wait for permission and instructions from the control tower.

A shiver ran up my spine as I thought about the disaster that would have occurred if our pilot had taken matters into his own hands. What if he had looked at his watch and said, "We were scheduled to leave Boston at 7:04 p.m. It's 7:45 and we still aren't airborne. I'd better hurry up and get this flight underway or we'll really arrive late in Atlanta. Some passengers have connecting flights, and they are depending on me to get them there in time to change planes. So, I'm taking off, with or without clearance."

What if the pilot had said, "This plane is ready to go. It has been refueled. All the instruments are working properly. The engines are humming. The flight attendants have made all the necessary preparations. Why wait around? Yep, I'm taking off, with or without clearance."

What if the pilot had said, "I am a well-trained, experienced, highly-respected pilot. I have both the authority and the ability to fly this plane. What right do the people in the control tower have to put me on hold? Don't they know who I am? I'm taking off, with or without clearance."

If any of the "what ifs" I imagined had taken place, Delta's flight 981 would have made front page news and I would not have written these words. Fortunately, the wise pilot yielded to authority and calmly announced, "We are waiting for clearance."

Those five words, which he probably said every time he prepared to takeoff, meant so much to me. They reminded me of something Jesus said, even though Jesus never said, "I am waiting for clearance." However, He did say, "But I do nothing without consulting the Father. I judge as I am told. And my judgment is absolutely just, because it is according to the will of God who sent me; it is not merely my own" (John 5:30).

He expressed a similar thought in another passage. "I don't speak on my own authority. The Father who sent me gave me his own instructions as to what I should say. And I know his instructions lead to eternal life; so I say whatever the Father tells me to say!" (John 12:49-50).

Reflections

If the Son of God and the well-trained pilot waited for clearance, shouldn't we? Yes! As we sit on the runways of life, ready to take off to wherever God directs us, we ought to say, "Father, I am waiting for clearance. I will go only with Your permission and in accordance with Your instructions." If we fail to wait for clearance, we invite disaster!

Johnnie Ann Burgess Gaskill

Quit Looking Where You've Already Been

I did not turn around to stare at the man and the preschool child he had brought into the store, but his command to the child captured my attention. "Quit looking where you've already been!" he said angrily.

Although I didn't like the harsh tone of his voice, his words intrigued me. If he had spoken the familiar, "Look where you're going!" I might not have given his words a second thought. But his "Quit looking where you've already been" stuck in my mind.

Though "Quit looking where you've already been!" is a negative command, it contains as much good advice as its positive counterpart. There is a difference between being aware of the past and of being fixated on it. The past, the place where we have already been, needs to be remembered and evaluated; however, we stumble in the present if we look too long at where we've already been instead of looking at where we are going.

The Apostle Paul decided to quit looking where he had aready been, though he used different words to express his decision. After mentioning his background and his accomplishments, Paul said, "I once thought all these things were so very important, but now I consider them worthless because of what Christ has done…Yes, everything else is worthless when compared with the priceless gain of knowing Christ Jesus my Lord…I don't mean to say that I have already…reached perfection! But I keep working **toward** that day when I will finally be all that Christ Jesus saved me for and wants me to be. No, dear brothers and sisters, I am still not all I should be, but I am focusing all my energies on this one thing: **Forgetting the past and looking forward to what lies ahead**, I strain to reach the end of the race and receive the prize for which God, through Christ Jesus, is calling us up to heaven" (Philippians 3:4-14, emphasis added).

Although Paul remembered how his religious zeal had initially caused him to reject Jesus Christ and to violently persecute those who believed in Him (1 Timothy 1:12-15), the sufferings he endured after becoming a Christian (2 Corinthians 11:23-33), and the joy of loving and being loved by those to whom he had preached the Good News of Christ (Acts 20:36-38), Paul knew that focusing too intently on them would cause him to stumble and to lose sight of the good things that lay ahead. Therefore, if Paul were to borrow the words the man spoke to the child, Paul would say, "Quit looking where you've already been! Focus on what's ahead, and you will avoid a lot of missteps."

Reflections

Conversations of Substance

A friend who volunteered regularly at my work place always regaled us with delightful stories and quotes as we performed our duties. One day she told the story of a group of monks who were allowed to speak only once a year. In order to maintain silence and solemnity, only one monk could speak each year.

The first year, one monk said, "I wish we didn't have to eat oatmeal."

After waiting 365 days to express his disagreement, a fellow monk replied, "I like oatmeal."

The third year, another monk had his long-awaited turn. "Oatmeal is okay, if it's not lumpy."

After years of waiting for his chance to speak, one of the monks said, "I like oatmeal whether it's lumpy or not. It's all this bickering I can't stand!"

When our laughter subsided, I said, "If I had waited an entire year to speak, I hope I'd be able to talk about something besides oatmeal."

That story made me see that many of us waste our thoughts and words on trivial subjects. Though we shouldn't discuss *only* serious, weighty matters, we do need to make sure the majority of our conversations have substance. Since being able to think and speak is a priceless privilege, we should express our gratitude by communicating in ways that build up rather than tear down. We ought to choose our words carefully and seize every opportunity to encourage, comfort, instruct, or affirm others.

The Psalmist knew that right thinking and talking must be a high priority. Therefore, he prayed, "Take control of what I say, O LORD, and keep my lips sealed" (Psalm 141:3).

The Psalmist didn't waste his time or that of his listeners/readers by discussing trivial matters. Instead, he chose to communicate wonderful truths about God: His forgiveness, His mercy, His tender care, His ability to rescue, His majesty, His power—to name only a few. Consequently, millions of people who have been instructed and blessed by the words of the Psalmist feel grateful that he didn't waste his words by bickering over the merits of oatmeal.

You and I may not be able to write or speak like the Psalmist or other excellent communicators, but we can follow the advice of the Apostle Paul. "Let your conversation be gracious and effective so that you will have the right answer for everyone" (Colossians 4:6).

Johnnie Ann Burgess Gaskill

A Verse to Remember

As I prepared to get out of her car, my friend handed me a piece of paper. "I thought you'd appreciate this," she said with a smile.

I read the neatly written words then started laughing. "This is our verse to remember, isn't it?" She nodded.

At that moment my friend and I enjoyed a special closeness that comes when two people who understand each other so well that they can laugh together about their weaknesses. My friend and I are both hopeless procrastinators—or so it seems. Knowing each other as we do and wanting to help each other overcome the mutual problems we face, we frequently share helpful suggestions we've discovered.

My friend and I aren't the only ones who procrastinate; at least I think we aren't, for almost every woman's magazine has an article that deals with it. One article I read placed procrastinators in four groups. The *perfectionists* fear they can't do the task perfectly, so they put off doing it at all. The *adventurers* rush into action at the last minute, enjoying that rush of adrenaline. R*ebels* delay in order to express their anger or resistance in a socially accepted way. *Decidophobics* procrastinate in order to avoid dealing with consequences of their decisions.

Whatever factors causes our procrastination, most of us procrastinators wait for perfect conditions before we take action. Yet, according to the verse my friend handed to me, that's exactly what we should **not** do. "If you wait for perfect conditions, you will never get anything done" (Ecclesiastes 11:4).

The Right Source of Power

The man expertly backed his tow truck up my driveway and aligned it with my car. He jumped from the truck, said a hurried hello, and began making some mechanical maneuvers that converted the silver flatbed of the tow truck into a ramp for my car. After he securely attached a chain to the rear of my Buick, he pushed a few buttons or levers on a little silver box that was mounted on the side of his tow truck. Doing that changed the ramp back into a flat bed, and my car was sitting high in the air on it.

"I'm intrigued by the device that you used to load my car," I said as I approached him with my check. "It must be something hydraulic."

"Yes, Ma'am. It's a hydraulic roll back."

I wanted to ask him how it worked, but I felt I shouldn't detain him. I assumed that the silver box located in the area where he'd done his mechanical maneuvers contained the control panel for the hydraulic system. If so, it was quite small—in relationship to the size of the truck and my car—yet powerful enough to move the larger objects with ease.

As he drove away, I thought about how much time and energy the man would have wasted if he had insisted on trying to load the car all by himself. He probably would have lost money too, for he would have had to ignore other calls for help while he struggled to load my vehicle. I concluded that any person who refused to use the hydraulic roll back (or something similar) and chose to depend on self-effort would be foolish indeed.

Seizing a teachable moment, the Lord said to me, "Johnnie, do you see how your conclusion relates to Zechariah 4:6? You've marked it in your Bible; you've quoted it; but, you have not applied it to your life."

Instantly, the verse flashed into my mind. "…It is not by force nor by strength, but by My Spirit, says the LORD Almighty."

Though the original message was given centuries ago to a man named Zerubbabel, I recognized that my name was on the recipient list also. I responded by whispering, "Yes, Lord, I see that I have foolishly depended on human strength and ability instead of relying on the power that Your Holy Spirit makes available to me. Forgive me. Each time I'm tempted to depend on my own strength instead of Yours, just send me a mental picture of how easily the hydraulic roll back placed my car on the tow truck."

Johnnie Ann Burgess Gaskill

Well-worn Bibles

A missionary from South Africa showed slides and told interesting stories about the people with whom he had shared the Gospel. The stories he told touched my heart and caused me to examine my own level of commitment to Christ (the Living Word) and to the Bible (the Written Word).

The missionary told of one woman to whom he had given a Bible that had been translated into her language. As she read and reread the precious truths contained therein, she used her finger to "keep her place." Within one year, she asked for a new one.

"She had worn out her Bible. There was not one page in the entire Bible that was completely readable. By moving her finger so often over each verse, she had rubbed the print right off the pages. When I saw her worn out Bible, I gladly gave her a new one."

As the missionary talked, I thought about my own Bible, the one I'd used for more than fifteen years. It was showing signs of use—underlining of key passages, notes in the margins, post-it-notes with additional bits of related information, and the like—but it was not worn-out—far from it.

I felt the same kind of painful shame I had at the time a friend said, "My mama read the Bible through twenty-three times. In fact, she continued to read it until she was too weak to hold it up."

I felt ashamed again when the missionary told us about how those enrolled in Bible correspondence schools memorized twenty verses of Scripture each week! I was struggling to learn two for MasterLife and one for Sunday School.

Reading and memorizing Scripture shouldn't be relegated to people who are old and sick or for folks in faraway places. You and I should commit to read it daily, to study it, to think about it, and to allow it to transform our lives. In fact, the writer of Psalm 119 listed many of the benefits that result from knowing and applying Bible truths. He pointed out that that knowing the Bible not only keeps us from sinning so much, but it also ministers to us when we grieve (v.28), helps us reverence God (v.38), makes us wiser than our enemies (v.98), provides guidance (v.105) and much, much more.

As the people in South Africa and my friend's mother knew, reading and obeying God's Word is not an unpleasant Christian duty. Rather it is an essential and enjoyable activity that brings the blessings mentioned by the Psalmist. The more we read the truth and obey it, the more intensely we desire to know more of the truths contained in the Written Word.

Reflections

May each of us make this promise to God: "I will study your commandments and reflect on your ways. I will delight in your principles and not forget your word" (Psalm 119:15,16).

Johnnie Ann Burgess Gaskill

"Planting" a Loved One

We walked slowly from the church to the nearby grassy slope. We said little as we gathered under the tent. The family sat in the chairs provided by the funeral home; our friends stood nearby. All of us looked at the closed coffin poised above the open grave.

I don't recall much of what the minister said that day. However, one sentence captured my attention and has continued to comfort me. At the time, his words sounded so strange that I questioned them. Perhaps my puzzling over them prevented me from remembering much else he said.

As the rain fell gently all around the tent and a cold wind blew, the minister said, "Remember we are not burying this dear one; we are planting her." Now I'd heard many ministers speak words of comfort to grieving families and friends, but I'd never heard the biblical truth about death and the resurrection expressed in those terms.

Even though the minister's words sounded foreign at first, I began to realize that the Apostle Paul had written a similar truth to the Christians at Corinth. In his letter to them, Paul reiterated his belief that death was not the end of life and that bodies will not stay in the grave forever but will be resurrected. Anticipating that his listeners would have questions about the process, Paul gave them an illustration they would understand. "When you put a seed into the ground, it doesn't grow into a plant unless it dies first. And what you put in the ground is not the plant that will grow, but only a dry little seed of wheat or whatever it is you are planting. Then God gives it a new body—just the kind he wants it to have. A different kind of plant grows from each kind of seed. And just as there are different kinds of seeds and plants, so also there are different kinds of flesh—whether of humans, animals, birds, or fish.

"There are bodies in the heavens, and there are bodies on earth. The glory of the heavenly bodies is different from the beauty of the earthly bodies...It is the same way for the resurrection of the dead. Our earthly bodies, which die and decay, will be different when they are resurrected, for they will never die. Our bodies now disappoint us, but when they are raised, they will be full of glory. They are weak now, but when they are raised, they will be full of power. They are natural human bodies now, but when they are raised, they will be spiritual bodies" (1 Corinthians 15:36-44).

Having said that the spiritual body will be just as real as the physical one, Paul explained why the earthly body must be exchanged for a spiritual one. "...flesh and blood cannot inherit the Kingdom of God. These perishable bodies of ours are not able to live forever. But let me tell you a wonderful secret God has revealed to us. Not all of us will die, but we will all be transformed. It will happen in a moment, in the blinking of an eye, when the last trumpet is blown. For when the trumpet sounds, the Christians who have died will be raised with transformed bodies. And then we who are living will be transformed so that we will never die. For our perishable earthly bodies must be transformed into heavenly bodies that will never die" (1 Corinthians 15:50-53).

Even though Paul did not say how the spiritual body will look and respond, he did emphasize that it will be far superior to the physical one. To help his readers understand that, Paul chose the analogy of planting a seed. The dry little seed the farmer plants in the dirt gives not even a *hint* of the appearance of the plant that will come from it. In like manner, the physical body that is planted in the earth does not reveal the glorious body it will become whenever it is raised from the grave.

The minister was exactly right. We had indeed "planted" the body of our loved one in the earth where it awaits the resurrection. One day it will come forth. I do not know what my sister will look like, but I am fully assured that her new body will be a glorious one, for God designed it and especially fitted it to live eternally in heaven. That comforts me.

Johnnie Ann Burgess Gaskill

A Time to Begin Again

As my two friends and I finished walking our second mile on the streets in our quiet, suburban neighborhood, Bob and I recalled the days when, as children, we swept our yards with the brooms our mothers made from broom sage. We laughed when Bob quipped, "If we ever saw any grass growing in the yard, we'd pull it up."

I immediately visualized the large yard in which I used to play. We swept it only during the dry weeks of the year, for the Georgia red clay turned to mud on rainy days. I'm not sure why we put up with dust half the year and mud the other half, but we did. To this day, I enjoy the smell created by rain falling gently onto thirsty ground, but I also like the sight of lush grass bordered by shrubs and flowers.

As we continued our walk, I ceased my "wool gathering," and Bob and I started to tease Jackie, for we knew that she, a city girl, had grown up with grass in her yard. Turning to Bob, I said, "She's not as old as we are, is she?"

"Yes, I am!" she protested. When Jackie told us she was forty-one, I was surprised to know I was only two years older than she was, because my recollections were like those of a much older person, since I'd grown up in a rural area, far removed from the progressive ways of "city folks."

Much to our surprise, Bob stated, "Well, I'm only forty-four!"

Before we could let him know we didn't believe that for one second, he hastened to say, "Well, at least I'd like to be forty-four again!"

Jackie said, "I'd like to be twenty-four, too!"

"I don't know about that," I mused. "I wouldn't mind having the health of a twenty-four-year-old, but I'm not sure I want to repeat some of the experiences."

For a few minutes, we walked on in silence. "You know," I said, "if we'd taken care of ourselves, like we do now, we could have younger, healthier bodies. Too bad we waited so long to start taking our health seriously."

They agreed. We spent some time discussing our regrets. "If only I'd eaten less." "If only I'd eaten better." "If only I'd exercised regularly." Oh, yes, we'd known what to do and we'd understood why taking care of our bodies was important. Yet, we had not taken our health seriously—until we started "falling apart."

Thankfully, the three of us had finally come to our senses and started doing those things we should have been doing for years. I think each of us realized that even though we could not turn back the clock, we could make a major change in the hours ahead.

As we continued walking, I said, "You know, it really is sad how we refuse to take things seriously. It seems that we wait until something precious is about to be taken away before we realize how little attention we've given to it."

After we returned to our own homes, I continued to think about how careless many of us are about the things that should concern us the most. Vital relationships wither and die from lack of attention. Children mature overnight, much to the surprise of their parents. Our neighborhoods deteriorate while we take few, if any, preventative measures. Our freedoms are slowly taken away, and we don't seem to notice, at least not enough to protest their removal.

Even our relationship with God often receives little attention. We wander away from Him a little bit at a time. We stay so busy with living that we set aside no time for the One who gives us life and sustains us. We are so intent on reaching *our* goals that we seldom seriously consider what He wants us to do and/or to be. Only when we see tell-a-tale signs that our lives are "falling apart" do we wish that we had lived differently.

Even though we can't retrace our steps, we can determine to make the rest of our lives better. Positive changes begin when we spend time alone with Him—reading His Word, talking with Him, seeking His will for our lives—and walk in obedience to Him.

God doesn't allow us to return to the past, but He does permit us to make new starts, to "do better" from this moment forward.

As we begin again, these words give us confidence: "Trust in the LORD and do good. Then you will live safely in the land and prosper. Take delight in the LORD, and he will give you your heart's desires. Commit everything you do to the LORD. Trust him, and he will help you" (Psalm 37:3-5). Doing so won't turn back the clock, but it will enable us to live fully, abundantly, and joyfully *now*, regardless of the mistakes we made in the past. Thank God, it's never too late to begin again!

Johnnie Ann Burgess Gaskill

Something Special About Him

From the moment he entered my office, I sensed something special about him. His greeting was warm and sincere, his smile genuine, and his voice gentle and pleasant. I immediately felt at ease in his presence.

We talked as I located the video tapes he wanted to borrow. I learned that he was eighty-four-years-old, though he appeared much younger, and that he was the father of six sons. As he called the names of his children, he spoke each name so lovingly that I could tell he considered each child to be a precious gift from the Lord.

While talking about his family, he mentioned his wife who had died a few years previously. I noticed a pensive, far-away look in his eyes as he remembered her. He said, "My, what sweet times we had together...praying for our children. We prayed that God would call at least one of our sons into the ministry. Now we have four sons who are deacons, one who is a minister, and one who is serving on the foreign mission field. As he went on to tell me about his grandchildren and great grandchildren, he rejoiced that all the members of his immediate family had accepted Jesus as their Savior.

We talked about many things during the brief time he was in my office—his garden, his chiropractor friend and his family, his church, and so forth. I did not hear him say anything negative. He spoke well of each individual and of each situation, and acknowledged each as a blessing from the Lord. And, he didn't do so in a phony or pious manner. He wasn't the kind of person who went around parroting the phrase "Praise the Lord! Praise the Lord!" Yet, praised flowed from his lips constantly and spontaneously. He could no more withhold his praise than a rose could withhold its sweet fragrance.

As the conversation shifted from one topic to another, the warm, gentle smile never left his face. Though tears often filled his eyes, the glow remained on his countenance. To be in his presence was such a joy, such a special blessing.

Later in the day, I told my daughter about him. "Jennifer, being in his presence was like being in the presence of an angel. He had such a sweetness about him...such a gentle spirit, such a tender heart, such a..." I couldn't find just the right words to describe him. Then I recalled a verse that helped me complete my description of him. After Peter and John (disciples of Jesus) had been arrested for preaching the Good News that Jesus had risen from the dead, they were brought before the Sanhedrin. "The members of [that] council were amazed when they saw the boldness of Peter and John, for they could see that they were ordinary men who had no special training. They also recognized them as men who had been with Jesus" (Acts 4:13).

Then I knew how to describe the godly man whose presence had been such an inspiration to me. *He, too, had been with Jesus.* Through many hours of talking to the Lord, through years of living in obedience to His Word, and through years of telling others about Jesus, this dear man had become like Christ: humble, gentle, kind, loving, sincere, positive, affirming, saddened by the evil around him, thinking of others before himself, ministering to their needs even before they were expressed, praising God, longing to go to the Father...

How we need more people who spend time with the Lord and reflect Him in their speech, in their attitudes, in their lifestyle, and in their faces. How we benefit from being in their presence. How we need to become that kind of person. And, such a transformed life is possible. The man proved that to me!

Johnnie Ann Burgess Gaskill

Prepared for Life and for Death

Just before ten o'clock on the morning of August 24, 1991, someone banged loudly and repeatedly on our front door. I immediately turned off the iron and ran upstairs. By the time I'd opened the door, our neighbor was already halfway across our yard and on his way back home. When he heard me open the door, he turned and said, "Johnnie, come quick. Jessie's hurt real bad. I think she may be dead."

We ran across the street and other neighbors joined us as they realized something was terribly wrong. After checking for a pulse and finding none, we waited for the paramedics to arrive and confirm what we already knew. Throughout the rest of the day, a steady steam of people came to the house. Many, many times we related the story of finding Jessie's body at the foot of the patio steps.

Late that night when things had settled down a bit, I paused to reflect on the happenings of the day. During those quiet moments, I had to face the fact that my neighbor and friend for eighteen years had died.

I remembered her as an energetic lady who looked younger than her actual age of eighty-three. I thought about her quick smile, her eyes that sparkled over little pleasures, her beautiful white hair that was always styled to perfection, and her neat appearance. I recalled how she always expressed her thanks for every kindness shown to her. She freely offered sincere compliments and always spoke well of others. She delighted in the neighborhood children and enjoyed watching them grow up.

My mind raced through many experiences we'd shared over the years. I recalled the time she came to visit me when I had been in the hospital in 1982. She brought me a tiny red rose bud encased in a tear-shaped, glass container that was still sitting on my kitchen window sill as a reminder of her. I remembered the many long talks we had had about so many subjects: the good old days, our families, decisions, ailments, death of loved ones, and, of course, the Lord.

While thinking about Jessie and the many things that made her special, I realized that one of the traits I most admired was her preparedness. I'd never seen her when she didn't look nice. Though she may have been wearing only a simple housedress or slacks and a sweater, she was always ready to be around people. Even when she'd spent weeks in the hospital, she still looked attractive.

Likewise, she kept her house immaculate. She never had to apologize when anyone dropped in unexpectedly. Even when she prepared meals, she never made a mess in her kitchen. She liked driving a clean car, too, and she kept the tank filled with her favorite premium gasoline.

Reflections

Thus, it was no surprise that on the day of her death her house was in perfect order. I knew that her spiritual life was in order also. She had told me that years ago she had trusted Jesus as her Savior and that He had become her closest, dearest friend. Therefore, she had made deliberate preparation for her "home-going," though she didn't know when she would leave this world.

As I considered how prepared she was and how much I admired that trait, I recalled a few of the many times the Bible instructs us to be prepared, to be ready. For example, Jesus told several parables that emphasized the necessity of being ready. And Paul encouraged young Timothy to be prepared at all times to preach the Gospel The prophet Amos urged the people to prepare to meet their God. (Amos 4:12).

I am grateful for such admonitions found in God's Word. I am also thankful to have had a precious friend who showed me that it is possible to be prepared in life and to be prepared in death.

Johnnie Ann Burgess Gaskill

When Weeping Won't Stop

"I am disappointed, so very disappointed," a friend said. My heart went out to him as I noticed the tears in his eyes. I knew the unexpected setback was hard to accept, especially when he had been moving "full steam ahead" in the direction he felt God wanted him to go.

After we'd talked a bit longer, I said, "I am sorry you are having to deal with this disappointment. However, I am glad you are not ashamed to admit your feelings. Many of us in the Christian community aren't honest or courageous enough to share our true feelings. Instead, we dry our tears, put on our fake smiles, and never let anyone know we are dying on the inside."

My friend managed a tiny smile. "I do love the Lord with all my heart," he said, "but I am also human. At this moment I do feel such tremendous disappointment."

"It's okay for you to feel that way and to express it," I answered. "Don't deny your feelings."

I reminded him of Job, a man who "was blameless, a man of complete integrity. He feared God and stayed away from evil" (Job 1:1). At the beginning of the biblical account of Job's life, he seems to have everything going for him. In addition to being a wealthy and prominent citizen, he was also the father of seven sons and three daughters. But, through no fault of his own, Job experienced a series of unexpected setbacks—tragedies, actually. All his children died. Job lost all his servants and his livestock. If that weren't enough to bear, Job's entire body was covered with sores that itched intensely and caused him great pain.

At that low point, Job's wife erroneously concluded that he was suffering because God was unfair and advised Job to "Curse God and die."

"But Job replied, 'You talk like a godless woman. Should we accept only good things from the hand of God and never anything bad?' So, in all this, Job said nothing wrong" (Job 2:10).

Job trusted God so much that he could accept whatever the Lord allowed in his life—either good or adversity, either joy or sadness, either prosperity or poverty. Yet, having such great faith did not mean that Job did not seek answers from God as to why suffering had come upon him.

Even though God never explained the reason for Job's adversities, the opportunity to openly discuss his feelings gave Job some measure of relief. Job did not hide his true feelings from his friends who came to comfort him or from God. He expressed his agony. "Why didn't I die at birth as I came from the womb? Why did my mother let me live? Why did she nurse me at her breasts? For if I had died at birth, I would be at peace now, asleep, and at rest…Why is life given to those with no future, those destined by God to live in distress? I cannot eat for sighing; my groans pour out like water…I have no peace, no quietness. I have no rest; instead, only trouble comes" (Job 3:11-26).

When we suffer, we can do what Job did. We can identify and deal with our feelings, then express them to trusted friends and to God. After all, our thoughts and feelings are not hidden from God, even if we refuse to acknowledge them.

David expressed it this way: "O LORD, you have examined my heart and know everything about me. You know when I sit down or stand up. You know my every thought when far away. You chart the path ahead of me and tell me where to stop and rest. Every moment you know where I am. You know what I am going to say even before I say it, LORD. You both precede and follow me" (Psalm 139:1-5a).

Knowing that there is a God who understands us and loves us brings comfort to us, even if we, like Job, never understand why God allows unexpected trials and tragedies. But whatever God chooses for us has a purpose, and God will cause all things to work together for His glory and our good, as the Apostle Paul says in Romans 8:28. Even when things don't make sense, we can also be fully assured of this great truth: "No good thing will the LORD withhold from those who do what is right. O LORD Almighty, happy are those who trust in you" (Psalm 84:11b-12).

As we deal with our difficulties and disappointments, we can take comfort in these words of the Psalmist: "Weeping may go on all night, but joy comes with the morning" (Psalm 30:5b). Until that joy comes, we can tell God all about the pain and the frustrations we feel—and fully trust Him all the while.

Johnnie Ann Burgess Gaskill

He's Just Remembering Me

I walked to the shelves to locate the videotape the man had requested. Upon finding it, I said, "I'm glad the video you wanted is in. Usually whenever someone needs a specific tape that will be the very one that's checked out."

The man smiled and said slowly, "Well, the Lord knows what I'm doing, and He's just remembering me."

Both his words and the easy manner in which he spoke them let me know that he trusted the Lord to provide everything he needed in order to do the work God had assigned to him. And I knew he had been given a big task: starting a mission church. Yet, I did not sense any stress, any tension, any agitation, or any uncertainty on his part as he obeyed God. Instead, there was a certain calmness about him, a quiet confidence, an assurance that God would supply *all* his needs. He was grateful, of course, but not surprised.

After he left my office, I continued to think about his statement: "Well, the Lord knows what I'm doing, and He's just remembering me." I considered the many times when the Lord, who also knew exactly what I was doing and what my needs were, remembered me. For example, when obeying God had become difficult, a stranger called to encourage me. If a friend had called, I could have passed it off as being an expected thing. But I knew beyond a doubt that God was involved when I answered the phone and heard an unfamiliar voice.

The lady who called could not have known anything about my struggle to obey God for we had never met nor did we have mutual friends. She knew me only through reading my weekly newspaper columns. She called to express her thanks and to let me know how God had used a particular column to bless her and some other ladies in her church.

God also knows what I'm doing and remembers me when I'm faced with a writing deadline. Sometimes He provides an unexpected block of time. For example, one morning my walking partner called to say she could not meet me at our regular time. Thus, I had an extra hour to write. Sometimes God's provision is in the form of the ability to stay alert even when I am exhausted. He always provides the inspiration and the ability to write.

Mentally recalling some of the countless times when God remembered me caused me to praise Him. My thanks and my praise increased all the more as I thought about these words of David the Psalmist: "You made all the delicate, inner parts of my body and knit me together in my mother's womb. Thank you for making me so wonderfully complex! Your workmanship is marvelous—and how well I know it. You watched me as I was being formed in utter seclusion, as I was woven together in the dark of the womb. You saw me before I was born. Every day of my life was recorded in your book. Every moment was laid out before a single day had passed" (Psalm 139:13-16).

Even before my birth, God knew all about me. Should I, then, be surprised that He still knows what I am doing and remembers me? Should I be surprised that He anticipates my needs and make provisions for me? Grateful, yes. Surprised, no.

Johnnie Ann Burgess Gaskill

The Side Effects of Self-Neglect

As the three of us walked along, the conversation shifted from one subject to another as rapidly as the ball being used in a professional tennis match. Near the end of our time together, however, we settled on one topic. As we began talking about people who worked long hours without taking a break, I began to share some insights I'd received from a psychiatrist who had spoken at a "Lunch and Learn" meeting I'd attended recently.

The speaker had said, "Women who self-neglect exhibit certain symptoms, among them: chronic fatigue, a feeling of emptiness, loss of pleasure, and body tension that manifests itself in physical ways, such as: grinding of the teeth, back problems, gastrointestinal disorders, and the like.

"Women who self-neglect frequently are angry with everyone. They have overriding physical complaints. Probably the most significant symptom is that they have difficulty in qualifying. By that I mean that they have no outer limits, no idea how much they should do. Therefore, they keep on working, working, working.

"For example," the psychiatrist continued, "women who self-neglect often suffer from recurring bladder infections because they refuse to stop working long enough to take bathroom breaks. Many women either delay lunch until two or three in the afternoon or skip it altogether, not because they are forced to do so but because they choose to work rather than to take care of themselves.

"When these women finally get into therapy and begin to understand the importance of taking care of themselves, they will try to make time for themselves. Even when they do spend a few minutes reading a book, soaking in the tub, or taking a walk, they usually do not delete any other activity from their hectic schedule. They simply add on the 'good' activity suggested by the therapist."

The psychiatrist had also explained why women self-neglect and she had mentioned various techniques used to help them learn to take care of themselves, but I didn't have time to share that information with my friends. Our walk was over.

When we arrived at my street, I said, "See ya in the morning," and started home.

As I walked up the hill, one friend called out, "Johnnie, we're going to call you at work today to see if you've taken your breaks and eaten your lunch at noon!"

"Don't do that," I yelled. "I only go to workshops to learn how to help other people!"

We laughed and said no more about the subject. However, I couldn't stop thinking about what I had said. Though I intended for my response to be funny—and the three of us *had* laughed at it—I realized that it contained a lot of truth—too much truth!

Late that night, I finally took time to sit down with my concordance and my Bible. I located the passage of Scripture in which the Apostle Paul described what people will be like during the "last days." He said that there would be people who would be forever following new teachings, yet be unable to grasp the truth. (See 2 Timothy 3:7.)

Gaining information, I realized, is an important part of the learning process but it is never the goal. Facts, insights, principles, and solutions must be discovered, then applied, experienced, and/or incorporated into our lives.

If we hear the truth and fail to allow it to change us, then this very sad phrase will apply to us: "ever learning, never doing."

Johnnie Ann Burgess Gaskill

A Remarkable Decision

When the lady handed me an annual report that had taken hours to prepare, I smiled and said, "Now that you've had so much fun with this, you're ready to celebrate, aren't you?"

I expected her to agree readily and to give me a play-by-play account of her struggles to prepare the report. (That's what others always did!) Instead, she smiled, looked me straight in the eye, and said, "I enjoyed doing it."

My face registered my surprise, for she explained, "I make up my mind to enjoy whatever task I have to do."

I thought, *What an unusual lady! What a remarkable decision*!

Long after she left the office, I continued to think about her words. The more I thought about them, the more they made sense, even though some tasks aren't enjoyable in and of themselves. For instance, I don't find cleaning bathrooms or washing endless loads of clothes particularly exciting. I can think of much more fun things to do on any given day, but since these chores have to be done, why not choose to keep a positive attitude while doing them?

While doing mundane chores, I try to follow the advice someone gave me years ago. As I wash the clothes, I thank God for providing them, and I thank Him for the loved ones who wore them. When I clean bathrooms, I thank God for indoor plumbing, for I remember what it's like to have to use an outhouse and to carry water from a distant spring. When I sweep wheelbarrow loads of pine straw from the driveway each Fall, I thank God for the beauty of the seasons even though each one brings added work.

When the load gets heavy at the office, I thank God for the privilege of serving Him in the position He has enabled me to have. I thank Him for health, and strength, and wisdom to do what is required.

I've noticed that when I have a thankful heart even the difficult tasks don't seem as unpleasant as they do if I do them with a bad attitude. However, I must admit that I don't always approach every task with an attitude of thanksgiving. Neither do I always enjoy each job. Nevertheless, I always have the option to choose my attitude toward the task at hand.

The Bible gives specific instructions regarding our attitudes toward work. In his letter to the Christians in Colosse, Paul advised, "And whatever you do or say, let it be as a representative of the Lord Jesus, all the while giving thanks through him to God the Father" (Colossians 3:17).

Later on in that same letter, Paul reminded them of this principle: "Work hard and cheerfully at whatever you do, as though you were working for the Lord rather than for people" (Colossians 3:23).

Reflections

Whatever our tasks—annual reports, laundry, yard work, relationships—we are to do each one as thoroughly and as thankfully as if we were doing them for the Lord Himself. After all, He is our Master. He is the one who will judge us and reward us accordingly.

Johnnie Ann Burgess Gaskill

Doubly Good!

One of our neighbors expressed his delight with a phrase I'd never heard anyone else use. For example, when we asked, "Did you get a good report from the doctor?" he answered, "Doubly good. Doubly good."

On more than one occasion he smiled and said, "I've got such good neighbors. Doubly good ones! My golfing buddies just can't believe it when I tell them what good neighbors I have. Doubly good. Doubly good."

Often I'd call and tell him what I was preparing, adding, "If you haven't eaten yet, I'll be glad to fix a plate for you." Then I'd smile as he said, "Why, that'd be doubly good. Doubly good."

He always expressed his thanks for every kindness shown to him, but when something was especially pleasing, he included "Doubly good" in his grateful acknowledgement. That was his highest compliment, one he used liberally but never indiscriminately.

Over the years we came to love him as if he were a member of our family. We cherished the things he said and did. We've heard him say "Doubly good!" so often during the thirty plus years he has been our friend, that we often use it, too. Whenever we do, we grin knowingly at each other, remembering pleasant memories of our former neighbor.

One day as I remembered his special phrase, a verse of Scripture popped into my mind. I located it in my Bible. "Taste and see that the LORD is good. Oh, the joys of those who trust in him!" (Psalm 34:8).

As I reflected on those words, I felt puzzled as to why I'd remembered that particular verse. I didn't see the connection between that verse and the phrase our neighbor had used.

Then I read the previous seven verses in that chapter and began to understand David had written those words of thanksgiving following one of the times when the Lord had delivered him from an enemy. "I cried out to the LORD in my suffering, and he heard me. He set me free from all my fears. For the angel of the LORD guards all who fear him, and he rescues them" (Psalm 34:6-7).

Because David felt such gratitude for what the Lord had done for him, he wanted the people to join him in praising the one who had delivered him. Therefore, he urged them to "taste and see that the LORD is good." David knew that when people experienced for themselves the goodness of the Lord, they would be so satisfied, so secure, so thrilled with the presence and power of the Lord that they would praise Him.

Like David, they would praise the Lord at all times. In both casual conversation and in worship services, they would continually magnify the Lord and exalt His name. That is, they would be eager to share what great things the Lord had done for them, thereby making him known to others and helping them to see His goodness and to desire to experience Him for themselves.

People who have "tasted" the Lord do understand that He is indeed good; or, as our former neighbor would say, "Doubly good. Doubly good."

Johnnie Ann Burgess Gaskill

The Highest Compliment

We attended a banquet honoring the eighth grade football players and cheerleaders. I listened attentively during the presentation of the certificates. I did that for two reasons: One, I wanted to be able to put faces with the names I'd heard mentioned during football season. Two, I wanted to hear the compliments paid to each player.

When the coach called out each name, he mentioned specific characteristics and skills that enabled that player to be an asset to the team. However, the highest compliment came near the very end of the program. One of the three coaches stood and said, "My wife and I have just learned we are going to have a son. I hope that he will have a heart like this young man." Then, after a long pause, he called out the name of the player. The applause was long for the young man, for everyone knew him, since he had truly had an outstanding year on the field.

For days after the banquet, I continued to think about the coach's words. One day as I was reading my Bible, these words from Paul's letter to the Christians at Philippi stood out on the page: "Every time I think of you, I give thanks to God" (Philippians 1:3).

I thought, *How marvelous it must be to be the kind of person for whom others give thanks to God. But does one have to be rich? Physically attractive? Successful? Famous? I don't think so.*

There are those about whom I say, "Every time I think of you, I give thanks to God." They are ordinary people. Yet, each one has had a positive impact on my life. Some have loved me unconditionally. Some have nurtured me. Some have encouraged me. Some have believed in me and given me opportunities to attempt things that "stretched" me. Some have been loyal and loving friends who have cried as well as laughed with me. Some have taught me how to live fully, while others have taught me how to face death courageously. Some, whose lives have been transformed by the indwelling Christ, have caused me to hunger and thirst after the righteousness that only Christ can give.

As I remembered the special blessings God sent to me via ordinary people, their names and faces flashed across my mind. There were too many to list, of course, though I wanted to thank each one publicly. However, God knows each one and what they contributed to my life and the lives of others.

As I thought about the host of individuals who had been so special, I asked myself several questions. *Am I the kind of person for whom others will thank God? Have I positively influenced the lives of others? Why or why not? In light of that answer, what changes do I need to make?*

Reflections

Those were difficult questions, yet they were important. If people do not say, "Every time I think of you, I give thanks to God," have our lives been of any real value? Have we wasted the precious years we were permitted to spend on earth? Have we brought honor to the Lord?

If we were honored at an event, such as the sports banquet I attended, what would those who worked alongside of us say? Would someone wish that their child might grow up and have a heart like ours?

If so, then we should rejoice!

Johnnie Ann Burgess Gaskill

Resting Like a Child

The mother who sat opposite me in the school office held in her arms a handsome little fellow who looked to be about age two. As the mom and I waited to pick up our children, I couldn't help but notice how soundly the child slept in his mother's arms. Apparently nothing disturbed him, not even all the noise in that busy place.

I smiled at the mother and said, "He's really 'sacked out,' isn't he?"

"He certainly is," she responded. Then, she picked up one of his small hands and held it in the air for a moment before letting it drop gently to his side. The little boy never stirred. The goings-on around him affected him not at all. No, he was asleep in his mother's arms, resting from all the things that normally would have concerned him.

A few nights later, I thought of the little guy as I read the words of David the Psalmist. "LORD, my heart is not proud; my eyes are not haughty. I don't concern myself with matters too great or awesome for me. *But I have stilled and quieted myself, just as a small child is quiet with its mother. Yes, like a small child is my soul within me*" (Psalm 131:1-2, emphasis added).

Wouldn't it be wonderful, I thought, *to experience that kind of peace and contentment? Wouldn't it be wonderful to have a 'quiet' heart, one that was calm and secure, one undisturbed by all the goings-on of life?*

I wondered, *How is this calmness achieved*? By rereading the words of the Psalmist, I discovered the answer. Obviously, the Psalmist knew the Lord, since he was talking to Him about his feelings. He stated that he had given up his pride and his arrogance and no longer concerned himself with matters that were too difficult for him, even (by implication) excessive ambition. And he, like the little boy, simply rested in the arms of the One who loved him, believing that he would take care of him in every situation.

Then I asked, "Based on what I know about the character of God, am I willing to trust Him to meet all my needs?"

Now, some folks think that only those who are weak or incompetent should answer "Yes" to that question. They believe that choosing to yield to God is nothing but a big "cop out." They have not learned the truth of Isaiah 30:15: "In quietness and confidence is your strength."

Each of us must decide whether we want to be a proud, self-seeking person with a life characterized by constant struggle and pressure or a person with a quiet heart who experiences peace and contentment in the arms of God. We cannot be both.

Reflections

Settling In

Oh, someone moved into the first house in the subdivision, I thought as I took my daily walk through the new development just behind our home. Every day I watched eagerly to see how quickly the new owners would settle in. Since their new house was so beautiful, I felt sure they wanted to get everything all fixed up as quickly as possible. I was wrong. Even after several weeks passed, the windows remained uncovered and several large cardboard boxes stayed stacked in front of an upstairs bedroom window.

Meanwhile, a family moved in next door to the first family. They did what I had assumed the first family would do. In just a short time, their house looked beautiful and inviting. Passersby like me knew immediately that they liked their new residence.

Perhaps the first family had good reasons for not settling in according to my timetable. Why they delayed was none of my business; but, as a casual observer, I noticed the difference between their settling in process and that of their neighbors.

I thought about how the settling in strategy differs from person to person. Whether we move into a new house, a new job, a new relationship, or whatever, we adjust to the newness in our own way and in our time. For some, settling in seems easy. No big deal. They just "move in" and do whatever is necessary to begin functioning in a comfortable manner. For others, settling in is a struggle. They do not "get with it," as expected. Observers wonder, *What is the problem? Why can't they get their act together?* Actually, such slow settlers are like the first family; they remain in limbo. They leave the old behind, but they don't make a strong commitment to the new. They do not strive to make the best of the new environment, nor do they receive maximum pleasure from it.

Even when we enter into a new relationship with Christ, a certain amount of settling in is necessary. When we receive from Him a new life, we discover that we "are not the same anymore, for the old life is gone. A new life has begun!" (2 Corinthians 5:17).

Surely, then, we grieve our Lord if we try to cling to our old habits, thoughts and feelings instead of committing fully to the new life He has provided for us. He wants us to "move" joyfully and eagerly into the new areas of service into which He leads us. And, He wants us to settle in quickly and begin to enjoy the "new life" we received when we became a part of the family of God.

When we get serious about our commitment to Him, settling into our new life becomes easier because He offers all manner of assistance to us. He helps us unpack our possessions and put them in the proper place. He even suggests the furnishing we need in order to make our hearts the kind of home He wishes to share with us.

When we've settled in, others will notice; and they'll be pleased to see that we like our new place.

Reflections

Here I Am!

While thumbing through my husband's high school yearbook, I noticed a 2½ x 3½ inch photo. *Goodness, there must be a hundred people in this picture!* I said to myself. The Seniors seated in the first few rows were recognizable, but those farther back probably could not have been identified by their own parents. Yet, one student had managed to locate himself and wanted others to know he was there. So, he had written his name in the white space surrounding the photo and drawn a line from his signature to his place in the group picture. His doing so said, "Here I am!"

That may be one of the most important messages we send to each other. In the midst of the crowd that surrounds us, we feel a great need to retain our individuality. We want others to know who we are and where we are. Feeling as if we're just another face in the crowd creates within us a desperate sense of loneliness, and we feel as if we are adrift in a sea of humanity, having no sense of distinction or direction. We do want others to notice us, to recognize us, and to be aware of our worth, even though we do not resorting to calling out, "Here I am!"

David the Psalmist found great comfort in knowing that God was totally aware of him as an individual. Read his words. Thrill to their message. Realize they are true for you as well. "O LORD, you have examined my heart and *[you] know everything about me*. You know when I sit down or stand up. You know my every thought when far away. You chart the path ahead of me and tell me where to stop and rest. *Every moment you know where I am*" (Psalm 139:1-3, emphasis added).

When you and I know that truth and believe it, we never have to say to God, "Here I am!" He already knows who we are and where we are …at all times!

Johnnie Ann Burgess Gaskill

Reflections About Pets and Nature

Johnnie Ann Burgess Gaskill

A Childlike Faith

One Tuesday, our fifteen-year-old cat whose health had been failing for several weeks, suddenly became too weak to stand. The vet said nothing could be done for Smokey; his body was simply worn out.

Our daughters, ages six and nine at the time, wept inconsolably when they learned Smokey had died. Neither of the girls could remember when that big gray cat had not been a part of their lives. In fact, when my husband and I brought each of our newborn daughters home, Smokey became their self-appointed guardian. He slept in our bedroom under the bassinet until we moved each daughter, in turn, into the nursery across the hall from our bedroom. Every night thereafter he slept in the hallway right outside their doors.

Wiping back tears, Jena, our six-year-old, said, "Why didn't God make Smokey better? I asked Him to!"

I prayed for wisdom to know how to answer that question, for I did not know how to explain the sovereignty of God to one so young, especially when I, myself, still had much to learn about that awesome truth. So I began, "Honey, God protected Smokey and gave him a good, long life, didn't He?" Jena nodded.

"And," I continued, "God let us love him and care for him. And we never saw Smokey sick or seriously hurt, did we?" She shook her head.

Stroking her beautiful red hair as she sat with her head against my chest, I said, "When it was Smokey's time to die, God was merciful even then, for Smokey didn't seem like he was hurting much, did he? Didn't he just grow weaker and weaker?"

Jena calmed down and seemed to be considering what I had said. After a few moments, she looked upward, beyond my face. Smiling radiantly, she said, "Lord, I love you!" I hugged her tightly and we sat together for a time as His peace flooded our broken hearts.

Johnnie Ann Burgess Gaskill

Monuments to Foolishness

What is that gray squirrel doing, I thought. *Is he really trying to enlarge the opening?*

He was! I watched in amazement and amusement as the shavings fell to the ground below the birdhouse that my husband had nailed to a tree in our front yard. I laughed as the squirrel contorted his body into some unusual positions as he attempted to find the angle that would best enable him to chew away at the small circular opening that was designed to admit small birds. He spent a great deal of time climbing all over the birdhouse. *I'll bet he's making mental calculations about how to proceed*, I thought.

He seemed fearful and uncertain as he worked, for every now and then he'd pause from his chewing and stiffen to attention. After a few seconds, he'd return with a vengeance to his work. From time to time, he'd scamper up the tree and play among the topmost branches.

Soon the opening was large enough to accommodate his head. That bit of success inspired him to work with an even greater zeal. As I watched his frenzied activity, I wondered, *What prompted him to try to nest in the too-small birdhouse? Why is he so determined to possess something so unsuited to his needs? Why has he spent so much time on such a worthless project?*

I shook my head. Then it occurred to me that, when we busy ourselves with accumulating possessions and positions which are unsuitable for us, we are much like that little squirrel. Though we struggle to make things work, we ultimately end up with exactly what the squirrel did—a monument to our own foolishness!

Reflections

The Snake in the Apple Tree

My husband thought he had come up with the perfect solution for saving the apples on the tree in our backyard. Actually, the scheme worked perfectly for weeks—until a smart little squirrel decided he was no longer afraid of the rubber snake my husband had draped on one of the bottom branches. As we lamented the loss of our apples, my husband said, "The trick might have worked if only I had repositioned the snake occasionally."

Be that as it may, we still had to admire that little squirrel. His intense desire for the fruit prompted him to take action. He may have tossed caution to the wind and headed straight for the apples, in spite of the presence of the snake, but I think not. I believe he had eyed his adversary carefully during those weeks before concluding that the snake had no power to harm him. That knowledge gave him the boldness to scamper out on the limb and pluck an apple.

Even though the squirrel figured his enemy was powerless, he stayed a safe distance away from the snake. The squirrel reserved his boldness for those times when he had to pass right by the snake in order to get up into the tree.

Like the squirrel, the victorious Christians are those who are no longer fooled by their adversary, the devil. They know that Christ, through His death, rendered the devil powerless. Yes, the adversary is present. Yes, he appears powerful. But, thanks be unto God, he is a defeated foe! Believers can move right past him and begin to enjoy eternal and abundant life.

Johnnie Ann Burgess Gaskill

C. C.'s Lesson

Before they left for school, the children fed the little stray kitten we named C. C. (Calico Cat). However, she must have still had a hungry spot in her tiny tummy for when she saw me walking down the driveway to mail some letters, she came running toward me. She meowed so pitifully. *She's just lonely and needs some attention*, I thought. So I sat on the front steps and played with her for a while before I went inside.

I settled myself on the sofa and prepared to spend the morning studying my Bible and writing my newspaper column. Immediately, I heard her familiar, plaintive "Meow! Meow! Meow!" I glanced up and saw her staring intently at me through the glass storm door and pleading for my attention.

Knowing she had been fed and petted, I tried to ignore her sad little face pressed against the glass. *She can't be hungry*, I thought. *Besides, she's not accustomed to being fed for another four hours.*

Nonetheless, she persisted with her shrill meowing and her beseeching expression. I put aside my work—rather resentfully, I confess—and took her a bowl of fresh food and clean water. But she smelled the food and then walked away from it.

"Well," I snapped, "we'll have to name you P.C. (Picky Cat), won't we?"

My aggravation diminished when I felt her soft fur brush against my ankles. I looked into her tiny face. She seemed to be saying, "Thank you for responding to my needs." Having thanked me, she hurried back to her food and began to devour it.

Her actions made me keenly aware of how wonderful it is to know that God is close by at all times and that He is both willing and "able to accomplish infinitely more than we would ever dare to ask or hope" (Ephesians 3:20). When He hears our persistent cries for help, He responds gladly, not grudgingly, as I had.

I wondered, *Does it grieve the heart of God when animals express to their caregivers a greater sense of gratitude than His children do to Him, their Creator and Sustainer?*

Reflections

Reacting to Everything

When Boo Boo was little, he entertained us for hours on end with his antics. For example, whenever our kitten saw his shadow on the kitchen floor or on the wall, he battled his enemy as if his very life depended on his skill as an attack cat. When we tossed a worn-out, stuffed kitten on the floor, he'd pounce on it. He'd bite that lifeless thing. He'd clutch it with his front feet and scratch it with his back feet. He'd wrestle it all across the floor. Then, tiring of fighting with his enemy, he'd pick up the stuffed kitten and carry it around the house as tenderly as his own mother had once carried him.

Every noise and every distraction attracted Boo Boo's attention. And since he reacted to each thing with equal intensity, he tired easily. But since he stayed home alone while the family was at school and at work, he had plenty of time to rest.

We laughed at Boo Boo's lack of discernment; however, I did not laugh when I recognized *my* inability to focus on the truly important things and to let go of other matters that *seemed* urgent but actually were not. That is one of the greatest dangers people face, according to Charles E. Hummel, author of **The Tyranny of the Urgent**, Some days—I'm ashamed to confess—everything seems urgent and important and I react much like our little kitten. My adrenalin level stays high as I deal with what I perceive to be high priority tasks. But, unlike Boo Boo, I can't curl up in a quiet, out-of-the-way place and sleep for hours. I have to keep going, and, as a result, my body becomes fatigued. Even so, at day's end, I realize that I have left undone most, if not all, of the truly important things.

I wish it weren't so difficult to distinguish between the important tasks and the lesser matters that seem so urgent. But it *is* difficult, dreadfully difficult. Year after year, the important things wait quietly while deadlines, daily chores, appointments, the phone, e-mails, and so-forth scream for attention. Like Boo Boo, I get so involved with them that I have little time and energy for the things of lasting value. As the years slip by. I grieve over all that I've neglected.

I studied the life of Jesus to see how He chose His priorities. I noticed that even Jesus did not meet all the urgent needs around Him. Neither did He do everything He might have liked to do. However, He did finish the important work of redemption that God had given Him to do.

What was His secret? He constantly sought guidance from His Father. In fact, in John 5:30, Jesus said, "But I do nothing without consulting the Father." In order to have time to talk with the Father, Jesus habitually woke up early to go to a quiet place to pray. At the end of the day when He was weary in body and mind, He took time to pray.

If God's Son needed to set aside time to talk to the Father, then I certainly do. I need to go before God, with paper and pen in my hand, and say, "God, I am totally Yours. This day is Yours. Now, please reveal to me how You want me to invest the life and the talents You have given me." If I've already written some things on my list, I need to say, "Now, Father, what about these? Are any of these a high priority?" If He says, "No," then I need to strike them from my list, no matter how urgent they seemed when I wrote them down. That's the only real way to ignore the urgent in order to accomplish the important.

Boo Boo and the Bacon

Boo Boo, our big gray cat, provided our family with daily doses of laughter. For example, Jena and Boo Boo sounded as if they were tearing down the house every time she'd get a long piece of narrow fabric and drag it behind her as she ran from room to room and up and down the stairs with Boo Boo in hot pursuit of the fabric. Soon they'd collapse—Jena from laughter, Boo Boo from exhaustion. After a brief rest, they'd go at it again.

Boo Boo made a wonderful playmate for the girls. In fact, in many ways he seemed almost human. He enjoyed sleeping on a soft bed. He loved to be petted. He showed definite preferences for food. And, as we discovered one morning, he had a bit of a conscience, too!

That morning I'd wrapped a few slices of leftover bacon in a paper towel and left them on the table while I drove Jena to school. When I returned home, I started to make a BLT sandwich to take to work with me. However, the bacon was gone and the paper towel was lying on the floor. *That's odd*, I thought.

I never suspected Boo Boo, for he had never taken anything from the table. But when I went upstairs to ask Jennifer if she could explain the mysterious disappearance of the bacon, Boo Boo was stretched out in the hallway and he had guilt plastered all over his face. He watched every move I made, as if waiting for his punishment. His guilt was so obvious that Jennifer and I exploded with laughter as we watched him slink around.

Although Boo Boo's responses were almost human at times, he was still a wild cat at heart. He enjoyed his creature comfort and he learned to be fairly civilized, but the animal nature was still present within him. For example, one morning as I opened a can of name brand cat food for him, I glanced out the window and saw him crouching in our neighbor's yard, ready to pounce on some unsuspecting creature that was underneath the azalea bushes. When Jennifer called, "Where's Boo Boo?" I quipped, "He's outside stalking big game!"

Remembering Boo Boo's two natures helps me understand how important it is for us to have our old sin nature replaced with a Christlike one. Until then, we'll remain a sinner at heart, despite efforts to refine and camouflage our old nature with religious trappings. God's Word expresses it this way "…throw off your old evil nature and your former way of life, which is rotten through and through, full of lust and deception. Instead, there must be a spiritual renewal of your thoughts and attitudes.

Johnnie Ann Burgess Gaskill

You must display a new nature because you are a new person, created in God's likeness—righteous, holy, and true" (Ephesians 4:22-24).

Reflections

Leaving the Nest Too Early

At first I didn't see what had caused Jennifer and Jena to stop suddenly and stare at the ground. Then I saw a baby bird that was almost concealed by the grass and a piece of bark. Only slightly larger than a golf ball and covered mainly with down, the young bird was unable to fly. Obviously, the fledgling needed to be returned to the nest—wherever that was. While the girls and I considered how we might help the baby bird, we noticed two robins that were chirping anxiously and circling the area. *At least we've found the parents*, we thought.

My husband gently moved the baby robin to a safer place. He placed him where the largest limb branched off from the trunk of the skinny dogwood tree. We hoped that the parents could manage to feed their young one, even though they had no way to return their little one to the warmth and security of the nest.

We felt sorry for the baby and the parents. Obviously, they wanted their baby safe in the nest until such time as he would be able to make it on his own. However, we doubted that would be possible, since the young one had left home before he'd developed the necessary skills to cope in a world hostile to him.

We did not know, of course, why the baby had left the nest. Had he, noticing the few feathers on his own body, assumed he was more mature than he actually was? Had that false assumption led him to venture out on his own? Had his parents misjudged his maturity and given him a premature push from the nest? Had a predator found the nest and dislodged the bird? Had he fallen out quite by accident?

Whatever the reason for his premature exit, the bird was now in a life-threatening situation. He kept calling to his parents who, though deeply concerned about him, were virtually unable to do anything to help their young offspring. We felt frustrated, too, as we stood by and helplessly watched the drama.

During the week that followed, I experienced the same feeling of sadness and frustration—only to a greater degree—as I heard about the results of a survey conducted by some local high school students. According to the survey, a number of students had engaged in premarital sex, had had abortions, had run away from home, and had contemplated and/or attempted suicide. As I heard these grim statistics, I immediately thought about how much the students were like the baby robin that had left the nest way too early.

I did not know why the students prematurely left the age of innocence. However, I did know that they, like the baby robin, were at risk. I also knew that many parents anxiously watched over their offspring, wondering what went wrong, longing to help, wanting to restore the family unit, but lacking the knowledge or the ability to do so.

During such times when we feel unable to give our young ones the help they need, we must rely on God's power, for He specializes in situations that seem impossible to us. How we rejoice to know that "The LORD is not too weak to save [us], and he is not becoming deaf. He can hear [us] when [we] call" (Isaiah 59:1).

However, we need to carefully consider the words that follow that statement of assurance. "But there is a problem—[our] sins have cut [us] off from God" (Isaiah 59:2). Therefore, it is essential that all of us—parents and children—confess any known wrongdoings and resolve to turn away from any thing that separates us from God. When we do that, God hears our cries for help. He intervenes. He forgives. He heals. He restores.

Reflections

Just Who Does He Think He Is?

When we lived in Austell, Georgia, we maintained a bird feed in front of our living room window. We also scattered wild birdseed on the upper end of our driveway. At first, only a few birds came, but soon we were feeding a sizeable portion of the bird population. Twenty-five pounds of birdseed barely lasted a month, but we felt that being able to see so many birds up close more than compensated for the expense of the food. We loved seeing the redbirds, the doves, the blue jays, the blackbirds, the brown thrashers, as well as a few squirrels, dine regularly on our driveway.

On the rare occasions when the birds had eaten all the seeds the evening before, they flew over their usual feeding place and then sat on the tree branches to wait for us to replenish their food supply. As soon as we went outside with the bucket of seed, the birds struck up what sounded like a symphony of praise. As soon as we went back inside the house, they flew down and began to eat.

Normally, the birds took turns eating—a few at a time. They ate quietly and quickly then flew away so as to make room for the next group of diners. However, one cocky redbird behaved quite differently. Whether he was prejudiced, selfish, or just generally afflicted with a bad attitude, he always chased away the same dove, refusing to allow her to feed at the same time even when there was ample food for both of them.

Watching that obnoxious redbird angered me. *Just who does he think he is? That food doesn't belong exclusively to him! He has no right to act in such a manner!*

Each time I fumed over his behavior, I had to remind myself, *The redbird is an animal. He operates instinctively rather than logically. He is not bound by moral, religious, or ethical codes.*

Then I'd ask myself, *What's man's excuse for acting unkindly and selfishly toward others? Don't we know that although God "richly gives us all we need for our enjoyment…[we] should give generously to those in need, always being ready to share with others whatever God has given [us]?"* (1 Timothy 6: 17-18.) When we do otherwise, we're behaving like the selfish redbird. Perhaps he has an excuse; we don't!

Johnnie Ann Burgess Gaskill

Laying Up Treasures

I smiled as I observed the little squirrel from my bathroom window. *He thinks his ship has come in*, I thought, as I watched him rushing to hide his nuts.

He executed a specific plan. He'd go to the pile of unshelled pecans we had poured onto the driveway the afternoon before, then he'd pick up one, twirl it in his tiny paws until he knew he was holding it just right, and scamper off with it. Next, he'd run to hide his pecans under some pine straw at the far end of the driveway.

I couldn't help laughing as I watched him work. He was so cute, so intent on his work, so eager to rake away the pine straw, deposit the pecan, cover it, then make another mad dash to the pecan pile.

He continued his frenzied activity—never stopping to rest—till the dozen or so pecans were gone. He did not seem to be as alert to danger as he normally was. Rather, he seemed oblivious to everything except making sure he stored those pecans before someone else discovered them.

As I watched, I realized that we are like that squirrel when we become greedy, only it's more serious for us. Our emphasis on accumulating more and more is such a gradual process that often we do not realize when we've gone beyond providing adequately for our basic needs and reached the point of excess and self-centeredness.

Because greed is so subtle, Jesus warns us to "Beware! Don't be greedy for what you don't have. Real life is not measured by how much we own" (Luke 12:15).

Greed causes us to put our priorities in the wrong place. To illustrate this point, Jesus tells a parable of a rich man who decided to tear down his barns and build larger ones in order to store his abundant grain and goods. Initially, the rich man's idea sounded reasonable. He did need adequate storage. However, what he said next revealed his selfishness. "And I'll sit back and say to myself, My friend, you have enough stored away for years to come. Now take it easy! Eat, drink, and be merry" (Luke 12:19).

Apparently, the rich man never considered sharing any of his goods with the less fortunate. Instead, he chose to hoard his possessions. And that proved deadly (no pun intended!), for God said to him, "You fool! You will die this very night. Then who will get it all?" (Luke 12:20).

Jesus concluded this story about the greedy man by issuing a warning that you and I would do well to remember: "Yes, a person is a fool to store up earthly wealth but not have a rich relationship with God" (Luke 12:21).

Reflections

No Longer a Captive

Boo Boo, our 17-pound cat, disappeared one Friday afternoon. My husband checked with our neighbors to see if they knew of Boo Boo's whereabouts. We searched every room in our house, the garage, the yard, and the woods behind our house. We drove up and down the streets in our neighborhood. I even called the animal shelter's "Lost and Found Department."

By Monday, we concluded that Boo Boo was gone forever. The only hope we had was that he might be trapped in someone's basement or crawl space. Even that hope diminished with each passing day.

Tuesday evening I gasped as I heard "Meow! Meow!" outside my bedroom window. The meowing grew louder and remained persistent. I hurried to open the door. Boo Boo almost knocked me down as he ran past me to his feeding dish.

"Look who's home!" I yelled to the family. We gathered around to watch him chow down on a freshly opened can of cat food. He gobbled down more than half of it before pausing long enough to rub around our ankles and purr "Hello!"

Even after satisfying his hunger and thirst, he continued to meow. "The big baby just wants to be petted," I said. So for hours the four of us took turns stroking him. Boo Boo, normally a rather standoffish cat, couldn't seem to get enough attention that evening. When we finally turned out our lights, Boo Boo lay in his regular place on our bedroom floor and purred so loudly that he sounded like a chain saw.

We never found out where he had been those four days, but we believed he was trapped somewhere, since he was starving but otherwise unhurt. Had he been able to tell us about his "captivity," he might have used words such as these: *confinement, deprivation, discomfort, loneliness, despair, abandonment, fear, hopelessness, frustration,* and *helplessness.*

His response to being home told us that the "captivity" into which he may have inadvertently placed himself was not pleasant. We hoped Boo Boo would think twice before allowing his curiosity to lead him into places where he doesn't really want to be!

As I listened to Boo Boo purring happily, I was glad he was home and able to experience the love and "creature comforts" he enjoyed. Yet, I thought about how my great happiness over Boo Boo's release was minimal when compared to the response of a person who has been set free from tormenting captors such as: food, drugs, alcohol, greed, fear, success, perfectionism, perversion, anger, the past…

Who can set people free from such "captivity?" Jesus! He used the words recorded in the Book of Isaiah as He described His mission: "The Spirit of the Lord is upon me, for he has appointed me to preach Good News to the poor. He has sent me to proclaim that **captives will be released**, that the blind will see, that the downtrodden will be freed from their oppressors, and that the time of the Lord's favor has come" (Luke 4:18-19, emphasis added).

That's good news!

Hidden Till Now

As I looked out my window and saw splashes of color everywhere, I remembered the words included in a note from a dear friend. The daffodils dancing in the wind and the flowering trees and shrubs proudly wearing their Spring wardrobe confirmed that "All the beauty we see just now was hidden even two weeks ago."

Indeed, the forsythia bushes looked drab, almost dead, a few weeks ago. Now, splashes of yellow indicated they had life and were doing their part in making Spring's debut a delight for the eyes.

The beauty surrounding me was part of an on-going process. It wasn't something that just appeared—unplanned and unscheduled. Even as I had looked at winter's bare landscape and longed for the beauty of Spring, nature was already preparing her annual display of colors. She worked secretly at first, and then the tell-a-tale signs began to appear. Though it seemed that Spring arrived suddenly, it actually had been on its way for some time.

Jesus mentioned this on-going process in a parable that He told to those who were having difficulty understanding what the Kingdom of God is like. He said, "A farmer planted seeds in a field, and then he went on with his other activities. As the days went by, the seeds sprouted and grew without the farmer's help, because *the earth produces crops on its own*. **First a blade** pushes through, **then the heads** of the wheat are formed, and **finally the grain** ripens. And as soon as the grain is ready, the farmer comes and harvests it with a sickle" (Mark 4:26-29, emphasis added).

We, like the farmer in the parable, do not understand how God will use all the "seeds" we sow to raise up a "harvest" of mature believers. Our work is to faithfully sow the seed—the Word of God. God's work is to produce the harvest. That is a work that God alone must do.

As we obey God by sowing the seeds (sharing His Word), we must learn to trust Him to do His work. Like the farmer who goes to bed at night and ceases from his labor, we must learn to wait upon God, to give Him time to do His work. And, like the farmer, we must wait expectantly for signs of the harvest. Just as the farmer gets excited when he sees the first tiny blade that has pushed its way to the surface of the ground, so also should we rejoice over every sign of God at work in hearts and lives.

The Apostle Paul became excited over the evidences of God at work. Paul knew that when God began a divine work in the hearts of people, He would complete it—that is, God would bring it to full maturity. One day, the harvest (the kingdom) will come—not unplanned and unscheduled, but as a culmination of an on-going process.

Both my friend's reminder that "All the beauty we see just now was hidden even two weeks ago," and the parable Jesus told encouraged me to trust the Lord. Even when I do not see what He is doing, God continues to work in my heart and in the hearts of others. At some point, God's work, which may seem to have been hidden, will be gloriously and magnificently revealed and will cause much rejoicing.

Reflections About Scripture

Johnnie Ann Burgess Gaskill

Reflections

The Painful Truth About Martha

"Martha, Martha," Jesus said tenderly, "you are too busy, too tense, too preoccupied with details."

"Well, someone has to be!" she retorted. "I've been in the kitchen since early morning and I've still got so much to do. Surely, You don't blame Me for being upset with Mary, do You?"

Without waiting for His response, Martha continued, "She's just sitting out there enjoying being with You and with the rest of our guests while I'm in here working myself to death! Well, I'd like to be out there, too, but someone has to get the food ready."

When Martha saw the look in His eyes, she hushed. She sensed that He could see into her very soul, that He knew the real truth about her, which, of course, He did. Looking intently into her eyes, Jesus said softly, "Martha, you are such a perfectionist, aren't you?"

That rebuke, spoken so lovingly, pierced her heart and brought tears to her eyes. She nodded mutely.

Jesus looked at her in His own inimitable way for what seemed to Martha an eternity. Then He said, "Martha, I must ask you this question. Have you made these preparations in order to please Me or have you done them to bring honor to yourself?"

"Why, Lord…You…know…I did them because I love You."

"Martha, don't delude yourself any longer. Your elaborate preparations do not impress Me. Rather, I am grieved that you think more highly of your reputation and your social standing than You do Me. I wish that you could let go of your need for the world's approval and simply take time to enjoy being with Me. If only you would sit at My feet and tell Me about your concerns. If only you would listen as I explain the truths of God to you, then you could change."

A part of her wanted to do just that. But another part of her wondered if she'd ever be able to break out of her old patterns of thinking and behaving. Knowing her thoughts, Jesus said, "Martha, the more you sit at My feet and the more you put Me first, the easier it will be to let go of your old ways."

His words made her feel hopeful, but still she hesitated and lowered her eyes so He could not see the struggle going on inside her.

"Martha," Jesus said softly, "because you are a take-charge-and-get-things-done person you've carried the weight of the world on your shoulders. Are you ready to give that burden to Me? Are you willing to be set free?"

(Based on Luke 10:38-42.)

Johnnie Ann Burgess Gaskill

What One Thing…?

Near the end of a busy day, I lay beside my nine-year-old on her bed. I was tired, but not too much to enjoy the sound of her sweet voice as she read a Bible story to me. However, I soon found myself struggling to stay awake—until one question from the story grabbed my attention.

Jena had been reading about the death of King David and the beginning of the rule of his son, Solomon. It was God's question to Solomon that woke me up. "What would you like Me to give you?"

I thought about that question and wondered how I would answer it. Would I ask God for a long list of things: happiness, health, wealth, popularity, success, easy living, etc.? Or would I focus on just one thing, as Solomon had. If so, what one thing would I request?

The young king, awed by the great responsibility of leadership placed on his shoulders, asked God for only one thing: "Give me an understanding mind so that I can govern your people well and know the difference between right and wrong. For who by himself is able to govern this great nation of yours?" (1 Kings 3:9).

That request pleased God, and He said to Solomon, "Because you have asked for wisdom in governing my people and have not asked for a long life or riches for yourself or the death of your enemies—I will give you what you asked for—riches and honor! No other king in all the world will be compared to you for the rest of your life! And if you follow me and obey my commands as your father, David, did, I will give you a long life" (1 Kings 11-14).

The same God who "is able to accomplish infinitely more than we would ever dare to ask or hope" (Ephesians 3:20) still wants to confirm what is the deepest desire in our hearts, so He asks, "What would you like Me to give you?" May we, like Solomon, have the wisdom and the grace to ask for that which will enable us to be obedient and pleasing to the Lord God whom we serve.

Arise!

Remember Eutychus? He's the young man mentioned in Acts 20:9 who came to hear the preaching of Paul, a noted evangelist. Eutychus sat on the windowsill and tried to listen to the rather long sermon. But as midnight approached, poor Eutychus began to fall asleep. Perhaps it was the flickering light from the lamps that lulled him to sleep or maybe it was the warm, crowded room. He might have been so tired that his body craved sleep. Whatever the reason, Eutychus dozed off to sleep and fell out of the third floor window. Though he interrupted the meeting, he managed to survive the fall.

I used to laugh whenever I read about Eutychus, and, admittedly, the story does contain a bit of humor. However, Eutychus deserves more than laughter. He deserves serious consideration, as do three others who fell asleep at an inappropriate time.

Peter, James, and John had had a long day. They were physically and emotionally exhausted. At their point of extreme weariness, Jesus asked them to accompany Him to a place called Gethsemane where Jesus struggled to come to grips with His imminent death. While He prayed, what did the three disciples do? They fell asleep!

I've often laughed about Eutychus; I've frequently judged the sleeping disciples. *How could they have slept? Didn't they love Him enough to remain awake and to pray with Him? Who needs a support group like that?*

Yet, as I get older and busier, I don't laugh at Eutychus or criticize the three disciples. Instead, I identify with them. I know how quickly fatigue prevents me from doing what I want to do, and I am comforted by His words to the sleepyheads: "Couldn't you stay awake and watch with me even one hour? Keep alert and pray. Otherwise temptation will overpower you. For **though the spirit is willing enough, the body is weak**" (Matthew 26:40b-41, emphasis added).

Although, Jesus understands the weakness of my body, I can't constantly use weariness as an excuse for not doing what I should, since, when I've rested a little, I'll hear Him say, "Arise! Let's get going. There's important work to do."

Johnnie Ann Burgess Gaskill

A Simple Question?

When our teenage daughters came home from an activity, I'd call out, "Is that you, Honey?"

One night, Jennifer, tired of hearing that inane question, responded, "No, Mama! I'm a burglar using the key to the front door."

I'm ashamed to say that many of my questions fell into the same category as "Who is buried in Grant's tomb?" or "What color was George Washington's white horse?" However, after Jennifer's little quip, I decided to try to refrain from asking questions with obvious answers.

Being sensitive to such questions, I noticed that Jesus often asked that type of question.

While reading the fifth chapter of the Gospel of John, I came to the account of a man who had been sick for thirty-eight years. He, along with a multitude of others who were sick, blind, lame, or withered, lay near a pool called Bethesda and waited eagerly for an angel to come down and stir up the water in the pool. Following the stirring, the first person into the pool would be healed.

One day Jesus approached the man and asked, "Do you wish to get well?"

Before I finished reading the rest of the account, I paused to reflect on that question. I wondered, *Why did Jesus bother to ask such a question? Wasn't the answer obvious?*

I thought about some reasons the man might have preferred to remain sick. He had many friends near the pool. In fact, they may have been his only friends. After all, they did have much in common. Perhaps, the man had grown accustomed to his condition and so accepting of it that he couldn't visualize being whole.

As I read verse seven, I wondered if the man had given up hope of being healed, for he said to Jesus, "I have no one to help me into the pool when the water is stirred up. While I am trying to get there, someone else always gets in ahead of me" (John 5:7). Certainly, he must have been discouraged and hopeless after years of struggling to receive physical healing. Who wouldn't be?

I considered yet another reason why the man might possibly have said no to Jesus' question. When the opportunity to be well and whole was within his grasp, he might have considered the changes that he would have to make. If he were made well, he would have to expand his circle of friends, go to different places, enjoy new experiences, and become more productive. All these changes would completely alter his lifestyle. He would talk about different things. He would have new goals.

His focus would shift. His entire outlook on life would be affected. Was he willing to change?

Apparently, he was. When Jesus said to him, "Get up, take up your pallet and walk," the man did just that. He accepted the healing that Jesus offered him. If he had any uncertainties about the future or any longings for the past, he put them aside in order to seize the opportunity to be made well.

I think I know why Jesus asked the man, "Do you want to get well?" He wanted the man to decide whether he wanted to remain in his present, hopeless condition or to be set free from the things that limited him. Jesus would not force him to accept healing.

Likewise, when the blind man mentioned in another story cried out, "Son of David, have mercy on me…" Jesus asked, "What do you want Me to do for you?"

The blind man gave Jesus a direct answer. "Lord, I want to regain my sight."

In that account, Jesus called upon the blind man to recognize his need, and to express his willingness to accept the healing Jesus was offering him.

Jesus still asks the same questions to you and me. "Do you want to receive spiritual healing?" That is not a frivolous question. Rather, it is one that merits a thoughtful answer, since the quality and the course of our life depends on the answer we give.

Although Jesus offers spiritual healing to us, He does not force it upon us. We can receive it when we are willing to admit how helpless and hopeless we are without Him. When we do that, then He will command us to get up and get moving, to stand up and begin a new life that will be infinitely superior to the old one.

When He asks, "What do you want Me to do for you?" He leaves the choice to us.

Johnnie Ann Burgess Gaskill

Spiritual "Smarts"

During the, "Wheel of Fortune" game show, the teenage contestant said she wanted to solve the puzzle. A hush settled over the audience as she carefully enunciated each word. "Given to Moses by God."

The game show host then gave the girl a chance to win some extra money if she could answer this question: "What was given to Moses by God?"

Even though she used all the allotted time to think about her answer, she was unable to make a response. The opportunity to answer passed to another contestant who said, "The Ten Commandments."

I could hardly believe what I had just seen and heard. The young girl who didn't know one of the most familiar Bible stories was obviously knowledgeable in other areas. In fact, she went on to win the game. During the introductions at the beginning of the show she had indicated that she had traveled abroad—to Germany, I think. Although no one would consider her "deprived," I couldn't help thinking she had missed out on the spiritual training that God commands parents to provide for their children.

Prior to the Israelites entering the land of Canaan that God had promised to them, Moses said, "…you must love the LORD your God with all your heart, all your soul, and all your strength. And you must commit yourselves wholeheartedly to these commands I am giving you today. Repeat them again and again to your children. Talk about them when you are at home and when you are away on a journey, when you are lying down and when you are getting up again" (Deuteronomy 6:5-7).

According to the Bible, parents themselves must love God supremely and be completely devoted to Him. They must think constantly about the commands of God and have the Word of God so incorporated into their lives that they provide their children with a daily example of godly living. When that happens, the teaching of the Word of God will be done constantly and continuously rather than at scheduled times.

Nurturing the faith of children is more than a privilege given to parents. It is a sacred obligation, a divine order. Parents who teach their children the commands of God and show them how to obey all that God requires can rest assured that their children will not be spiritually deprived. Rather, they will experience prosperity because God blesses those who know Him and obey Him. However, the blessings God gives are not necessarily monetary ones, but they are far more satisfying and enduring than the biggest prizes won on television game shows. And the parents who provide spiritual instruction and nurture are blessed as well.

They, like John, can say, "I could have no greater joy than to hear that my children live in the truth" (3 John 1:4).

Johnnie Ann Burgess Gaskill

Never Alone!

One day the prophet Elijah acted boldly and was very much God's man-of-the-hour. All that changed when the queen threatened to take his life within the next twenty-four hours. Elijah became afraid and ran for his life. Feeling hopeless, defeated, and alone, he asked the Lord to take his life.

How the Lord ministered to Elijah is one of my favorite stories from the Bible. Instead of scolding him or asking, "Don't you trust Me anymore?" God allowed Elijah to get some much-needed sleep. Twice an angel of the Lord touched Elijah and instructed him to get up and eat the bread and water that had been miraculously provided for him.

For the next forty days Elijah walked toward Mount Horeb (Sinai) where God had given the Ten Commandments to Moses. Once there, he found a cave in which to live. Then the Lord asked, "What are you doing here, Elijah?"

That question gave Elijah the opportunity to express his feelings. He said, "I have zealously served the LORD GOD Almighty. But the people of Israel have broken their covenant with you, torn down your altars, and killed every one of your prophets. I alone am left, and now they are trying to kill me, too" (1 Kings 19:10).

Elijah's assessment of the situation was accurate except for the phrase, "And I alone am left." God was still very much present with Elijah and still powerful, as evidenced by the strong wind that broke rocks into pieces, the earthquake, and the fire that Elijah observed. Later on in the conversation, God reminded Elijah that there were 7,000 others who had not participated in pagan worship (verse 18). Most assuredly, then, Elijah was not alone.

That story contains many truths, among them the fact that God is always with us in every situation. God had been with Elijah during the time when Elijah was bold; God stayed near when Elijah was depressed and discouraged.

Other Biblical accounts verify God's nearness at all times. Sometimes He is near even when people wish He weren't. For example, after Adam and Eve sinned, God was near them. "Toward evening they heard the LORD God walking about in the garden, so they hid themselves among the trees. The LORD God called to Adam, 'Where are you?'" (Genesis 3:8-9).

As Adam and Eve learned, there is no place we can go where God is not. David expressed the omnipresence of God with these words: "I can never escape from your spirit! I can never get away from your presence! If

I go up to heaven, you are there; if I go down to the place of the dead, you are there. If I ride the wings of the morning, if I dwell by the farthest oceans, even there your hand will guide me, and your strength will support me" (Psalm 139:7-1).

God is near us when we succeed and when we fail. He is near us when we are happy and when we are brokenhearted. God is near us when we are bold and when we are cowardly. He is near us when we are strong and when we are weak. God is near us when we please Him and when we grieve Him. God is near us when we delight in His presence and when we reject Him.

Even more amazing than His nearness at all times is His constant love for us. Whether we are saints or sinners, whether we are bold or defeated, whether we are God's man-of-the-hour or the wimp-of-the-week, the eternal, ever-present God loves us unconditionally.

Johnnie Ann Burgess Gaskill

When God Is Nearby

I've always liked the word *because*. I especially enjoyed it when the girls used a variation of it when they were young. In response to my "Why did you do that?" they'd grin and say, "Just 'cause!" As Jennifer and Jena matured, they used *cause* less often, but I continued to look for *because* phrases in my reading because they usually provided the reasons why something was done or said.

For example, I found a *because* phrase when I studied Luke 19:41-45. I felt grateful that Jesus used it. Had He omitted it, people could not have understood why Jerusalem was going to be destroyed.

As Jesus made His way to Jerusalem where death by crucifixion awaited Him, He stopped outside the city. When He saw it, He wept over it and said, "I wish that even today you would find the way of peace. But now it is too late, and peace is hidden from you. Before long your enemies will build ramparts against your walls and encircle you and close in on you. They will crush you to the ground, and your children with you. Your enemies will not leave a single stone in place, **because** *you have rejected the opportunity God offered you*" (Luke 19:42-44, emphasis added).

Jesus had walked the streets of Jerusalem. He had worshipped in the Temple. He had taught the people and preached the Gospel to them. Yet, they had not really understood who He was or the nature of His mission. Even His disciples, who knew Him best, were often confused by His words and actions.

Indeed, He spoke strange words. The principles He taught them were in direct contrast to popular thought. For example, I imagine the elite people had trouble with these words of His: "For the proud will be humbled, but the humble will be honored" (Luke 14:11). And Jesus really blew them away when He said, "'But if you are willing to listen, I say, love your enemies. Do good to those who hate you. Pray for the happiness of those who curse you. Pray for those who hurt you'" (Luke 6:27-28).

Never had they known anyone with such amazing insight into their true character. Never had the religious people experienced such open rebuke. Consequently, they refused to believe that Jesus was the Son of God, the One who had come to save them.

Therefore, Jesus wept as He looked over the city of Jerusalem. How different the future of the city could have been if only the people had recognized what one Bible translation calls "the time of their visitation." If only they had understood who Jesus was and what He came to do, they and their beloved city could have avoided destruction. The opportunity had passed, however; and death and devastation awaited them.

How sad, how incredibly sad, to have been visited by the Son of God and not to have recognized Him and followed Him. Yet, that still happens today, doesn't it?

How often have we been comforted in grief and remained unaware of the presence of the Comforter? How often have we enjoyed the beauty of the earth and refused to believe in the Creator and give praise to Him? How often have we been wonderfully and undeservedly blessed and considered not the Source? How often have we been healed and then neglected to thank the Great Physician?

Can it be that we, too, "have rejected the opportunity God offered [us]?" Can it be that Jesus looks at us and weeps because He knows what blessings could be ours if only we would recognize the time of our visitation, if only we would accept the opportunities God offers us?

For Jerusalem, the opportunity to recognize and respond to Jesus had passed. Destruction lay ahead. However, our future can be different. God's Word tells us how. "Today you must listen to his voice. Don't harden your hearts against him" (Hebrews 4:7b). In other words, do not close your mind to the truth. Do not shut your eyes to God's revelation of Himself. Do not cover your ears when the Word of God is proclaimed. Instead, respond to Him when He speaks. Recognize the time of your visitation. Accept the opportunities God offers you. Then you will be assured of eternal life "**because** your sins have been forgiven **because** of Jesus…[and] **because** you know Christ, the one who is from the beginning" (1 John 2:12-13, emphasis added).

Johnnie Ann Burgess Gaskill

Know the Author!

A friend recommended a certain book to me. He assured me that it was a classic, one of the best books about Sunday School teaching. I took his advice, ordered the book, and waited eagerly for it to arrive. The day it came to my office, I hurried home that afternoon to read it. But, honestly, the book disappointed me. It was boring. No matter how hard I tried to read it and make notes, I simply couldn't "get into it." Time and time again I tried to read it, but doing so was like taking bad-tasting medicine that the doctor prescribed. I knew the book was supposed to be good for me, but I longed for a more palatable way to get the instruction I needed.

After repeated attempts to read the book, I put it aside. *Maybe someday I'll be able to tolerate it*, I thought.

That day came sooner than I expected and in a way that I never dreamed of. I met the author at Ridgecrest, North Carolina, during a Sunday School conference. The class he taught was a brief one—only one hour long—but as I watched him and listened to him, I knew he was a master teacher!

I had a few moments after class to ask him a question. During that brief conversation, he helped me more than I'd ever dreamed possible. I walked away with a specific method for dealing with a teaching problem that had puzzled me for years.

When I returned home and retrieved his book, I was amazed that the ideas in it made sense. I took pages and pages of notes, and when I'd finished doing that, I compiled a skeleton outline of the entire book. Each time I read from his book, I gathered new ideas for making Sunday School a more meaningful experience for my class members.

Knowing the author does make a difference, I concluded. But simply *meeting* him was not what altered my response to his book. It was more than that. It was getting to know him by observing the skill with which he taught us, by being assured that he could help me with a problem, by feeling his concern…Those things made the difference! In other words, the author became more than a name and a face. After I became aware of the kind of person he was, one who could help me, then I wanted to hear what he had to say and to incorporate his ideas. And guess where I found them? In the very book that I had tossed aside.

So it is with God's Word. Until we come to know the Author—not just about Him—but come to know Him personally, the Bible doesn't appeal to us nor does it make very much sense. It bores us. It doesn't seem relevant. We view it as a good book—for someone else—but not for ourselves.

All that changes, however, when we come to know the Author. Then, we have a hunger to know more about His thoughts that are recorded in the Bible. The Apostle Paul explains how God's book can be the very source of inspiration we need. "All Scripture is inspired by God and is useful to teach us what is true and to make us realize what is wrong in our lives. It straightens us out and teaches us to do what is right. It is God's way of preparing us in every way, fully equipped for every good thing God wants us to do" (2 Timothy 3:16-17).

When we know the Author, we want to read His book! And, it is *the* best!

Johnnie Ann Burgess Gaskill

Reflections About This 'n That

Johnnie Ann Burgess Gaskill

Reflections

"Miss Blue"

All efforts failed to repair our Oldsmobile station wagon. All weekend "Miss Blue's" engine remained unresponsive, except that her headlights burned. On Monday morning, I called for a tow truck. The driver expertly parked his vehicle in front of "Miss Blue's" half of our side-entrance, two-car garage. That maneuver was complicated by the size of his vehicle and the location of a tree close to the driveway. However, the driver coped with both problems then began to attach cables to the back of "Miss Blue."

I watched as he stepped to the control panel that was on the side of the tow truck. Slowly and cautiously he inched "Miss Blue" onto the silver bed of the truck. At one point, she stood nearly erect, causing her front bumper to nearly scrape the floor of the garage as he pulled her out. Meanwhile, I kept a close eye on the cable that held onto her, for I knew that if the cable snapped "Miss Blue" would demolish our house.

Soon "Miss Blue" was in place on the bed of the tow truck. I commended the driver for his expertise in handling such a difficult situation and commented, "You have a lot of faith in that cable, don't you?"

"Yes," he replied confidently. "It'll pull up to ten tons!" Then I knew that he never doubted the cable's ability to hold onto "Miss Blue." Our station wagon wasn't going anywhere except onto the truck!

While reflecting on that experience, the title to an old hymn written by George Matheson came to mind: "O Love That Will Not Let Me Go."

I thought, *God's love must be like that cable—strong and always able to hang on to me even when, like "Miss Blue", I'm broken down and in a difficult situation*. Then, I experienced another "Aha!" moment as I recalled these words: "Can anything ever separate us from Christ's love? Does it mean he no longer loves us if we have trouble or calamity, or are persecuted, or are hungry or cold or in danger or threatened with death?…No, despite all these things, overwhelming victory is ours through Christ, who loved us.

"And," continues the Apostle Paul, "I am convinced that nothing can ever separate us from his love. Death can't and life can't, and demons can't. Our fears for today, our worries about tomorrow, and even the powers of hell can't keep God's love away. Whether we are high above the sky or in the deepest ocean, nothing in all creation will ever be able to separate us from the love of God that is revealed in Christ Jesus our Lord" (Romans 8:35-39).

With an assurance like that, it's time to stop worrying and start thanking Him for His "love that will not let [us] go," no matter how dreadful the difficulties!

A Distressed Sheep

I laughed as I looked at the card a friend had mailed to me. On the front, a fluffy, white sheep was, shall we say, in a dilemma? Though she was in an idyllic environment—cloudless blue sky, lush green grass, and a stream of clean water—the poor sheep needed someone to rescue her. Her hind legs were caught on the top rail of the fence she was attempting to jump; her chin was on the ground; and one of her front legs pointed east, the other west. The bewildered expression on her face said, "Okay. What do I do now?"

The pre-printed message on the inside of the card said, "Everything that happens to you matters to me!" My laughter changed to tears when I read the handwritten note from my friend. "How I wish I could bear all these things for you. Better still, I'll pray earnestly for you…and leave my petitions at His feet for His handling according to His will for you."

I gave God thanks for providing a poor, distressed "sheep" like me with a wise and loving friend who understood my troubles. Though unable to solve my problems herself, she knew our Shepherd and she went to Him on my behalf, fully confident that He would surely get me on my feet again. (See Psalm 138: 8.)

Johnnie Ann Burgess Gaskill

A Lesson from the Trees

One cold November night I lay in bed and listened to the wind as it roared around our house. After a bit, I got up to look out the window. I saw that the trees in the backyard were taking a beating as the wind whipped around them. Hour after hour those trees endured the pressure the wind placed upon them. Every now and then dead branches and small limbs snapped and fell to the ground; but when the wind finally subsided all the trees were still standing.

I felt a keen appreciation for those trees. During Winter they bowed low with loads of ice and snow. In Summer they endured heat and drought. The fruit trees even endured severe pruning. Yet, year after year they stood in their places and continued to grow and to produce.

I thought, *There's a lesson to be learned from the trees. Haven't we felt the weight of seemingly unbearable responsibilities? Hasn't everyone experienced intense emotional heat brought on by conflict? Who among us has not desperately longed for something that was being withheld? Can't we identify with the pain of pruning, with having to give up something or someone who has been a vital part of our lives?*

Yet, as the seasons of life come and go, each taking their toll, each demanding something of us, we can endure. Like the trees, we may be a bit worse for the wear, but we can endure. Not only that, but we can also remain productive. How? The secret is found in Jeremiah 17:7-8, "…blessed are those who trust in the LORD and have made the LORD their hope and confidence. They are like trees planted along a riverbank, with roots that reach deep into the water. Such trees are not bothered by the heat or worried by long months of drought. Their leaves stay green, and they go right on producing delicious fruit."

Reflections

My God Has Died

I remember hearing the story of a football coach whose team had gone to the play-offs and then soundly defeated their long-standing archrival. The coach, who expected to experience an emotional high after such a sweet victory, plunged into a deep depression. His explanation? "My god has died."

When I first heard those words, I thought about how concise and insightful they were. I realized that the coach was neither the first nor the last person to experience the death of a god. Others have also given themselves to a person or a thing they considered to be of supreme value, only to find themselves left with nothing of substance.

Many things may assume the form of a god: a particular job, a desired goal, a specific achievement, an important position, a significant honor, an impressive house, a beautiful body, an opulent lifestyle, a close relationship, and so forth. An individual may have more than one god, more than one thing in which he invests his time, energy, and talent. The tragedy comes when that thing—whatever it may be—proves to be unworthy of the investment in it.

For many people, finally obtaining the thing they so highly desired or so highly prized is as disappointing as eating cotton candy. It looks good and tastes sweet at the moment, but it does not last. It has no real substance.

A child quickly recovers from his momentary disappointment with cotton candy. However, an adult who has invested years of his life in something he thought would bring him ultimate satisfaction does not readily accept his disillusionment. In fact, his emotional reaction may be comparable to grief—painful, intense, deep, and long lasting.

Is there any way to avoid this trauma? Yes, according to the Apostle Paul. "…don't look at the [things seen] right now; rather…look forward to [things]…not yet seen. For the [things seen] will soon be over, but the joys to come will last forever" (2 Corinthians 4:18).

Paul knew that as wonderful as family, friends, jobs, possessions, prestige, money, perfect bodies…are, all will pass away some day. If we idolize any of these—that is, if we focus excessively on them—we will experience great emotional pain when they slip away from us. Then we will hear the coach's words coming from our own lips: "My god has died."

Therefore, we must choose our focus carefully, as Paul did. He said, "…everything else is worthless when compared with the priceless gain of knowing Christ Jesus my Lord. I have discarded everything else, counting it all as garbage, so that I may have Christ and become one with Him" (Philippians 3:8).

The Christ that Paul knew will never die, neither will He disillusion those who worship Him and serve Him. He is a God of substance, a God of infinite and <u>eternal</u> worth.

Reflections

Don't Fall Off the Runway!

After two stressful days of preliminaries, it was time to announce the nineteen pre-teen girls who had been chosen as semi-finalists in the beauty pageant. An expectant hush fell over the crowd assembled in the ballroom as the 106 girls and their well-wishers listened to the Master of Ceremonies read the list.

By the time he finished, a long line of excited semi-finalists extended across the platform. Excitement and hope surged within them as they realized that the coveted crown and prizes lay within their grasp.

Before the judges made their final decision, the contestants were instructed to walk to center stage, turn around, and then walk slowly down the runway. One by one, as their names were called, the girls made their final appearances before the judges who sat at long tables parallel to the runway.

One young girl was so determined to impress the judges that she looked over her shoulder and smiled beautifully at them. Unfortunately, she forgot to watch where she was going and nearly tumbled off the end of the runway. Had it not been for the person who was standing beside the steps to assist the contestants as they exited the runway, that semi-finalist would have fallen on her pretty face. (I don't know if her less than graceful exit influenced the judges' decision. However, she did not win the coveted title.)

I felt truly sorry for what happened to her, but I also felt grateful for the lesson she unknowingly provided for me. Her mistake is one many of us make. While intently trying to impress others, we fail to take note of our position. Often we, like the contestant, are not aware of the pitfalls ahead. When we stumble and fall along life's path, how grateful we should be to those who keep us from making a total spectacle of ourselves!

Citing the goofs made by well-intentioned but overly confident people of the past, Paul warned the Christians at Corinth to avoid making the same kind of mistakes. "All these events happened *to them* as examples *for us*. They were written down to warn us...If you think you are standing strong, be careful, for you, too, may fall into the same sin" (1 Corinthians 10:11b-12, emphasis added). To put it another way, "Watch where **you** are going! Don't fall off the runway!"

Johnnie Ann Burgess Gaskill

Are We On the Right Road?

Steady, heavy rain cascaded down the windshield as we traveled the unfamiliar road to our vacation destination. The blackness of the night surrounded us, making it impossible to see more than a few feet ahead. "Are you sure we're on the right road?" I asked.

"I don't think we've missed our turn," my husband replied, "but it'd certainly be nice to see a road sign."

Indeed! But he had to drive for miles, or so it seemed, before we saw a sign that let us know we were traveling in the right direction. How we appreciated that sign. Though it didn't stop the rain or push back the darkness, it did assure us were on the right road. Just knowing that helped us relax and begin to enjoy the trip once again.

Life's a lot like that, isn't it? Somehow the circumstances are easier to deal with if we can just know for certain that we are on the right path. But how can we be sure?

First, we must come to know Jesus for He said, "I am the way, the truth, and the life. No one can come to the Father except through Me" (John 14:6).

Second, we must believe and obey God's Word. "Trust in the LORD with all your heart; do not depend on your own understanding. Seek his will in all you do, and he will direct your paths" (Proverbs 3:5-6).

Third, as we travel down's life's unfamiliar roads that are filled with uncertainties, we must learn to listen to God's voice for He will direct us, as Isaiah 30:21 says, "You will see your teacher with your own eyes, and you will hear a voice say, 'This is the way; turn around and walk here.'"

And the way God directs us will always be well marked. The cross of Jesus will point the way to our heavenly home!

Reflections

Choosing the Best

Decisions! Decisions! Decisions! Sometimes I wish I didn't *have* to make them, though I am grateful for the ability as well as the freedom to choose. Actually, it's all that pre-decision thinking that wears me out. For me, even small decisions like what to cook for dinner are often tough to make since I want to make sure each person gathered around the table has a balanced meal, even finicky eaters.

Naturally, when big decisions come my way, I struggle. I really, really do. I contemplate how my decision will affect other people. I try to predict the outcome by asking, "If I do this, then this may happen. But, on the other hand, if I do this, then this or that may happen."

Sometimes the choices are so obvious that I can immediately select the good one and reject the bad one. However, when I am faced with more than one good option, then I must ask some serious questions. "God, which of these will enhance my relationship with You? Which will enable me to be more obedient to You? Am I willing to choose the one You want for me or will I insist on having things my way? Will I make up my own mind and then ask You to approve my choice?"

Answers to such questions don't come easily or quickly. But they do help me choose between better and best. As I pray and seek God's will, I agree with the Apostle Paul when he said, "I really don't know which is better. I'm torn between two desires" (Philippians 1:22b-23a).

Every time I come to God with a sincere, seeking heart, He guides me, especially when I say, "God, open wide the door to whichever option is from You. And, please close the door to the choice that is not according to Your will for me at this time. Keep me from being anywhere or doing anything that is not for Your glory and my good."

Johnnie Ann Burgess Gaskill

Carl

As I dressed hurriedly, I made mental notes for the day's schedule. Because I was so preoccupied, I scarcely paid any attention to the sportscaster as he recapped recent athletic events.

However, without really knowing why I snapped to attention, I heard him say, "Carl is not selfish. He always thinks of the team before he thinks of himself."

Of course, I had no idea who Carl was or even the particular sport he played, but I assumed he was a talented athlete of some sort. After all, he had been singled out for special mention by that sportscaster. However, I was glad I heard that little bit about Carl, for it started me to thinking about the value of being a team player.

It must be real tough, I thought, *for a person with exceptional abilities to be just one of the team*. Most of us just "go for it" and get all the attention we can. We forget the other guys, especially those less capable than we are. However, we need more people who are willing to be like Carl. We need people who take seriously the advice found in Philippians 2:3: "Don't be selfish; don't live to make a good impression on others. Be humble, thinking of others as better than yourself. Don't think only about your own [interests], but be interested in others, too, and what they are doing."

Imagine how changed our world would be if everyone did that! What would happen to power struggles? Would we devote our energies to getting the job done rather than to making a name for ourselves? Would we see more of a balance in our society, particularly in regard to education, economics, health care, housing and so forth?

The Carls of this world do make a difference, a significant one. If you and I agree our world needs more Carls, are we willing to become one?

Reflections

The Golden Rule

For years I thought I understood the Golden Rule: "Do for others what you would like them to do for you" (Matthew 7:12). I'd always believed that following the Golden Rule involved some kind of bartering system. For example, if I want people to be kind to me, I should treat them kindly. The verse ***does*** mean that; however, there's more to the Golden Rule than simply treating others the way we want them to treat us, or so I learned.

While preparing to lead a conference for those who teach Adults in Sunday School, I came across the insight that changed my thinking regarding the Golden Rule. In **Teaching Adults the Bible**, authors Michael Fink and Ross West point out that teachers must consider the learning styles and preferences of their students and use methods that best enable them to learn instead of the teacher always using instructional methods that he or she prefers.

That new slant caused me to analyze my own teaching methods. I am a visual learner; therefore, when I teach, I tend to write on the board, make charts, use outlines, color code information that is on overhead transparencies, etc. That is all well and good, up to a point. But, as a teacher, I must remember that not all my students are visual learners. Some learn best through creative activities, such as role playing or writing and presenting dramatic monologues and skits, etc. Since adults (and children, too!) have different learning styles, a teacher who follows the Golden Rule will not teach them the way she wants someone to teach her. Instead, a good teacher will teach to meet the needs of her students rather than her own.

The new insight into the Golden Rule carried over to other areas of my life. I began to see that the way I express love should be determined by what the recipient needs rather than by what I would need or want if I were in a similar situation. For instance, when I am sick I want my family members to stop by the bedroom frequently and check to see how I am doing. I like for them to ask me if there's anything I need. I appreciate their sitting beside me for a few minutes and just "visiting." Such little gestures make me feel loved and cared for.

My husband, on the other hand, dislikes all that attention when he is ill. He much prefers being left alone. When he feels better, he will rejoin the family. Until then, the most loving thing we can do for him is simply "let him be." That's so hard for me to do because I want to care for him like I want him to care for me when I'm sick.

So, I've learned that I am to make diligent effort to understand others and to treat them in a way that pleases them, for I want those people, in turn, to treat me in the way that pleases me. That biblical principle works well not only within the classroom but also in every situation in which we interact with others.

Reflections

A Tranquil Heart

During my morning quiet time, this verse grabbed my attention: "A relaxed attitude lengthens life…" (Proverbs 14:30). As I reflected on what it meant, I knew that I had felt differently the past few weeks, for I had slowed down (somewhat!) and had taken time to read my Bible, to pray, and to write in my journal before going to work. I knew that if I continued to do those things I would experience even more tranquility in my mind and emotions. I felt that such a change in my "inner person" would improve my physical well-being also.

As I dressed for work, the phrase "a tranquil heart" kept going through my mind. I yearned for one, and I knew that it was possible to have one. I envisioned how wonderful it would be for my mind, my emotions, and my will to be undisturbed and at a peace regardless of what was going on all around me.

"Father," I said, "will You help me have a tranquil heart this day?"

Upon arriving at work, I began completing the tasks on my to-do list. The first one was to find a replacement for a conference leader who had called to say she could not lead a training session that was to take place in five days.

I made one call, two calls, three calls, and more, but all to no avail. Each of the persons I called was already scheduled to be somewhere else. However, each one apologized for not being able to come to my rescue. Each suggested names of others who might be available.

As I tried again and again, my heart remained tranquil, which was unusual for me. I'm usually "churning" on the inside, even though I appear calm. Although few people notice that I am stressed, I know it and my body feels it!

The hours sped by as I made one unsuccessful phone call after another. At lunchtime, I went outside the building and enjoyed the crisp Fall air. I took time to praise God for the beauty so characteristic of that season. Then I said, "Father, I am going to trust You to handle this crisis. You know how important it is that I find not only a replacement but also someone who will do an excellent job. I will continue to pursue all the leads I've been given, but I am just about all out of names."

When I left work that afternoon, I still had not found a conference leader. Nevertheless, I remained calm. I didn't dismiss the situation from my mind, but neither did I allow it to create undue stress. Instead, I believed that God would help me find someone.

That evening a conference leader for whom I had left a message earlier in the day called me. "I already have a commitment for that night," he said, "but I'll see if I can juggle my schedule."

"I do appreciate your being willing to do that, but I don't want you to complicate your life in order to help me."

We talked a bit more, and then he gave me the name of someone who had once led a conference for him. As it turned out, that person could come and was excited about being asked.

During what turned out to be a three-day enlistment process, the Lord helped me to have a tranquil heart, even as I was getting right down to the wire! My tranquil heart felt so wonderful that I decided not to wait until the next crisis to ask for one.

Reflections

Where Jesus Wants to Go

Though I wanted to be attentive to the minister's words, my mind took a slightly different track. The pastor had asked, "Where have you taken Jesus lately?" Then he had mentioned some of the wrong places where people might have taken Him.

I agreed with what he said, but another question, closely related to his, popped into my mind. "Where have I NOT taken Jesus recently?" That question proved more painful to answer than the one the minister had asked.

I immediately thought about the people I knew who needed to be invited to Bible study so that their lives could be transformed as we learned what God wanted us to do and to be. Jesus would like me to take Him to visit them.

I thought about neighbors and friends who were dealing with aging bodies and problems associated with that stage of life. They would enjoy seeing the smiling face of someone who'd come to lend a hand or just to visit with them. Jesus would like me to take Him to visit them.

I remembered some friends who were struggling with heavy burdens: single parenting, loss of a spouse, addiction, divorce recovery, rejection, unemployment, financial problems… Jesus would like me to take Him to visit them.

I contemplated those who were weary of caring for others: those who worked with the poor, the mentally ill, the imprisoned, the handicapped, their aging parents or their young children… Jesus would like me to take Him to visit them as well as the people to whom they ministered.

I remembered dear friends I hadn't been in touch with in a long while. At one time our friendship was one of the joys of my life, but circumstances had taken us down separate paths and we no longer communicated heart-to-heart and encouraged each other. Jesus would like me to take Him to visit them.

I remembered many others who had not yet accepted Jesus Christ as their personal Lord and Savior. They needed someone to tell them the Good News. They needed to know how they could be born into the family of God. Jesus would like me to take Him to visit them.

Many others crossed my mind that Sunday morning and in the days that followed. Though I mentally listed several places Jesus would like to go, I did not take Him there. Instead, I took myself where I needed to go: to work, to the stores, to places of rest, to meetings…Now, these were not necessarily *wrong* places, for Jesus wanted to be there, too. And I knew He could reach out and touch people through me wherever I took

Johnnie Ann Burgess Gaskill

Him. However, on that Sunday morning He reminded me of places He wanted me to take Him. I sensed He wanted me to stop being so devoted to my own agenda and to become more sensitive about where *He* wanted to go.

Reflections

Exteriors and Interiors

The bananas looked perfect. Not a single dark spot marred their thick, yellow-green peel that told me they had reached what I considered the perfect stage of ripeness. I could hardly wait to eat one.

The one I selected looked so perfect, even after I peeled it. But when I began to slice it, I saw that the lovely banana was rotten on the inside, all the way down, from top to bottom. I tossed it in the trash and peeled another one, assuming that it would be just fine. But, alas, its condition was the same as the first. The third banana was like the others. By salvaging the best parts of them, I managed to get enough to add to my bowl of cereal.

As the day passed, I thought about those bananas. *Their external appearance certainly fooled me*, I thought. Each time I passed by the rest of that bunch of beautiful bananas lying on the countertop, I felt a twinge of disappointment as well as a bit of anger at having been deceived.

Even in small matters, I strongly desire that the inside be as good as the outside, perhaps even better. I don't really care if there is a blemish on the *peel* of my banana, but I do expect the inside to be free from any rottenness. Likewise, a book may have a plain cover and a ho-hum title, but I want its content to be superior. In summary, it's not the external appearance—the packaging—that matters most to me.

By taking that thought a step further, I began to see that the kind of person we are on the inside cannot remain hidden. The true self **will**, at some point, be revealed. And if people discover any rottenness there, they will be feel both disappointed and deceived, regardless of how attractive the external appears.

Speaking to those who took great pains to appear pious and pure, Jesus said, "How terrible it will be for you teachers of religious law and you Pharisees. Hypocrites! For you are so careful to clean the *outside* of the cup and the dish, but *inside* you are filthy—full of greed and self-indulgence! Blind Pharisees! First wash the inside of the cup, and then the outside will become clean, too.

"How terrible it will be for you teachers of religious law and you Pharisees. Hypocrites! You are like whitewashed tombs—beautiful on the *outside* but filled on the *inside* with dead people's bones and all sorts of impurity. You try to look like upright people outwardly, but inside your hearts are filled with hypocrisy and lawlessness" (Matthew 23:25-28).

(And they thought they had fooled Him!)

When we begin to see ourselves as God sees us, we will realize what a mess we are. Then we'll ask God to forgive us and to cleanse us…from the inside out. Once He makes our inner self pure and clean, we will no longer disappoint others when they look past our outer layer and see our true self. All hypocrisy, all deception, will be gone. What others will see is exactly what we are.

Reflections About Myself

Johnnie Ann Burgess Gaskill

Reflections

Two Vital "C"s

A ten-day stay in the hospital forced me to depend on other persons to meet my needs for even simple things such as a cup of crushed ice. I had to swallow my pride, put aside my independence, and allow others to do those things for me. The doctor insisted on strict bed rest for me, since I had a blood clot in a deep vein in my right leg. He said, "Every step you take increases the likelihood that it will dislodge and move toward your vital organs." Of course, I did not want that to happen, so I stayed in bed as per his orders.

As the medical staff cared for me, I knew that my life depended, in part, on their competency. I watched what they did, and I felt scared, almost paranoid, actually, when anyone deviated from following the procedures to which I had grown accustomed, especially those involving injecting medicine directly into my bloodstream.

In addition to needing competent care, I also needed and appreciated compassion. I felt so grateful to those who sensed my needs and met them without my having to ask for help. I welcomed compassion from people at all levels—from the doctor who gently wiped the perspiration from my face following a painful procedure and from the maintenance man who changed a light bulb in my bathroom and then, several days later, asked how I was doing when he saw me taking my first steps outside my room.

Competency is critical in many situations, but so is compassion. Competency may enable us to survive physically, but who wants to live if not treated with compassion?

Jesus understood that. Not only did He heal every kind of disease and sickness, but when He saw the crowd that followed Him everywhere, He also "felt great [compassion] for [them], because their problems were so great and they didn't know where to go for help. They were like sheep without a shepherd" (Matthew 9:36).

That rare mix of competency and compassion—of power and pity—drew multitudes of hurting people to Jesus. Now I know why!

Johnnie Ann Burgess Gaskill

Speak, Lord; I'm Listening!

I normally did not sit alone in my den at 4 a.m., especially when the day ahead promised to be of the "get-up-early-and-collapse-late" variety. Yet, instead of getting some much-needed rest in my comfortable bed, there I sat. Why? Four days earlier I had decided to follow a "guaranteed-to-work" suggestion. Since then, I made "Speak, Lord, for Thy servant is listening" my last conscious thought before I drifted off to sleep.

As the Lord honored my decision to be attentive to His voice, I began to notice a difference. I sensed He was giving me additional strength and guidance. Ideas and solutions to problems came more easily to my conscious awareness—something I might not have noticed were it not for my nightly request: "Speak, Lord, for Thy servant is listening."

Naturally, I felt very grateful for God's willingness to communicate with me during "normal business hours;" however, I must admit that I rose rather reluctantly from my bed in the wee hours of that morning! But, as I sat quietly before Him, I sensed God saying many things to me. For instance, He assured me of His love. He reminded me of the two specific things He wanted me to do: teach His word and write inspirational material. Thus it was, that during those pre-dawn hours I sensed anew His call upon my life.

Over the years I'd learned that when God speaks to me through thoughts and feelings, He also validates the messages through His written Word. Therefore, I opened the Bible and re-read the account of God's speaking to young Samuel.

Since Samuel had not heard the Lord's voice before, he naturally assumed the voice calling him belonged to Eli, the aged priest who had taught and cared for Samuel since his mother weaned him and brought him to live in the house of the LORD. Twice Samuel ran to Eli, only to discover that Eli had not called him.

"So now the LORD called a third time, and once more Samuel jumped up and ran to Eli. 'Here I am,' he said. 'What do you need?'

"Then Eli realized it was the LORD who was calling the boy. So he said to Samuel, 'Go and lie down again, and if someone calls again, say, "Yes, LORD your servant is listening."'" (1Samuel 3:8-9).

Samuel did as Eli told him. As soon as God had Samuel's attention, He asked Samuel to warn Eli of God's impending judgment upon him and his family. Though Samuel was afraid to deliver that message, he did tell Eli everything that God had revealed to him. That was the first of many assignments the Lord gave to Samuel, for he served for many years as a prophet/spokesperson, for God.

Reflections

Like Samuel, I'm learning to say, "Speak, Lord, for Thy servant is listening, ready to hear and then to obey." Such time spent in listening is never wasted, even if God chooses to speak in the wee hours of the morning while all is quiet and still.

Johnnie Ann Burgess Gaskill

What a Week!

What a week! And it wasn't over! My watch told me that it was 12:30 a.m. that Saturday, but my body believed it was still Friday night for it hadn't slept yet. Though I was exhausted, I continued to sit in what my children call "Mama's study corner" and to enjoy a few moments of solitude as I waited for the clothes dryer to complete its cycle. It felt good to be in my special place and to recline on the sofa—pen in one hand and Bible in the other—and to have my beloved books nearby.

In the stillness of the night, I reflected on the events of the past few days. What a week! I'd stayed in touch with a friend whose husband was critically ill. I'd gone to the funeral home to express sympathy to a mother whose daughter had died in an automobile accident. Sharing their concern and grief increased my emotional stress. Then there had been back-to-school shopping for my two daughters, completing a long-term project at work, fulfilling some PTA responsibilities, and squeezing in two days for a family vacation.

One morning that week I felt especially weary. I thought my brain had shifted into neutral, but as I automatically went through the routine of getting dressed for still another busy day, this question popped into my mind: "My God, my God, why have I forsaken You?"

Startled to alertness by such an unexpected, disturbing question, I began to argue against the truth. "But I haven't forsaken You!" I said to that inner voice. "I've read the Bible every day. I've prayed for those who needed You so desperately."

Though my words were true, I knew—deep in my heart—that they were a cover up. I knew, and God knew, the *real* truth. Yes, I had read His Word, but more out of a sense of "oughtness" or habit rather than from a desire to hear God speak to me. Yes, I had prayed, but mainly because I had several "somethings" I wanted Him to do, including heal my friend's husband and comfort the grieving mother.

I began to see how I had indeed temporarily forsaken Him as I allowed my activities—necessary and appropriate though they were—to consume precious moments normally reserved for intimate communication with God. Feeling somewhat like the prodigal son described in Luke 15, I admitted my sin and returned to my heavenly Father, and He welcomed me with open arms. Once again there was joy in His heart and in mine!

I recalled all of that as I sat quietly in "Mama's study corner," thinking, *What a week! What a night! What a God!*

Sleeping Soundly

The fire alarm sounded in a nearby dorm, but I did not hear it. Neither did I hear voices of the girls who ran into the room Linda and I shared in order to see what was going on outside. The following morning I felt more than a little embarrassed as I listened to them recount the arrival of the fire truck.

Years later another episode reminded me of how soundly I slept. When my husband returned home quite late from an Atlanta Falcons' football game, he made lots of noise. He raised the heavy garage door that was below the bedroom, parked the car, and lowered the door. He entered the house, fixed himself a snack, and took a hot shower to thaw his frozen body. But I heard nothing. Actually, I did not know he was anywhere around until he slipped into bed beside me and placed his cold feet against my warm ones.

When I was expecting our first child, I wondered, *Will my sleeping so soundly prevent me from hearing the baby*? However, I need not have worried. My eyes opened wide and my senses went on red alert each time Jennifer cried. In fact, most of the time I heard her stirring and grunting before she ever started crying.

I still did not hear other things when I slept, things like my husband's alarm clock and heavy thunder, but I always heard and responded quickly to Jennifer's signals. I did the same when Jena was born. Even when the girls were teenagers I heard them if they got up to get a drink of water or to let the cat out.

Why was I able to hear the children and not other things? I don't know. Perhaps God gives mothers a sixth sense, a heightened sensitivity to the needs of their children.

Likewise, in spiritual matters, I find I must pray, "Lord, give me the sensitivity I need to hear Your voice and the cries of those around me. Wake me up, Lord. Open my eyes. Put my senses on red alert. Help me to respond."

Johnnie Ann Burgess Gaskill

Keeping Everything Clean

A friend and I talked about how difficult it is to maintain a clean house. Since we had neither big blocks of leisure time in which to do our own cleaning or money to pay someone else to do it, we had to clean a little here and a little there in whatever time our busy schedules allowed. We lamented the fact that we were seldom able to thoroughly clean our entire house on any given day. "Even if we did," my friend said, "the house wouldn't stay clean for very long. The sink would fill up with dishes. There'd be dirty clothes all over the place."

What we needed, we decided, was someone to come in every day and clean for us. Then we'd sit serenely and enjoy our clean surroundings. We pictured ourselves sitting on the patio and enjoying a cup of coffee in the morning or sipping a glass of iced tea in the afternoon. We also imagined we'd have time to stretch out and read a few chapters in a book or thumb through a magazine. Best of all, we decided, we could walk through the house without feeling guilty and stressed out over the things that needed to be done.

As we talked, we described the house we wanted: clean windows framed by freshly-laundered curtains, vinyl floors so clean and sparkly they looked dangerously slippery, carpets without stains, sterile bathrooms, dust-free furniture, empty laundry baskets, toys sorted and shelved, the smell of bread baking in the oven...and ourselves calm and serene, beautifully manicured, casually but elegantly dressed, and able to invite an unexpected guest into our home without any embarrassment whatsoever. Admittedly, a gap existed between the current condition of our houses and the way we'd like them to be. But, to our credit, my friend and I were trying to reach that illusive goal.

Reflecting on that conversation, I realized our spiritual lives need daily attention as well. Even though Jesus cleansed us thoroughly of our sins the moment we trusted Him as our Savior, we need daily cleansing, for we are prone to clutter up our lives with bad attitudes and actions. Often we leave a trail of unkind words or deeds behind us. We forget to put priorities in their proper place. We can no longer find the picture of the person God wants us to be.

Without daily confession and cleansing, our sins accumulate faster than dirty dishes in the sink. Like David, we need to say, "Wash me clean from my guilt. Purify me from my sin...For I recognize my shameful deeds—they haunt me day and night...Create in me a clean heart, O God. Renew a right spirit within me" (Psalm 51:2,3,10).

Reflections

A Friend Like Linda

A phrase from one of the songs we sang often at Tift College frequently comes to mind. "Remember the friends you made here…" And I do! I remember one friend above all others: Linda, my roommate. She was and still is my encourager, my counselor, and my friend. Though we were total strangers the first day we arrived on the campus in September 1964, we liked each other instantly. From the beginning I cherished her friendship, but even more so as the years pass and I gain a greater appreciation for one of the many unselfish things she did for me.

Traditionally, the President of the Senior Class played the role of King Arthur in the annual ceremony known as "Round Table." As time drew near for the reenactment of King Arthur knighting the Knights of the Round Table, the speech professor who would be directing the ceremony summoned me to her classroom. After some preliminary remarks, she got right to the point. "Johnnie Ann, I wonder if you've considered letting someone else play the part of King Arthur?"

Of course, I hadn't. The Senior Class President had always been King Arthur. Although a casting committee decided on the roles the other Seniors (all female) would play, there was never any doubt about who would be King Arthur.

I held back the tears until our meeting ended and I walked across campus to the room I shared with Linda. Then the tears flowed freely. I realized the professor was right. Someone else should play King Arthur. But, my, oh my, how it hurt to acknowledge that!

When I told Linda what the professor had said and that I had decided to step down, she became angry. "You will not! You are our President and you will be our King Arthur!"

"But," I protested. "You don't understand. The professor wants someone who has a better voice, someone who can project and enunciate well, someone who can speak eloquently to the large audiences we'll have each night of the performance."

Linda could do all that. The professor knew it. I knew it. Linda knew it. But Linda refused to assume the role that was mine even though I was willing to give it to her.

"You will be King Arthur," she insisted. "I'll help you!" She kept her promise. Hour after hour she helped me memorize pages and pages of script. She coached me as I struggled to swap my Southern accent for one that sounded a bit more King Arthur-ish.

The ceremony was beautiful as knights and ladies in medieval costumes marched in and sat around the huge table in the gymnasium.

During those nights of pageantry, we felt as if we'd been transported back in time to the days of the real King Arthur. It was a ceremony never to be forgotten.

No wonder I think of Linda whenever I sing the song, "Remember the friends you've made here..." and also whenever I read these words of Jesus: "I command you to love each other in the same way that I love you. And here is how to measure it—the greatest love is shown when people lay down their lives for their friends" (John 15:12-13).

Although Linda did not die for me, as Jesus did, she did lay aside her opportunity to be cast in the leading role and she did give of her time and talents to help me do my best in the role that could so easily have belonged to her.

Having a friend like Linda helps me understand the One who did indeed lay down His life for me.

Reflections

Regaining Control of a Runaway Horse

When talking with a friend who had a job similar to mine, he asked, "How's it going?"

I laughed. "I feel as if I'm on a runaway horse!"

We laughed together. "Say no more," he said. "I know exactly what you mean."

Unfortunately, as most of us race through life on our trusty steed, we sense that he often carries us faster and farther than we really want to go. Being successful in the workplace requires that we adjust our speed from a trot to a full gallop if we are to fulfill the ever-increasing demands placed on us. While we race on several tracks in one day, our children grow up before we've had time to train them as we should. While moving at breakneck speed, we have time for little more than a fleeting look at our parents (and at our image in the mirror) and realize that the years are slipping away from us.

Riding a horse that can take us the fartherest distance in the shortest amount of time is a risky endeavor, even if we control the direction the horse takes us. However, if we should lose control of the horse and allow him to take us wherever he wishes, defeat is certain. (Has any jockey every ridden a runaway horse to victory?)

If we're on a runaway horse, how do we regain control? How do we get him back on the right track and keep him moving toward the finish line? Better yet, how do we keep from having a runaway horse in the first place?

In my search for answers, I read books on time management and goal setting. I took pages of notes about making choices and determining priorities. I read about people who had learned to do ten things while on the telephone!

How wonderful it must be to be so efficient, I thought. *Maybe someday I can do that.* But even that brief surge of hope turned to despair as I continued to understand and follow what seemed like "99 Steps to Regaining Control of Your Life."

As I kept searching for answers, I happened to hear part of an interview James Dobson conducted with a lady named Gert. Though I missed the introduction to the radio program, I surmised that Gert's life had not been easy. Even so, she had managed to carry out many successful ministries.

When Dr. Dobson asked her how she managed to accomplish so much that was meaningful, she answered, "I ask myself two questions every hour, on the hour."

Well, I tuned in at that point in the interview. Two questions seemed wonderfully simple when compared to the "99 Steps for Regaining Control of Your Life." I eagerly awaited Gert's method of establishing priorities and managing her time.

"The first question I ask is, 'How is my relationship with Jesus?' I do nothing until I make sure that all is right between the Lord and myself. Then, when I look all my activities, I ask, 'Is what I am doing for Gert or for the Lord?' If it's for Gert, I don't do it. If it's for the Lord, I give it all I've got."

As Gert continued to talk, I realized she had discovered the secret to dealing with a runaway horse. Get him back on the right track and under control with two simple questions: How is my relationship with Jesus? Who is the focus of my service? If we remember to ask often enough ("every hour, on the hour"), we may never again feel as if we're speeding through life on a runaway horse.

Reflections

Moving Beyond the Comfort Zone

"That walk was a killer," I exclaimed as I headed for the nearest chair.

Now, I was accustomed to walking. In fact, my neighbor and I had maintained a regular walking program for several weeks. We had started out slowly, but had gradually increased both our speed and our distance.

But on the night I returned home exhausted, my neighbor had been unavailable for our evening exercise; so, I'd said to my daughter, "Walk with me, Jennifer."

Before we reached the end of our street, I started doubting my ability to keep up with her. However, I determined to do my best to match her pace so that she could get maximum benefit from the exercise time rather than be hindered by her not-yet-physically-fit mother.

As we walked, I gave up talking in order to have enough oxygen to breathe. Only a few times during the 30-minute walk did I have to ask Jennifer to slow down. On the level places and on the down slopes I kept her pace, but when we started up the hills, I begged for mercy!

Whenever we finished the first lap, I checked the stopwatch and was pleased to see that we had trimmed three minutes off my normal time. Encouraged by that, we set off on the second lap. Exhausted though I was, we walked a fast pace and finished that one almost as quickly as we had the first. I was elated! My body had potential that I had not yet tapped. All I needed was for someone to set a faster pace, someone to challenge me to a new level of performance. Though it nearly killed me, I needed it!

That's true not only of physical challenges but also of spiritual ones. We need people who will walk with us, while encouraging us to stretch ourselves to reach new levels of achievement. As we persevere and put forth extra effort, we feel elated as we attempt things for God that we might never have tried had we not had someone to challenge us.

Whenever I think of spiritual challenges, I always recall the Apostle Paul's words to Timothy, his young disciple, who had worked with him to reach people with the Good News about Jesus Christ. By observing the life of Paul, Timothy had seen what God could do with a life surrendered to His use. Timothy had also learned that serving the Lord didn't guarantee a life free from problems and trials of all sorts. Yet, he had also seen how one could rejoice while persevering in the midst of difficulties.

Having set a godly example for Timothy, the Apostle Paul felt free to challenge his young disciple. Paul left a "tall order" for Timothy: be strong, suffer hardship, focus on Jesus, be a workman who needs not be ashamed, flee youthful lusts, preach the word…

Paul summarized his commands to Timothy with these words: "…keep a clear mind in every situation. Don't be afraid of suffering for the Lord. Work at bringing others to Christ. Complete the ministry God has given you" (2 Timothy 4:5).

Those words encourage me. As I face the challenge of reaching my God-given potential, I will have to persevere, to push myself out of my comfort zones. But each time I become weary, God graciously provides an encourager, someone who says, "Fulfill your ministry. Be all that God wants you to be." Sometimes doing so nearly kills me, but meeting the challenge surely does feel wonderful.

Reflections

Running on Empty

My eyes widened and my pulse quickened when I looked at my gas gauge. "Good grief," I mumbled, "I can't believe I'm running on empty."

As I drove to the school, I reprimanded myself all the while for forgetting to gas up the car over the weekend. Naturally, I had good excuses for not having done so, but none of them made me feel better that morning. I still had a near-empty tank and four excited children who did not want to be late for the first day of school.

As my two daughters and their friends talked "a mile a minute," I took a calculated risk when I bypassed a gas station in order to get Jennifer and her friend to high school on time. As I drove there, I watched the needle on the gas gauge. When it moved to the right, I relaxed—a little. When it dropped all the way to the left, I leaned forward slightly, fearful of hearing the engine sputter and die on me.

Thankfully, we made it to the high school and then I drove to the nearest gas station. The price of the gas did not concern me. I would have paid anything the owner asked.

Once I'd filled the tank, I drove confidently to the middle school to drop off Jena and her friend. Since my attention was no longer riveted on the gas gauge, I concentrated on the children as they talked excitedly about their first day in the new school.

Several days later when I had more time to reflect on the experience of running on empty, I still could not believe I had let my car get that low on fuel. I certainly knew better. My only excuse for having taken such a chance was that I'd been too busy. Always in a rush to get somewhere, I'd look at the indicator, assure myself that I had plenty of gas to get to my destination, and resolve to fill up the tank on the way home. However, since I was always in a hurry to get home, too, I never took the time to fill up.

I've found myself running on empty in other ways—physically and emotionally, as well as spiritually. When my warning signal appears, I keep hoping that I'll have enough resources for one more task. Unless I force myself to stop and refuel, my life registers *empty* and I have nothing left to give, no matter how important the situation.

When in such a drained, depleted condition, I feel fearful and anxious. I tend to focus on the negatives in myself and in others. I am unable to see beyond my own needs, my own emptiness.

All of that changes dramatically as soon as I take time to refuel. When I rest and when I spend quality (and quantity!!) time with God, He so faithfully fills my empty tank with the fullness of His divine presence

(Ephesians 3:19). All that He is and everything He provides (love, peace, strength, wisdom, goodness, joy…) become available to me. No longer running on empty, I confidently and eagerly participate in the exciting adventures of the life He has given me.

Reflections

Warm Fuzzies

For as long as I can remember, I've saved personal notes, awards, certificates of appreciation, and the like. At times I've wondered why I do this. Is it because I've tucked away in my subconscious a notion that one day I'll be famous, and people will search through all my possessions to retrieve interesting bits of information about me? Is it because I have too much pride? Too little self-esteem?

I received an answer when a friend expressed his appreciation for a note I had sent him, a note affirming his ability as a teacher. He said, "After I read your note, I dropped it in my 'warm fuzzies' folder." Smiling, he said, "I always keep such notes of affirmation. Then when I'm feeling discouraged, I take out the folder and read everything in it! Before long I'm feeling better and ready to face the challenges of the day."

His words relieved me. *Maybe*, I thought, *I don't have a personality quirk after all. Perhaps, I've been doing something sensible by treasuring the kind words that have been extended to me.*

I realized that affirmations are to be cherished and used to encouraged us at the moment we receive them as well as at future times when we are discouraged. Sincere praise elevates our self-esteem and increases our motivation, for it assures us that we have something to contribute.

Soon after my conversation with the man, I received notes from three friends who had no idea about the issues with which I was struggling. Yet each of these friends spoke to me at my point of need and encouraged me to keep on keeping on.

What did I do with each of the notes? After I'd read them again and again, I put them in my warm fuzzies folder, for I knew there would be other days when I'd need to read again those precious words of affirmation and confirmation.

Biblical writers knew the value of giving a sincere compliment or a word of praise to a friend. In his letters, the Apostle Paul frequently mentioned people who had enriched his life and ministry in a variety of ways. As I read about their characteristics and contributions, I thought, *I'd like to be that kind of person.*

One of my favorite affirmations is the one John, the beloved Apostle, sent in a letter to Gaius. "Dear friend, I am praying that all is well with you and that your body is as healthy as I know your soul is. Some of the brothers recently returned and made me very happy by telling me about your faithfulness and that you are living in the truth. I could have no greater joy than to hear that my children live in the truth" (3 John 1:2-4).

How I wish those same words could be said to me and of me.

If I were to receive a note like that from a spiritual giant like John, I wouldn't put it in my warm fuzzies folder. Instead, I'd keep it with me at all times so that I could read it often, for there is no greater affirmation than that one lives by the truth—that one walks in obedience to the Word of God.

Reflections

All the Difference

As Jena and I talked with Richard, he shared with us how lonely he had been much of the time since he had come to America from his home in Barbados. He said that the daytime hours passed quickly for him since he was busy learning technical information to take back to Barbados, a beautiful island in the Caribbean. However, time weighed heavily on his hands during the evenings and weekends as he sat alone in his motel room.

But those hours of loneliness had served a purpose in God's plan for Richard's life. "I have had time to pray and think," he told us. "At home I could hardly find any time to be by myself, but here I have had many hours to look at my life."

As Richard continued to talk, I realized God had indeed done a marvelous work in his life. At one point in our heart-to-heart conversation, I said, "Jesus does make a big difference, doesn't He?"

Richard's reply pierced my soul. With his dark eyes brimming with tears of joy, he looked me directly in the eye, and whispered, "He makes **all** the difference."

The impact of his simple, yet profound, words stunned me. Whenever I recovered, I said humbly, "Thank you for correcting me. You are exactly right. Jesus does make all the difference."

Richard did not intend to cause a storm in my soul; he spoke only the truth of his own relationship with Jesus. However, the Holy Spirit of God used his words to convict me of the shallowness and the superficiality of my own relationship to Jesus. I realized that I had allowed Jesus to impact certain areas of my life—to make a big difference; whereas, Richard had invited Jesus to permeate all of his life—to make all the difference.

Long after Richard left our home that Saturday in July, I continued to think about his words. I prayed that the five words he spoke would permanently change my relationship with Christ.

I considered also the life of the Apostle Paul, for Jesus made all the difference in his life, too. After his conversion on the Damascus Road, Paul's life was never the same. Jesus changed Paul's priorities, removed his racial and religious prejudices, used him mightily to spread the Gospel he had once despised, gave him a love for people which did not "count the cost," and enabled Paul to experience joy in the midst of great suffering and persecution. To Paul, as to Richard, Jesus made more that a big difference. He made all the difference.

If Jesus is indeed our Lord, we will allow Him to revolutionize rather than simply modify our thinking and our service. If Jesus makes all the difference in our lives, His impact is felt every day, not just on Sundays and Wednesdays when we assemble to worship Him and to fellowship with other believers.

When Jesus makes all the difference, we can sing Will L. Thompson's beautiful hymn, "Jesus Is All the World to Me," with deep conviction of the truth of its words. "Jesus is all the world to me/My life, my joy, my all;/He is my strength from day to day,/Without Him I would fall./When I am sad to Him I go./No other one can cheer me so;/When I am sad, He makes me glad,/He's my Friend."

Reflections

Focus on the Center

Several years ago when a man named Richard was visiting us from Barbados, my husband and I, along with our daughter Jena, took him bowling. Though he had never been bowling before, he learned quickly and even managed to score a strike and several spares.

Of course, I don't remember all the details of what happened that afternoon, but I do recall one thing that Richard did. It happened during Jena's turn to bowl. She had knocked down eight pins and was attempting to get the remaining two. However, her bowling ball was running right along the edge of the lane, dangerously close to the dreaded gutter. I took my eyes off her ball momentarily and turned to say something to Richard. Whatever I had intended to say left my mind, for I saw him trying to keep Jena's ball on course by waving his hand in the direction the ball needed to go.

He surprised me by doing that, though the gesture was one I often used. Yet, there he was, thousands of miles from home and having his first experience at bowling, and instinctively trying to direct the ball with a hand signal.

Later that afternoon as Richard and I sat at the kitchen table and talked, the conversation shifted to knowing and doing the will of God. Richard explained that he had a difficult time determining exactly what God wanted him to do. I agreed with him. Choosing between good and evil is fairly easy. Choosing the best from the good is often very difficult.

As we talked, I sensed Richard's intense desire to be in the center of God's will. I surmised that he felt a certain uneasiness about missing God's best for his life.

"Richard, do you remember what you did at the bowling lanes? Do you recall how you desperately wanted Jena's ball to stay out of the gutter in order to knock down those two remaining pins? When the ball ran into the gutter anyway, do you remember how you encouraged Jena?"

He nodded.

"Well," I continued, "I believe there's a lesson we can learn from that. God has a specific target or goal in mind for each of us, which can be compared to the center pin. He wants us to aim at the center pin and strike it with much force because that's the key pin. If we hit it, it will impact the pins around it, adding to our success. However, just as in bowling, we often give it our best shot but still miss the center pin. That is, we often miss God's ideal plan for our lives."

"When our hearts are focused on doing God's perfect will, and we miss it, I picture God watching the scene ever so intently and trying to redirect our misguided efforts so that we will hit the target. Yet, when we experience gutter balls or balls that knock down only a few pins, God does not become angry with us and give us a tongue-lashing we won't forget. Rather, he encourages us to try again, knowing that if we keep our focus on the center pin, we will eventually hit it.

"In that process of trial and error, of success and failure, we will not always have a perfect score. Even experienced bowlers have occasional gutter balls. But failure doesn't keep them out of the game. Rather, they just get up and try harder the next time."

I smiled at him. "So should we," I said gently. "God is for us. He wants us to know His will and do to it. Yet, whenever our efforts don't produce the results He desires, He forgives us."

When I finished my mini-sermon, Richard was smiling. "I like that," he said. "I'm going to remember that illustration."

So will I.

Reflections

Life Will Trash Your Treasures

During a radio broadcast, Dr. James Dobson stated, "Given enough time, life will trash your treasures." That remark concluded the following story he had had shared with the listeners.

When Dr. Dobson had arrived on a college campus to begin his freshman year, one particular trophy captured his attention. Being an avid and an excellent tennis player, he noticed that that trophy bore the names of those who'd won the yearly tennis tournaments. He determined right then and there that he wanted his name on that trophy. He went on to become the school's best tennis player for three out of the four years he was enrolled there.

Many years later a college friend's son salvaged the trophy from the trash and brought it to Dr. Dobson. As he looked at what he had once considered a trophy among trophies, Dr. Dobson's became distressed. Not only had someone trashed the trophy, but someone at the college had neglected to inscribe his name on the trophy following his final victory. That's when Dr. Dobson realized, "Given enough time, life will trash your treasures."

I've never forgotten Dr. Dobson's statement. In fact, I've come up with a few illustrations of my own that verify his conclusion.

Back in the early 1970s, my husband and I bought a brand-new Monte Carlo. We were so proud of that car. We showed it to all our friends and let them swivel around in the leather bucket seats. We washed it at least once a week and waxed it so often that it probably had wax buildup!

However, one day a drunk driver crossed a median and plowed into the side of the car. When the insurance company decided to total the car rather than repair it, our pride and joy ended up in the junkyard.

Likewise, I've seen pictures of the ruins of far-away and long-forgotten cities and castles. Though once well-fortified and bustling with activities during their moments of glory, the ruins that remain testify of their existence. Archaeologists now sift through the sands of many places where a proud people once prospered and enjoyed unparalleled achievements and an opulent lifestyle.

Yes, illustrations abound which prove Dr. Dobson's conclusion: "Given enough time, life will trash your treasures." That isn't a new truth; in fact, Jesus had this to say about cherished possessions: "Don't store up treasures here on earth, where they can be eaten by moths and get rusty, and where thieves break in and steal. Store your treasures in heaven, where they will never become moth-eaten or rusty and where they will be safe from thieves. Wherever your treasure is, there your heart and thoughts will also be" (Matthew 6:19-21).

If we focus mainly on accumulating material possessions, we will weep when we discover that our riches have rotted, our garments have become moth-eaten, and our gold and silver have rusted. (See James 5:1-3). And that will happen, for "Given enough time, life will trash [our] treasures."

Reflections

Due and Payable Upon Receipt

Every now and then I have to relearn some very basic truths. Believe me, I do not like having to repeat simple lessons, for relearning is so humiliating…much like being a college graduate who is forced to return to kindergarten in order to take fundamental courses all over again.

One week I had to relearn a lesson that a mature woman should have mastered long ago. Which lesson? This one: Sooner or later all bills become due and payable.

Keeping track of my spending is fairly easy if I use only the cash in my wallet or write a check. Either way, I can tell at a glance how much money I have left. Whenever I hand over the credit cards, I inadvertently spend more than I realize.

Since I do not have accountant blood flowing through my veins, I do not feel compelled to total the amounts on my copies of the charge receipts. I just stick the little slips of paper in a folder labeled "Receipts." Out of sight. Out of mind. Right? Yet, whenever the monthly bills come in, I'm shocked at the amount due. (Those small charges—a little here and a little there—do add up, don't they?) After I recover from a fainting spell at the mailbox, I walk slowly to the house and place all the mail, including the bills, on the table.

My anguish increases as I wait for my husband to come home and reach for the mail the moment he puts his briefcase down. I do not want my patient, hard-working husband to see the bills, yet he must because they are now due.

Normally, I stay well within our monthly allowance, for we always pay each bill in full every month. Even so, he urges me to spend even less and to save more, which I promise to try to do. But the day a large credit card bill arrived, my husband surprised me when he said angrily, "Johnnie, if you insist on spending the money, then **you** figure out how to pay these bills. **You** juggle the checkbook!"

I shrank from his blunt words. Yet, I needed to hear them. I needed to understand that even though he earned an adequate living, we did not have unlimited funds. So, he, in effect, sent me back to kindergarten to relearn a basic truth: Sooner or later, all bills become due and payable, even those that include those "forgotten" charges.

Credit card bills are not the only ones that become due and payable upon receipt. For example, someone called a radio talk show and expressed her sorrow over being unable to conceive a child due to scar tissue that had formed following an abortion she had had when she was a teenager. Like me, she was surprised and grieved at the amount of her "bill" that was due and payable.

Often when a medical diagnosis is given, a patient sees the high price he or she must pay for self-inflicted physical neglect. The charges for insufficient exercise, improper diet, and unhealthy habits have been added to the enormous health bill that has become due and payable.

In regard to finances, I've learned that a "pay-as-you-go" policy works best. That way, I avoid accumulating any charges that will increase my bill-a-phobia. Plus, keeping a careful eye on my spending guarantees fewer fainting spells at the mailbox. Likewise, I try to act responsibly and take into account the "spending" I do in other areas of my life, since all bills do become due and payable.

Reflections

The Debtor

I closed the storm door with extra force that morning as one of our daughters left for school. Instantly, I regretted allowing her to leave without our resolving the conflict that I had initiated. Immediately, I felt ashamed for not having behaved in a Christ-like manner.

True, the matter I had brought up needed attention, but not during the early morning rush. However, I'd brought it up anyway. I'd been through a stressful, exhausting week and then on my one day off I faced an unending list of chores. So, I gave it my best shot; I began complaining about how nobody cared about me, how nobody volunteered to help, how everybody expected me to make our family life run smoothly…During the pity party I was staging for myself, I became even angrier when no one paid attention to the guest of honor!

No wonder my daughter became angry. The charges I'd made were greatly exaggerated, though I felt they were wholly true—at that moment. I do have a cooperative, supportive family. Whenever I need help, all I have to do is ask. Even if they complain or procrastinate, they do come through for me. However, that particular morning, I felt so totally drained that I need someone to take the initiative rather than grudgingly accept job assignments.

Although the matter did deserve attention, I should have waited until we had time to discuss it. I should have allowed myself time to put things into proper perspective. After all, I was not the only one who had had a tough week. At least I had a day off; no one else did. I should have chosen my words carefully in order to present the situation as objectively as possible while refraining from making "global" statements.

What concerned me even more than my lack of foresight was my unwillingness to let go of my anger. Consequently, I felt immediate shame when I slammed the door and allowed my daughter to leave for school with the unresolved anger still between us.

As I tackled my long to-do list, I thought about how unreasonable I'd been, how I'd held onto my anger as if it had been a precious thing instead of a deadly poison. As the Lord dealt with me, He reminded me of a passage of Scripture I'd studied many times before.

I stopped my work so that I could read Matthew 18:21-35, a story Jesus told in order to illustrate the importance of forgiving one another. At the beginning of the story, a servant who owed the king millions of dollars was brought in and told to repay the debt. Of course, the poor servant could not, so he begged the king to forgive the debt, which the king did.

When that servant left the presence of the king, he went to a fellow servant who owed him a few thousand dollars and demanded immediate payment of the debt. The servant begged for mercy, promising to repay the debt as he could.

The servant whom the king had forgiven a huge debt had his fellow servant thrown into prison because he was unable to pay a small debt, by comparison.

"Oh Lord," I wept, "You have forgiven me of so much. You have forgiven me of my ingratitude to You and of my unwillingness to do my share as a member of Your family. You have forgiven me for thinking of myself instead of You and of the people for whom Your Son gave His life. I ask You now, once again, to forgive me for being angry and unforgiving with my daughter. Since You have forgiven me of such huge debts, why am I unwilling to forgive so little?"

Shortly after I prayed, my daughter called from school to share a bit of good news with me. Though I was tremendously pleased with the news she shared, I hastened to take the unexpected opportunity to ask her to forgive me. Then I paused to thank God for not only forgiving me but also for not making me wait until the end of the day to set things right with my daughter.

Reflections

More Religious Than Righteous?

When I took my eyes off the road long enough to glance at the woman, I saw that she was standing beside a new grave, a tiny one. A Styrofoam cross covered with pink flowers marked the head of the grave; a spray of lavender and white flowers covered the length of it.

The woman looked so alone, so in need of someone to stand beside her. I wondered if she had anyone to comfort her, anyone to weep with her. *I don't know her*, I thought, *but I'm going to go to her and see if there's anything I can do.*

I glanced at the clock. 10:52 a.m. *Oh no! If I take time to stop, I'll be late for my 11:00 appointment.*

My "dutiful" self chided me. "You told the Minister of Education you'd meet him at the church before 11:00. He's expecting you. What will he think about you if you don't keep your promise to meet with him?"

My "compassionate" self whispered, "The woman needs you now. Go to her."

My "dutiful" self won. As I drove on to the appointment, I tried to relieve my guilt. *If I keep the meeting brief, maybe she will still be here when I pass this way again. Then, I will stop and stay as long as she needs me. I'll be able to give her my undivided attention because I won't have to be concerned about the time.*

On the return trip, I slowed as I neared the cemetery. The woman was not there! I noticed that someone had placed a cluster of artificial red rosebuds on the grave. In my mind's eye, I saw her solitary form bending low to place them on the tiny grave of the child she loved.

My "compassionate" self asked, "Why didn't you stop? She needed you."

I was ashamed to answer, reluctant to admit that I had been more concerned with my "image" and my "duties" than I had been with the woman's grief.

Once again, I tried to rationalize my decision. *She probably wouldn't have appreciated a total stranger approaching her at a time when her grief was so new. She might have told me to go away and mind my own business.*

Late that night, after everyone was in bed and I had time alone to do some serious thinking, the Lord dealt with me regarding the wrong choice I had made. He reminded me of a conversation Jesus had with a certain lawyer who had asked what he must do in order to inherit eternal life.

Jesus answered the man's question with a question. "What does the law of Moses say? How do you read it?" (Luke 10:26).

The man replied, "'You must love the Lord your God with all your heart, all your soul, all your strength, and all your mind.' And 'Love your neighbor as yourself'" (Luke 10:27).

When Jesus agreed with him, the lawyer asked, "And who is my neighbor?"

In order to answer that question, Jesus told a parable about a man who was beaten by thieves and then left for dead. Both a priest and a Levite (highly respected religious leaders) saw the wounded man and passed on by, presumably to carry out their "church work," just as I had done. Later on a Samaritan, a man who was despised and rejected by the religious elite, stopped and took care of the injured man.

At the conclusion of that story, Jesus asked the lawyer, "Which of these three proved to be a neighbor to the man who had been beaten by the thieves?"

The answer was obvious to the lawyer. "The one who showed mercy toward the man."

Jesus said, "You go and do the same thing."

Having read and reflected on the parable, I couldn't miss its message. The words reverberated in my soul. "If you love Me as much as you say you do, then you will show compassion to those in need, even if they are strangers. You will delay your 'duties' and risk being misunderstood or rejected in order to reach out to someone who is hurting."

"Yes, Lord. I see that I was more religious than I was righteous today. Please forgive me."

Reflections

His Will or Mine?

Late one Wednesday evening I learned that a friend's mother was near death. I decided that I'd go to the hospital the following morning.

I hurried with my early morning chores and then sat down for my daily quiet time with the Lord. I prayed for several persons and situations, including my friend and her mother. Afterward, I read passages from the Bible. One verse seemed to express what I felt at the moment, so I wrote it at the top of the page in my journal. "I take joy in doing your will, my God, for your law is written on my heart" (Psalm 40:8).

The test of whether or not that was a true statement for me to make came as soon as I got up from my place of prayer and Bible study. I began to alter the day's agenda. I said to myself, "Instead of going to the hospital first, I'm going to write my newspaper column. The house is quiet; now is the perfect time to write. Besides, when I go to the hospital, I'll stop by the newspaper office and hand-deliver the column. Maybe I'll have a chance to say 'hello' to the editor."

I sat down at the computer and prepared to write. I mulled over several ideas, but not a one of them "burned in my heart." I struggled for a few minutes, knowing that I needed to do two things: write a column and go to the hospital. Since I couldn't do both at the same time, I vacillated between "Yes, God, I'll go right now" and "No, I won't go there first."

Feeling frustrated by the conflict going on within me, I pushed myself away from the computer. As I spun around in my swivel chair, my eyes alighted on my opened journal and I read: "I take joy in doing your will, my God, for your law is written on my heart."

Ouch! Those words hurt. I knew God wanted me at the hospital, and I did intend to go—at a more convenient time. At that point, I had to ask myself, "Do I truly take joy in doing what God wants me to? Do I delight to do His will?"

I struggled to make an honest response. I knew from previous experiences that obeying God does bring such joy, such unexplained peace. *Why then*, I asked myself, *do I resist doing what He wants me to when He wants me to do it? Why do I feel I have to take His plans and make them fit into my agenda? Why do I even consider delaying my obedience to Him? Why don't I just do what He asks of me?*

I felt miserable as I forced myself to deal with those questions. I seriously doubted that I delighted to do God's will, even though I knew I should. However, I received some comfort when I remembered that the Apostle Paul had struggled with knowing what to do but failing to do it. He wrote: "It seems to be a fact of life that when I want to do what is right, I inevitably do what is wrong. I love God's law with all my heart. But there is another law at work within me that is at war with my mind. This law wins the fight and makes me a slave to the sin that is still within me. Oh, what a miserable person I am! Who will free me from this life that is dominated by sin? Thank God! The answer is Jesus Christ our Lord. So you see how it is: In my mind I really want to obey God's law, but because of my sinful nature I am a slave to sin" (Romans 7:21-25).

After admitting his own struggle to obey, Paul encouraged all believers who identified with the struggle between *flesh* and *spirit*, between *self will* and God's will. "But you are not controlled by your sinful nature. You are controlled by the Spirit if you have the Spirit of God living in you" (Romans 8:9).

Believers, having been set free from the power of the sin nature that once controlled us, are no longer forced to disobey God. Rather, we are free to choose to obey Him in every circumstance. Yes, my wishes often come up against God's will. But I can exercise my freedom to choose to do His will. And that's exactly what I did. I turned off my computer and headed for the hospital—in obedience to Him—even though I did not know why He had so strongly impressed me to go at that particular time.

Shortly after I arrived at the hospital, however, I found out why God's plan was better than mine. I learned that my friend, whose mother lay dying in a room on the second floor, had fallen and was being brought to the emergency room. Because I had obeyed God, I was able to sit with my friend while she waited to find out whether or not she had a broken leg. Had I gone later, as I had planned, I would have missed the privilege of expressing to her the love and compassion God wanted her to have.

As I reflected upon that experience, I realized that I do indeed delight to do God's will—once I choose to override my own desires and plans.

Reflections

I Will Help You

My watch told me that one a.m. was fast approaching; my body confirmed the lateness of the hour. Wearily, I gathered my purse and briefcase and made my way toward the door. Before turning out the lights, I took one last look at the room.

You're going to make it, I reassured myself. *Everything will come together. Right now you need to go to bed and get some rest.*

As I walked slowly toward the elevator, I couldn't help but notice how attractively the other conference leaders had decorated their classrooms and doorways. I forgot the reassuring words I'd said to myself just moments before.

As I rode the elevator to the third floor, I thought, *Girl, you've really done it this time. You are not only going to embarrass yourself but also the lady who asked you to lead this conference. You are way out of your league. Why did you ever agree to do this?*

Those same negative thoughts and questions ran through my mind as I prepared for bed. Though I normally go to sleep quickly and sleep soundly, I did neither that night. Instead, I tossed and turned. I mentally rearranged the tables and chairs in my conference room. I reviewed my teaching outlines. I tried to figure out how I could add more visual appeal to the room. In other words, I "worked" all night.

As I dressed for the day, I felt exhausted and depressed. I did not want to teach for six hours. All I wanted to do was to go home, although that was not one of my options.

Before leaving the room and joining the faculty for breakfast, I sat down to read the Scriptures. Normally, I eagerly read God's Word, but that morning my spirits were so low that I reluctantly opened the purse-size Bible that I'd recently purchased. With a level of enthusiasm equivalent to that one feels when going for a root canal, I began turning the pages, some of which were still stuck together. "Even this Bible is hard to deal with this morning," I muttered.

Not wishing to increase my frustration, I decided to quit struggling with the pages. "I'll just read something right here," I said as my fingers slipped between two easily-opened pages. My eyes focused on God's words that were found in Isaiah 41:10, "Don't be afraid, for I am with you. Do not be dismayed, for I am your God. I will strengthen you. I will help you. I will uphold you with my victorious right hand."

I knew immediately that those words, written centuries before, were intended for me. After thanking God for His wonderful promise to strengthen me and help me, I picked up a pen and wrote in the margin the date and the place where I was that day.

Near the end of the all-day conference, I shared my story with my students. "The Lord will help you when you go back to your churches and teach them the things I have taught you. You will not need to fear or feel like your best will not be good enough."

After the conference ended, I rejoiced as I read the evaluations. "Conference leader was great! She did a wonderful job. Johnnie was very well-informed and presented the material with ease, showing she was well-prepared…"

I had spent many hours preparing for the conference, but I would have been a dismal failure if the Lord had not come to my rescue. I remember that frequently, most especially when I see the date and the place written in the margin of my Bible.

Can't Earn Life

The seven of us made our way to the pew where my mother-in-law sits every Sunday. After we'd settled in, a woman I've known for many years sat down in her regular place directly in front of me. She immediately turned around to greet us. We chatted for a few minutes. Then, she looked at all of us and teased, "I'm jealous."

I knew she wasn't jealous. Being the loving person she was, she was happy that my mother-in-law had so many of her family members seated with her on that day. However, I sensed that seeing all of us, particularly me, had stirred bittersweet emotions within her.

Her daughter and I had been good friends in college. And whenever my husband and I visited his hometown and went to church with my mother-in-law, I knew I'd get to talk with my friend and her husband for they always sat directly in front of us.

Those little visits ended abruptly when my friend and her husband died in an automobile accident about six years after our college graduation. Since then, I always felt very sad and a little uncomfortable each time I saw the empty places on the pew in front of us. However, my friend's mother always greeted us warmly.

As I sat behind her once again on that Sunday morning, I hurt with her and for her. Only God knew the many times she had longed for her daughter and son-in-law to sit beside her. Only God knew the tears she had shed over the years. I felt distressed as I considered how much pain she surely felt when she saw my mother-in-law enjoying what she herself longed for but would never again experience. I felt guilty for being happy and alive.

Yet, as I sorted through my feelings, I began to realize that my life is in God's hands. Just as He determined when my life began, He will also decide when it will end. I do not know why God has given me a longer life than He gave my friend and her husband.

Length of life is not based on personal merit any more than salvation is. I cannot *earn* life any more than I can *earn* salvation. Both are gifts of God. (See Ephesians 2:8-10.)

Johnnie Ann Burgess Gaskill

Rest? Yes!

For weeks I struggled to know whether or not I should take the MasterLife course that was going to be offered at my church. I wanted to participate, for I'd seen how others had matured spiritually as a result of practicing the disciplines the course required: daily prayer and Bible study, fellowship with other Christians, and witnessing and ministering to people. However, I felt I had no time.

Two days before the twenty-six week course began, the MasterLife coordinator called to ask what I'd decided to do. "I really do want to, but I'm not sure I have the time to do all that will be required. I'm already maxed out. Maybe I should wait until the next course begins."

She chuckled. "Johnnie Ann Gaskill, you will always be busy. If you wait until you're not, then you'll never take MasterLife!"

The night before the first session, the leader of the class called. When he asked about my decision, I explained to him about my busy schedule. He said he understood, but still encouraged me to attend.

Finally, I said, "These next two weeks are going to be extremely busy ones. If I can keep up with the MasterLife requirements during that time, I should be able to finish the other twenty-four weeks. So…if it's okay with you, I'll join the class on a trial basis. If it doesn't work out, then I'll just drop out."

He accepted my provisional commitment. However, he was more at ease with it than I was. I wanted a closer relationship with the Lord, but I didn't know what to give up in order to have additional time. I enjoyed all my involvements and felt that each was too important to abandon.

Near midnight I stopped doing the household chores and sat down, intending to spend some quiet moments reviewing the Sunday School lesson I was to teach the following morning.

As I read the words the Lord God had spoken through the prophet Isaiah to the nation of Israel, I felt that the message was intended for me as well. "In quietness and confidence is your strength" (Isaiah 30:15).

As I read those familiar words, I knew God was reminding me to slow down and learn to be quiet before Him. Like the Israelites who had turned away from God as their source of strength and had begun to seek their help from Egypt, I had not been willing to give God first place. The Israelites had mistakenly sought swift horses to use in battle; I had foolishly depended on my own strength to carry out a whirlwind of activities instead of setting aside sufficient time to communicate with God in order to know Him, to learn how to obey Him, and to receive strength from Him.

Reflections

Through that passage of Scripture, my Heavenly Father let me know that He did not require me to work harder in order to please Him. Quite the contrary! In fact, He had said, "In quietness and confidence is your strength."

Those words reminded me of the ones spoken centuries later by Jesus. "Come to me, all of you who are weary and carry heavy burdens, and I will give you rest. Take my yoke upon you. Let me teach you, because I am humble and gentle, and you will find rest for your souls. For my yoke fits perfectly, and the burden I give you is light" (Matthew 11:28-30).

I realized I didn't need to work harder. Rather I needed to come to Him and rest! Maybe MasterLife was for me, after all, even though I'd have to let other things go.

Johnnie Ann Burgess Gaskill

What Hinders Me?

Our MasterLife leader asked, "Name one thing that hinders you from knowing Christ better?" A thoughtful silence followed.

"I can share something that used to be a hindrance," I said. "Just before and then immediately after the birth of my first child, I spent several hours each day watching soap operas. I missed being around adults, so I invited my 'TV friends' into my home. When the last show went off each day, I felt sad, as if I'd just said goodbye to company.

"I continued watching the 'daytime dramas' until someone shared a verse of Scripture with me. "Above all else, guard your heart, for it affects everything you do" (Proverbs 4:23). Then I realized I was not guarding my mind as carefully as I should. So, I stopped watching soap operas."

The MasterLife leader said, "Since you took time to watch the soaps, you could have used that time for Bible study and prayer, couldn't you?"

I nodded.

"Just think," he continued, "how much further along you would be now as a Christian if you had used all those hours to study the Scriptures and to pray."

I knew he was right. His comment made me think about other blocks of time I could have used to foster Christian growth and development. When the children were in kindergarten, I went shopping, ran errands, did household chores, and talked with other stay-at-home moms during the hours when I could have had uninterrupted quiet time.

When I had been confined to bed during the last three weeks of my second pregnancy, I hadn't used those long hours to study and pray. Instead, I'd watched game shows on TV (not soaps!), read books or magazines, talked on the phone, and fretted about being forced to stay in bed. Eight years later when a blood clot in my leg kept me in the hospital for ten days and on the sofa for many days thereafter, I failed to use that time to get to know Christ better.

During the MasterLife class I realized that I had become a time-waster. Even though I had been a Christian since I was eleven years old, I knew little about making the most of the time God had given me (Ephesians 5:16). Neither did I understand that I was to renew my mind, to allow the Word of God to transform my life from within rather than to permit the world to shape me into its mold (Romans 12:2).

I can't reclaim the wasted hours, but I try diligently to make the most of my time and to constantly renew my mind. When I am doing routine chores, I no longer put my mind in neutral or listen to unwholesome or trivial words on radio or TV. Instead I listen to Christian radio or to inspirational music. Often I just thank God for all He's done for me, or I'll think about a sermon I heard at church, or else I'll spend time reflecting on the meaning and application of Bible truths.

Although I've identified many of the time-wasters from the past and have eliminated many of them, I still find it helpful to ask, "What *currently* hinders me from knowing Christ better?"

Johnnie Ann Burgess Gaskill

Revealing the Wounds

Friends as well as strangers showed instant concern when they noticed the orthopedic shoe on my right foot. "What happened?" they asked.

"I had foot surgery," I replied. However, that simple explanation was never enough. They asked other questions. "When did you have your surgery? Who was your doctor? What did you have done? Are you in pain? How long will it be before you can wear a regular shoe?"

I appreciated their concern, for it made me feel loved, and I did not mind answering their questions or hearing their stories of similar operations or hearing them say they needed foot surgery, too. Actually, I rather enjoyed talking with people about a subject that we probably would never have discussed if my temporary handicap had not been so obvious.

Even though I was grateful for every expression of compassion, I couldn't help thinking of those times when my emotional pain had been much greater than the pain I experienced following foot surgery. However, since I concealed my emotional suffering, no one expressed compassion. Neither did I bond with others as we discussed solutions to our common problems. In other words, I felt very lonely and unloved, as perhaps others did.

I'm not sure why I kept my emotional distress to myself. Perhaps I chose to suffer alone rather than to risk rejection. Perhaps I felt ashamed to be having problems whenever it seemed that no one else was. Perhaps I felt that they would not understand. Perhaps I knew that people often look the other way whenever they see persons with serious disabilities or with intense emotional pain. Since they don't know what to say or do, they prefer not to get involved, even on a conversational level.

Since I tend to suffer silently, as do many other people, I'm so thankful my Father graciously provided a Savior who sees the teeming masses of humanity, just as He did years ago when He lived upon this earth in a physical body. Jesus feels great compassion for each of us, for He knows that our problems are great and that we do not know where to go for help. He sees that we are "like sheep without a shepherd" (Matthew 9:36) and like hurting people who have no physician.

Jesus knows how I feel even when I think I have no one to care for me, no one to meet my needs, no one to help me get back on my feet again, no one to lead me in the right path. Knowing my helplessness, Jesus offers to become my shepherd. As such, He comes and ministers to me individually, one-on-one.

Reflections

   As my shepherd tenderly cares for me and restores me to wholeness, He says, "Because you know what it feels like to have a deep hurt that you do not feel free to share, be sensitive to those all around you who also suffer silently. Have compassion on the distressed and the downcast. Don't look the other way. Instead, be willing to open up to them. Show them your wounds and scars. Tell them about your pain. Tell them how I lovingly minister to you as you suffer. Tell them how you are being healed. People will tell you their stories if you'll just show them that you, too, need help in managing your pain."

Johnnie Ann Burgess Gaskill

Just As I Am

Normally, my pride would have kept me from entering my daughter's school. However, on Friday morning, March 29, 1991, I abandoned my pride and ran into the building. I automatically stopped by the school office to check-in, as visitors were required to do, and stayed just long enough to wave at the vice-principal and the secretary, both of whom knew me. Then I hurried to the seventh grade hall to locate my daughter.

Jena's class had already assumed the "duck and cover" positions in the hallway, but I immediately spotted her beautiful red hair. I knelt in the vacant spot that was nearest to her. Though we did not speak, she looked relieved to see me.

The students, faculty, and staff remained in the hallway from about 8:40 a.m. till ten o'clock. During the time of greatest danger, hardly anyone spoke. Once I heard one of the teenagers whisper, "I hope my Mama's okay. She's real scared of storms." My eyes filled with tears as I listened to the concern she expressed to whomever might care. That precious child, who was in a life-threatening position herself, was thinking about her mama's well-being.

As we continued to wait for the tornado to touch down, I looked down the long, wide hallway and saw hundreds of students kneeling and waiting…waiting…waiting. "Oh, Father," I prayed, "may no lives be lost today. Please, Father, no lives today."

God answered that prayer. Soon we were instructed to sit up, put our backs against the lockers, and wait quietly for additional instructions. As the minutes dragged on, the person nearest to Jena moved down the hall to a spot where there was more room. I scooted over next to my daughter.

Jena whispered, "Oh, Mama! I'm so glad you are here. I was worried when I thought you were driving home in the tornado."

"Well, I started to go home after I dropped you off, but then I heard that a funnel cloud had been spotted in this area, so I came back. I hope I haven't embarrassed you by coming in here looking like this."

"No, Mama. I'm *glad* you're here."

Jena may not have been embarrassed by my appearance, but I was. Everyone else had groomed for the day. But I had put on sweat pants and a tee shirt for I intended to drop Jena and Kristi (our neighbor) off at school and come right back home. Since I planned to write my newspaper column, clean house, and do the laundry, I had not bothered to put on makeup or to shampoo my hair.

Reflections

Normally, I would *never* have gone into the school looking the way I did that morning. However, my need for safety forced me to abandon my pride and seek shelter. When I'd heard the warning of impending disaster, I did not take the time to try to improve my appearance or to review my plans for the day. I simply ran for shelter.

That, I think, is how we must come to Jesus. In 1834, Charlotte Elliott wrote, "Just as I am, and waiting not/To rid my soul of one dark blot,/To Thee whose blood can cleanse each spot,/O Lamb of God, I come! I come!"

As the hymn writer so beautifully expressed, we should come to Jesus just as we are. Jesus will receive us, for He said, "…those the Father has given me will come to me, and I will never reject them" (John 6:37). He only asks that we come to Him, regardless of our appearance, regardless of our condition. We must not worry what others will think or say. We must not let pride hinder us from coming to Jesus. And we must not delay! Whenever He calls us, we must gladly and unashamedly say, "O Lamb of God, I come! I come!"

Johnnie Ann Burgess Gaskill

Returning Ownership to the Owner

In an effort to cheer up one of the girls, I wrote this message on a note and slipped it into her lunch sack: "Today is a new day...an opportunity to make a new start. And it is a day that the Lord has made. Let's be glad in it. Love, Mama."

When I tucked the note inside her napkin, I had no inkling that the day would hold a new beginning—for me! So, I simply started doing the usual chores. I sorted what looked like a ton of laundry, started one load in the washer, and then loaded the dishwasher. While my appliances did their work, I settled down for a time of Bible study and prayer before I started writing my weekly newspaper column. My morning routine was so familiar that not once did I consider the new day as an opportunity for a new start—for me!

Even as I completed my assignments in the "Experiencing God: Knowing and Doing the Will of God" workbook, I had no idea that God wanted to do something in my life that very day. However, as I used a colored pencil to highlight two main ideas in the last portion of the day's assignment, I began to weep uncontrollably.

I frequently shed tears—happy ones as well as sad—but I seldom sob. That morning, however, the sobs came unexpectedly and uncontrollably from deep within my soul. I heard myself say, "It's all Yours, God. It's all yours! It has never been mine."

After the sobs finally subsided, I reread the two sentences that God had used to speak to me. "God speaks when He is about to accomplish His purposes. What God initiates, He completes." Those two sentences from the workbook impacted me so strongly because they touched one of my sensitive areas.

As I sat quietly before the Lord, I recalled how He had spoken to me years ago and told me to write a book. I began writing that very day, and the Lord graciously and faithfully helped me. He provided opportunities for me to sharpen my writing skills. He brought to my mind the experiences and the truths He wanted me to share with readers. He opened doors so that the weekly columns could be shared with thousands of potential readers.

Although He was faithful to me as I tried to be obedient to Him, somewhere along the way I assumed ownership of the book. Finishing the book had become *my* job. Finding a publisher had become *my* responsibility. Marketing the book had become *my* challenge. Because I often despaired of ever completing the assignment God had given me, I made only sporadic attempts to finish the book.

Reflections

When I read, "What God initiates, He completes," I saw clearly that the book had never been mine. God had called me to do a work for Him. The idea was His, not mine. The ability to write the book came from Him, not from within me. The end result was His, not mine.

Why had I carried the burden of ownership? God had not forced it upon me. In fact, He never intended for me to carry it. He simply wanted me to take small steps of obedience and leave the results to Him.

I decided to do that. "Father," I said, "forgive me for assuming the ownership that belongs to You, ownership not only of the book, but also of all the things that You have allowed into my life. I especially thank You for sending loved ones who have brought me such joy, but they are not mine. They belong to You. Help me release them to You. Even the material things that make life easier and more comfortable belong to You. Show me how You would have me use them."

Returning rightful ownership to God brought such freedom. The realization that "…everything comes **from him**; everything exists **by his power** and is intended **for his glory**" (Romans 11:36, emphasis added) set me free from the burdens associated with ownership. Experiencing that made me rejoice in the new day that He had made and motivated me to give special thanks for yet another personal encounter with the Living God, the Sovereign Lord of all.

Johnnie Ann Burgess Gaskill

A Meeting with Myself?

Noticing I was getting dressed up, Jena asked, "Mama, aren't you off work today?"

"Well, this *is* my day off, but I have to attend a meeting at the office."

My daughter shrugged her shoulders.

I smiled at her and said, "That's big news. Right?"

Jena nodded and said, "You have so many meetings, I'm surprised that you haven't scheduled one with yourself!"

We laughed as she hurried out the door to meet the bus. Jena probably thought nothing else about the conversation, but I certainly did. I realized she was right. My job required that I attend day meetings, night meetings, weekend meetings, and even occasional out-of-town conferences. Therefore, my family was accustomed to hearing me say, "If you need me, I'll be at..." And although I constantly adjusted my schedule to accommodate all the meetings, I'd never considered scheduling a meeting with myself, as Jena had jokingly suggested.

When I returned from the meeting late that afternoon, I settled down for a minute with a book (**Honest to God?**) I'd borrowed from a friend. As I read it, I learned how I could schedule a meeting with myself. The author, Dr. Bill Hybels, said that nearly all the authentic Christians he knew had one thing in common: they kept a journal. He defined journaling as the daily habit of examining our lives—in written form.

The author admitted that he had been reluctant to try journaling because blank sheets of paper scared him. (I identified with that, since, as a writer, I often think 8½ x11 sheets of paper look as large as bed sheets.) Despite his fear of blank pages, Dr. Hybels decided to try journaling, for he said he frequently repeated the same mistakes over and over and often went to bed with regrets about his actions. When he considered that, he realized that he was living an unexamined life. Failing to evaluate his mistakes or his progress was keeping him from becoming more Christlike. He wondered how he could become more Christlike if he never examined his character, his decision-making, his ministry, his marriage, or his parenting.

As I read that part of Dr. Hybel's book I began to see the importance of examining *my* life. Previously I'd had a daily quiet time during which I read God's Word and prayed, but, I must admit, I spent hardly any time evaluating my mistakes or my progress.

With the importance of doing that fixed firmly in my mind, I eagerly read more about journaling. Dr. Hybels begins each day's page in his spiral notebook by writing the word *Yesterday*. Then, as the heading implies, he writes a brief description of what happened the previous day—how he felt, decisions he made, high and low points, etc. Having done that, he analyzes *Yesterday* by asking himself a series of questions. What should I have done differently? How did I manage my time? Did I make good decisions?

Dr. Hybels then writes out a prayer, using the acrostic *ACTS* as a guide. He writes at least one paragraph each of adoration, confession, thanksgiving, and supplication (requests).

Following *Yesterday* and *ACTS*, is a section devoted to *Listening* to what God has to say. Recording His thoughts not only provides a record of what He said but it also, when reviewed periodically, enables the journal-er to see if he or she is doing what God said to do.

All that sounded like a lot of work, but I felt impressed to incorporate those ideas as soon as I scheduled a meeting with myself. I discovered that following Dr. Hybel's suggestions did take time, especially since I wrote a lot in each category (particularly in the *Yesterday* and *Confession* sections), but I considered the time well spent.

Although the Psalmist didn't call his writing "journaling," that's basically what much of it was. In one of his "entries," David made a request that helped him avoid what Dr. Hybels calls the unexamined life. "Search me, O God, and know my heart; test me and know my thoughts. Point out anything in me that offends you, and lead me along the path of everlasting life" (Psalm 139:23-24).

When we schedule a meeting with ourselves we, like David, need to ask God to help us evaluate our lives. Not only must we ask for divine help, but we must also set aside the time to allow God to report the results of His findings! When we finally get serious about being honest and authentic, we'll say, "God, please show me my wrongdoings. Help me to see my true motives. As I wait quietly before You, tell me how to make corrections and adjustments so that I will be what You want me to be."

Johnnie Ann Burgess Gaskill

Physical Bankruptcy

I didn't respond truthfully when someone asked, "How are you?" Instead I smiled and said, "Fine, thank you."

Truth was I felt fatigued. Exhausted. Tired to the bone. Stressed. Sleepy. Worried. I didn't like feeling that way. Yet, because I had almost overdrawn my time and energy account, I found myself on the brink of physical bankruptcy the week we learned that my husband needed eye surgery—immediately.

The long wait the day of the surgery and the all-night vigil that followed nearly depleted my energy reserves. Afterward, my balance dropped dangerously close to zero when the responsibilities I'd temporarily put on hold demanded attention.

Feeling like someone with a fistful of bills and no money with which to pay them, I wondered where I'd get the necessary time and energy to meet my obligations. However, people spontaneously began to make deposits to my overdrawn account. A security guard helped me carry some things into the hospital. Our pastor waited with me during the surgery. Nurses urged me to rest on the extra bed in my husband's hospital room. Neighbors brought dinner the day he came home from the hospital. Co-workers assumed extra responsibility during my absence. The editor extended the deadline for my newspaper column. The children voluntarily helped out more around the house. A friend took my turn in the carpool.

I felt so grateful for each one who helped out, especially when I realized that they transferred resources from their time and energy account in order to make a deposit to mine. These gracious folks willingly shared in order to keep me from physical bankruptcy.

While thinking about how people helped me in my time of need, I recalled a favorite Scripture. The Apostle Paul, writing to the Christians in Corinth, urged them to give money to the Christians living in Jerusalem who were trying to cope with the financial reversals that had come upon them as a result of their turning to Christianity.

Paul explained the necessity of sharing with others. "If you are really eager to give, it isn't important how much you are able to give. God wants you to give what you have, not what you don't have. Of course, I don't mean you should give so much that you suffer from having too little. I only mean that there should be some equality. Right now you have plenty and can help them. Then at some other time they can share with you when you need it. In this way, everyone's needs will be met. Do you remember what the Scriptures say about this? 'Those who gathered a lot had nothing left over, and those who gathered only a little had enough'" (2 Corinthians 8:12-15).

Paul urged them to balance the accounts in order that there might be equality. That's what my family and friends did when they transferred some of their resources to my account at a time when I was needy. Not only were my needs met, but I also saw more clearly the truth in Paul's words: "And when we take your gifts to those who need them, they will break out in thanksgiving to God. So two good things will happen—the needs of the Christians in Jerusalem will be met, and they will joyfully express their thanksgiving to God. You will be glorifying God through your generous gifts…and [the Jerusalem Christains] will pray for you with deep affection because of the wonderful grace of God shown through you" (2 Corinthians 9:11b-14).

I said a heart-felt "Amen!" to Paul's words. Also, I began to tell the truth when asked, "How are you?" I said, "I am very tired, but also very thankful for friends who willingly increased their load in order to lighten mine."

Johnnie Ann Burgess Gaskill

Narrowing the Gap

"I need to put my bathroom scales in the closet or under the bed," I said. My friend laughed and nodded sympathetically.

"I'm tired of dieting and walking and then seeing so little progress," I whined. I'm just going to do what I need to do and not worry about the results. The weight will come off if I eat sensibly and continue to walk two miles each weekday."

A few days later, the scales were still in the bathroom, and I continued to step on them every morning. Sometimes I was delighted with what I saw; other mornings I was so discouraged that I was tempted to give up. Even when I had been "good" for days, the weight indicator didn't move, not even the width of a hair.

In addition to that stubborn little indicator, there was another feature on the scales that intensified my early morning emotions. On the outer rim of the round dial, there were five small moveable triangles that served a variety of functions. However, I used only two of them. I placed the small red one at the spot where the indicator stopped to mark my current weight. I moved the white triangle to mark my desired weight.

By using those markers, I was able to see at a glance the distance between where I was and where I needed to be. But when the gap remained the same or widened, I wanted to forget the diet. When the gap closed, I got so excited. "Minus one!" I'd yell to anyone who happened to be around. Then I'd move the little red triangle one notch closer toward my desired weight.

Even though I did consider hiding the scales or buying digital ones that only revealed my current weight, I needed to be aware of the gap—the distance between reality and goal. The more I was aware of the gap, the harder I worked to close it.

That same principle applies to spiritual matters. The Bible is much like my scales. When I read it, I learn where I am spiritually and where I need to be. I'm sad to say that the gap there is even wider than the one on my scales. I can envision the day when I reach my desired weight, but I know I can never be where I ought to be in Christlikeness, at least not during this earthly life.

However, knowing I am so far from spiritual maturity should not stop me from trying to become Christlike, but it sometimes does. That's why I like to read the assurance John was inspired to write to fellow believers. "Yes, dear friends, we are already God's children, and we can't even imagine what we will be like when Christ returns. But we do know that when he comes we will be like he is" (1 John 3:2-3).

Until then, I should be aware of and attempt to close the gap between where I am now and where I will someday be. Rather than being discouraged by the distance in the gap, I am encouraged that spiritual maturity will one day be a reality. In the meantime, I must persevere—sometimes losing a little ground, sometimes making progress, but always striving to become more and more like Christ, realizing that one day the gap will be forever closed!

Johnnie Ann Burgess Gaskill

Reflections About Various Places

Johnnie Ann Burgess Gaskill

Lest We Forget

Even though more than forty years have passed since the opening of the Henry Grady Elementary School in Ellijay, Georgia, I still recall the sense of awe I felt as I entered the new building.

For those of us who had known only the white-frame, one-room school, the new one seemed the finest in the entire world. Why, it contained six classrooms, a lunchroom, office space, a stage, and even a closet-size room that served as a store where we purchased pencils and paper before school and ice cream during recess.

As a seven-year-old child, I remember being particularly impressed with the indoor plumbing, especially the water fountain. My first experience at drinking from it left me slightly embarrassed but laughing, nonetheless, as the water as cold as that from a mountain spring splashed all over my face rather than into my mouth. But I quickly learned the art of proper positioning and found that new way of drinking to be far superior to the old method at the previous school: a metal bucket, a tin dipper, and an assortment of glasses—some pint canning jars, some "jelly" glasses—we brought from home.

At the new school, we enjoyed the large playground with its swings, the merry-go-round, the exercise bars, the ball field, and the grassy area where we could search for four-leaf-clovers or simply sit and talk with our friends. Despite getting our knees and elbows skinned, we had great fun learning to roller skate on the sidewalk that ran along the entire length of the front of the long building.

Even though we were thrilled with the new school and its wonderful features, we soon grew accustomed to its wonderful amenities and began to take them for granted. As the memories of the crowded, uncomfortable, old building faded, so did our appreciation of the new one.

That tendency to take benefits for granted didn't originate with the students at the Henry Grady School. No, God, speaking through Moses, found it necessary to remind the people to "Beware that in your plenty you do not forget the LORD your God and disobey his commands, regulations and laws. For when you have become full and prosperous and have built fine homes to live in, and when your flocks and herds have become very large and your silver and gold have multiplied along with everything else, that is the time to be careful. Do not become proud at that time and forget the LORD your God, who rescued you from slavery in the land of Egypt. Do not forget that he led you through the great and terrifying wilderness…" (Deuteronomy 8:11-15).

May the admonition to "Beware lest you forget the LORD your God" ring in our ears. May we always recognize God as the Source of all our blessings and praise Him for who He is as well as thank Him for all He gives us to enjoy.

Reflections

A Prepared Place

One October day we loaded our luggage and headed South for a much-needed vacation in Florida. As we neared the resort area, we passed several condos—nice ones—but we kept going.

A few miles on down the road we located the multi-story condominium where my husband had made our reservations. He drove up to the main entrance; I went inside to check-in. When I told the clerk my name, she smiled warmly and said, "Yes. We're expecting you."

Within minutes my family and I entered a spacious, luxuriously-furnished condo on the seventh floor. From our balcony, we could see two heated swimming pools, two whirlpools, and several picnic areas—all facing the white sands and the emerald green water of the Gulf of Mexico. In addition to providing and maintaining outdoor amenities, the management had even stocked the kitchen with orange juice, a dozen eggs, muffins, jelly, paper towels and the like. The management's careful attention to detail impressed us and conveyed to us this message: "We're glad you've chosen to stay here. Enjoy yourselves."

And enjoy ourselves we did. We rested and rested and then rested some more. We jumped in the waves. We walked along the water's edge and left our footprints in the wet sand. We let the wind play with our hair. We lay on the beach and absorbed its sights, sounds, and smells.

In that pleasant environment, school and work seemed like a part of the distant past. No clocks. No deadlines. No demands. No need to hurry. It was wonderful, absolutely wonderful.

There was time to reflect. And, as I did so, I remembered a thought one of our former pastors loved to express. "Heaven," he'd say with a smile, "is a prepared place for a prepared people." Indeed, it is, for Jesus Himself said, "I am going to prepare a place for you. If this were not so, I would tell you plainly. When everything is ready, I will come and get you, so that you will always be with me where I am" (John 14:2b-3).

Our vacation ended years ago, but I continue to rejoice in the thought that when my life is over, I have a reservation in Heaven, that "prepared place for a prepared people," that place infinitely more wonderful than even the best of the best vacation resorts.

Johnnie Ann Burgess Gaskill

A Safe Harbor

Like a thirsty wanderer who'd found an oasis in the desert, I drank in the beauty of the view. I absorbed all of it—the sights, the sounds, and the smells. Spellbound, I continued to watch the boats leave the harbor and make their way out into the Gulf of Mexico. Shrimp boats, charter boats, motorboats, sail boats—all headed for a day on the sea. They stayed pretty much in single file until they reached the end of the jetties. Then each went separate ways—some to work, some to sail, some to catch the "big one."

What a sight they made! From where I sat on my seventh-floor balcony, all of them looked white—brilliantly white—as they made their way through the emerald water. The motorboats, racing ahead with their noses out of the water, seemed to bounce along over the waves. The larger boats moved slowly, as if plowing through the water. I thought, "They look so regal, so stately."

Many boats left the harbor that October morning. I watched them as they moved onward and outward till they looked like tiny white dots on the horizon. As they disappeared from my sight, I felt so sad. Their departure had been so beautiful…each boat moving to its destination in its own way. *But*, I consoled myself, *they'll return when evening comes. That sight will be just as beautiful.*

Later, as I reflected on the scene and my feelings, I recalled the thoughts expressed by H. L. Gilmour in the song, "The Haven of Rest." In that beautiful hymn, Gilmour said he had anchored his soul in Jesus, the Haven of Rest; and although others might choose to sail the wild, stormy seas, he would choose to keep his soul peacefully and safely anchored in Jesus.

Thinking of his words, I whispered, "Oh Jesus, help each of us to know that, regardless of where and why we've sailed, we can return to You. In You we find a safe and peaceful harbor, a place to anchor our souls. In You we can rest from the struggles of the day and take on new strength for the challenges ahead."

Reflections

The Way Out

Several years ago we stayed often at our friend's chalet located between Gatlinburg and Pigeon Forge, Tennessee. Each time we visited there, out anticipation built as we left the main road and began going down the narrow, unpaved road to the vacation hide-away. Down, down, down we'd go before rounding the sharp curve that afforded us our first glimpse of the gray chalet nestled in the trees at the foot of the mountain. A short distance onward, we'd cross the one-lane rickety bridge that spanned Little Pigeon River.

After going up a small hill, we'd turn into the driveway that is so steep that the car seemed to stand on its nose as we made our descent. I always held my breath as my husband inched slowly down the steep embankment and backed into the narrow parking space, for all that kept us from plunging into the river was a few logs the owner had placed along the side of the graveled parking space.

Normally, we'd unload the car, collect the fishing gear, and scamper down the steep path to the river. There we'd fish, collect rocks worn smooth by the water, or photograph the wild flowers until we grew tired. Then we'd climb onto the huge rocks along the river's edge where we'd bask in the sun and fill our lungs with clean, fragrant mountain air. At night we'd be lulled to sleep by the river that sounded as comforting as a gentle rain falling on the tin roof.

Our last trip there was different. The melting of the nineteen-inch snow that had blanketed the area a few weeks before, coupled with several days of steady rain, had caused the river to be near flood stage. Yet, despite being denied previous pleasures provided by the river, we spent three wonderful days at the chalet.

On our last night there, as I was drifting off to a peaceful sleep, a disturbing question flashed through my mind. *If the bridge gets washed away, how will we ever get out of here?*

The following morning I breathed a sigh of relief and offered a prayer of gratitude as we crossed the bridge safely and began our trip home. As we traveled, I couldn't help thinking about those times in our lives when we seem to be trapped in valleys of despair because mountains of difficulties have so surrounded us that we can see no way out.

The Psalmist experienced such a situation, but he found a way of escape. "But in my distress I cried out to the LORD; yes, I prayed to my God for help. He heard me from his sanctuary; my cry reached his ears…He reached down from heaven and rescued me; he drew me out of deep waters. He delivered me from my powerful enemies, from those who hated me and were too strong for me…He led me to a place of safety; he rescued me because he delights in me" (Psalm 18: 6, 16-17, 19).

The Lord God continues to be the bridge, the way out of difficulties! He will always be there.

The Former Days

Escape? Yes, that's exactly what I wanted to do, but a sense of "oughtness" forced me to walk into the nursing home. Mother, who was seventy-one at the time, walked beside me. We said little as we made our way toward Daddy's sister's room, for memories of Daddy's death exactly six years ago on that day filled our minds. We braced ourselves for yet another painful experience.

All too soon for me, I heard Mother whisper, "Here's her room." I knocked and we entered hesitantly, unsure of what we'd find.

The dramatic change in Aunt Delia's appearance shocked me. Gaunt and too weak for conversation, she lay in her bed and appeared to be asleep. But when her daughter asked me to help her reposition Aunt Delia, she looked up at me, but gave no indication that she recognized me. That hurt—deeply.

I fought the tears as I remembered the way she used to be: plump (not fat), with snow-white hair gathered neatly into a bun on the crown of her head, energetic, a hard worker, and someone who always had time for the group of kids who gathered at her house to play. Now, she was totally dependent on her caregivers, her strength all but gone, and unable to recognize many of us who loved her.

I didn't want to face the truth, for doing so hurt too much. Instead, I wanted to turn back the clock and make Aunt Delia and all the other special people in my life the way they used to be.

A few days later as I continued to experience an intense longing for the past, God spoke to me through His Word, as He so often does. I read in Ecclesiastes 7:10 that it is not wise to ask why the good old days were better than today. Yet, I found it hard not to do so, even though my present life was full and rewarding.

A few verses farther down the page, I found out why it isn't wise to long for either the times that are past or the times that are yet to be. "Enjoy prosperity while you can. But when hard times strike, realize that both come from God" (Ecclesiastes 7:14a). As the Psalmist said, "**This** is the day that the LORD has made. We will rejoice and be glad in it" (Psalm 118:24, emphasis added).

So, the bottom line is: *Each day—this day—*is a gift from God, a day in which He will accomplish His purposes. Thank Him for the good times. Trust Him during the difficult ones. He's in charge. He knows what He is doing—and why!

Johnnie Ann Burgess Gaskill

Only *One* Point?

One afternoon I took our two daughters and a couple of their friends to the local bowling lane. After I'd settled in as the scorekeeper for the group, I snatched a moment to observe the players around us. To my right, I saw a man—I assumed he was the father—a teenage boy and his date, two younger boys, and a preschool girl.

I smiled as I watched the little girl. She wasn't strong enough to hold the bowling ball properly so she cradled it in her arms as one might carry a watermelon, carried it to the line, placed it gently on the floor, and gave it a hard push. Slowly, ever so slowly, the ball traveled toward the pins. Amazingly enough, that technique worked well for her. In fact, she seldom rolled a gutter ball.

She was so cute, so determined to give it her best despite her immaturity. For a while she seemed pleased with her success; then she began to notice how skillful the other four children were. And they *were* good—really expert bowlers. Their balls whizzed down the lanes and made quite a noise as they crashed into the center pin, knocking the others over. Scoring strikes and spares became routine for the older children.

Once when the little girl used her usual bowling method, her ball knocked down only one pin. While she waited for the machine to reposition the others, she walked up to the man and looked up at him. Disappointment was written all over her angelic face. He smiled tenderly at her and, using the same positive voice he'd used throughout the entire game, he said, "You got *one*."

She was not at all encouraged by his affirmation. She remained dejected, so much so that she made no attempt to finish her turn. Her facial expression said, "One? What good is one?"

The man looked directly into the eyes of his adorable little girl and said, "But that one is *yours*!"

He didn't say, "You'll do better next time," or "Don't worry. Someday you'll be a great bowler," or "You're doing great, for a beginner." Instead, he showed his wisdom by trying to teach her to be proud of what she was able to do at the moment. So what if she wasn't the high-scorer for the day? By careful effort, she'd earned that one point. *It was hers*!

That episode reminded me of one of the parables Jesus told. One slave received five talents from his master, while another slave received two and another servant received only one. The servants who received five and two pieces of money each doubled their gifts, while the slave who received only one talent hid his in the ground, afraid that he might incur his master's anger if he did not return at least the original amount to him.

When the master returned and demanded an accounting, he was equally pleased with the two who had doubled their money. He made no distinction between the two men, though one man had ten and the other four talents to present to him. To each he said, "Well done, my good and faithful servant. You have been faithful in handling this small amount, so now I will give you many more responsibilities. Let's celebrate together!" (Matthew 25:21,23). However, the master reprimanded the servant who had been afraid to do what he could with the talent that was given to him.

Would that each of us could learn to do our best and then celebrate whatever measure of success we achieve, regardless of how our accomplishments compare with those of others. We are gifted on an individual basis; we are evaluated individually.

Johnnie Ann Burgess Gaskill

A House with a View

Soon after I went off to college, Mother, Daddy, and my sister moved into a house on top of a hill. To get there, we turned left off the main road and inched our way up a long, narrow, rutted driveway. The house was nicer than our previous one, but still rather ordinary. I liked it instantly because it had a floor-to-ceiling picture window on the east side of the living room.

From any point within that room, we could see a portion of the beautiful North Georgia mountains off in the distance. The view was breathtaking, particularly in late Spring and early Fall. It was in that very room that I learned to appreciate what I call a "house with a view." Actually, all houses except those that are totally enclosed provide some kind of view, but I especially like those with panoramic views. I find there's such a sense of peace and well-being that comes over me whenever I sit and look out at an unspoiled landscape.

Many years later while my husband and I, along with our two daughters, lived in a split-level house in the suburbs West of Atlanta, GA, I often thought, *If we ever decide to move, I want us to try to find a house with a spectacular view. The house itself won't need to be anything grand, but I do want one with a view like I've dreamed about all these years*. But then I'd say to myself, *Come to think of it, our present house has provided some amazing views. Through these windows I've watched our children change from toddlers to teens. I've seen our neighbors grow old gracefully and with dignity.*

Through these windows I've watched eagerly for family or friends to arrive and then I've cried as I watched them go. Through these windows I've seen squirrels and birds enjoying the bounty God provided for them. I've seen glorious sunsets and awesome storms. I've seen brilliantly white snow and jewel-tone leaves covering the lawn like a carpet.

Agreed, this house does not provide the panoramic view I've always desired, but I've seen life and loved ones through the windows of my house. I am very thankful for having had such a lovely view!

(I wrote this in 1988 while living in Austell, Georgia, in the house we built in 1970 and occupied till 1997).

Reflections

Shining Lights

As I looked through the windows of our van, I saw the shining lights of the city. The scene was breathtakingly beautiful, totally different than it had been two days before when we had driven that same route at midday. During daylight hours, we noticed little that was distinctive about the city, other than it was quite large. Because it was just one of many located along the interstate, we had paid little attention to it.

But that night the sight of that same city filled me with awe as I saw literally thousands and thousands of lights punching holes in the darkness that surrounded the entire area. As I gazed at the exquisite scene before me, I realized that it was the contrast between the light and the darkness that had transformed the view from ho-hum to spectacular. Sure, lights burn in the daytime, but their effect is not as striking then as it is when contrasted against the blackness of the night.

The sparkling lights of the city illustrated so beautifully the words spoken by Jesus to His followers. "You are the light of the world—like a city on a mountain, glowing in the night for all to see. Don't hide your light under a basket! Instead, put it on a stand and let it shine for all to see" (Matthew 5:14-15).

Even though the world is full of sin and darkness, Christians can and do make a real difference in the total picture when we (Yes, "we" includes you and me!) remain in our particular places of service and let Jesus shine forth in all we do and say.

The greater the darkness, the more essential [is] the light. The greater the darkness, the more obvious [is] the light. Decrease the darkness by increasing the light.

Johnnie Ann Burgess Gaskill

Ebb and Flow

While vacationing in Sanibel Island, Florida, I got up early one morning and sat on the balcony that overlooked the Gulf of Mexico. As I sat there and listened to the pounding surf, I thought about the bounty of seashells the tide was bringing in. I could hardly wait for our daily trip to the beach to see what new treasures the tide had brought for us.

As I enjoyed the quietness of the moment, a memory surfaced and I started to smile. I could almost feel the sensation of standing on the beach at the point where the water lapped the sand. With my feet firmly placed on the wet, hard sand, I felt secure—at least for a moment. Then I felt the tide pull my secure footing from me as the salt water demanded sand in return for shells. Instinctively, I curled my toes around the little bit of sand I thought was mine. Yet, no matter how tightly I held on, I was powerless to keep it. The water brought its treasures and took from me what it wanted because its force was greater than mine.

As I sat on the balcony, I thought about how the events of life seem similar to my experience on the beach. Life brings its treasures to us: love, family, friends, health, and happiness—to name a few. However, the same life force that brings such cherished blessings also takes them away. Naturally, we feel panic and frustration rising within us when we realize that what we thought was ours forever is being removed. Yet, regardless of how hard we hold on, we cannot control the situation, for a power greater than our own determines what comes and what goes.

While on the beach, I noticed that all I had to do to regain my footing and experience the firmness of the sand underneath my feet was to take one step in the right direction! Likewise, when you and I move closer to Jesus, we experience greater security even as the tides of life come in and go out all around us. Standing on a firm foundation and feeling His arms around us, we can focus on the treasures life brings rather than on what it takes away. It is the presence of Jesus that enables us to anticipate the discoveries made as life daily ebbs and flows.

Reflections

A Hiding Place

Immediately upon getting out of the van, we felt the force of the hot current of air. As we walked toward the Little Grand Canyon in Arizona, we giggled as the scorching wind pushed us along like Fall leaves on a blustery day. However, we did not laugh as we returned to the van. With each step, we pushed against an unseen, yet powerful barrier.

As the wind intensified, it gathered particles of sand and jabbed us with them. In every place the grains came in contact with our skin, we felt a sting akin to a pinprick. To keep the sand out of our eyes, we closed them as tightly as we dared and walked blindly toward the van, opening our eyes only briefly in order to determine our direction.

Frightened by such an unexpected assault, Jena screamed, "Mama!" As she did so, she got a mouthful of dust and sand. I grabbed her and clutched her to my chest. I turned our faces away from the wind and we walked backwards toward the van.

Once safely inside, we poured cold soft drinks and turned the air conditioning on full blast. Though the wind continued to blow and to plague other travelers, the four of us relaxed in our "haven on wheels" as my husband drove on to the Grand Canyon (the big one!).

I looked out the window at the barren land. No trees, only scrub brush, grew in that desolate place made bone-dry and dusty by the relentless wind and the scorching sun. Against such a bleak and inhospitable backdrop loomed an occasional huge rock formation, providing about the only variety in the landscape. I noticed that many of them had openings large enough to accommodate several people. As I visualized travelers, weary from battling the relentless forces of nature, seeking refugee in the clefts of those giant rocks, I recalled the words of Fanny Crosby's beautiful hymn, "He Hideth My Soul."

Having seen and experienced the dry, thirsty land she mentioned in the song, I understood more fully the need for refuge, and I realized I did not have to be in a geographical desert to be reminded of the importance of having a shelter available. I only have to face a tough issue, one that makes me feel as if I'm walking into a relentless wind. During such times when moving forward is especially difficult and slow, confusion, uncertainty and emotional pain make progress even harder. When I feel as if I can no longer go on, Ms. Crosby's words describe my emotions. "A wonderful Savior is Jesus my Lord,/A wonderful Savior to me;/He hideth my soul in the cleft of the rock,/Where rivers of pleasure I see./He hideth my soul in the cleft of the rock/That shadows a dry, thirsty land;/He hideth my life in the depths of His love,/And covers me there with His hand,/And covers me there with His hand."

What a Savior! What a hiding place! What a welcomed refuge!

Reflections

Climb On! Stay On!

After we returned from our trip out West in 1988, folks wanted to hear about what we'd seen and done. Each one of us had our favorite highlights to share. Jena always told about going horseback riding at the Sky Corral Ranch. Each time she told about her first horseback riding experience, I cringed inwardly, dreading the inevitable question. "Well, Johnnie, did you go horseback riding, too?"

Rather than risk embarrassing myself any more that I absolutely had to, I condensed my shameful saga. "I mounted. I dismounted. End of story."

Each time I offered that brief explanation, I hoped it would satisfy the persons with inquiring minds who wanted details, but it never did! So I had to tell them that I finally got up the courage to climb on the horse, then spent what seemed an eternity half-mounted—my left foot in one stirrup, my right foot dangling—because I could not bring myself to swing my right leg across the horse's broad back. I had to tell about how the wranglers encouraged me, as did the owners of the ranch—thinking it would be time for lunch before I ever got ready for what was to have been an early morning ride up the mountain.

At long last, I summoned what was left of my pride and used it to supplement my dwindling supply of courage. With every bit of spunk I could muster, I swung my right leg over the horse's broad back. Just about the time I was straight in the saddle, the huge horse shifted its weight. When that happened, my fear would not have been any greater had I been perched precariously on a limb overhanging a precipice! In about three seconds I had dismounted, vowing never to go near a horse again.

Though everyone encouraged me to try again, I refused. With tears in my eyes and a lump in my throat, I watched as my husband and our two daughters rode toward the mountain that was just behind the ranch. Despite being inexperienced riders, they conquered their fear and rode off to enjoy a wonderful new experience, one they would long remember.

In retrospect, I realized that I, too, could have had a different story to share if I had not allowed my fear to control me. Intellectually, I knew the horse could be trusted, for "Bluebell" was the owner's personal favorite. I knew she would never choose an unsafe horse for herself and certainly not for an inexperienced guest rider. However, I permitted my fear to override my intellect. Though I saw others able to overcome their fears and develop new skills, I was unable to do the same.

In a similar way, I often want to trust God fully, but am unable to cast doubt and fear aside and believe that God is able to carry me safely through new experiences. True, God will take me over some paths that will cause me to be apprehensive, but during that time of moving on to higher ground, my perspective will change. During my journey with God, I'll view life from new heights and unfamiliar vantage points. Therefore, the things that once seemed large and important become smaller and less significant.

Now, if I really learned my lesson at the ranch, I'll tell myself: "Go with God, no matter how fearful you may be. He can be trusted. Don't draw near and then pull away from him. Don't be left behind while others embark on an incredible, life-changing journey of faith. Give Him a chance. He can and will carry you safely."

When Morning Gilds the Sky

As I lay on a comfortable bed in Sapphire Valley, North Carolina, and watched the dawn arrive, I thought about these words found in an old hymn: "When morning gilds the skies,/My heart awaking cries,/May Jesus Christ be praised!"

In the early light, I praised the Lord and considered His greatness. That feeling continued as my husband and I took an early morning walk around the resort. Fog shrouded the majestic mountains, yet such a thick veil could not hide their massiveness or keep me from feeling small as they towered over me.

As we strolled leisurely along, we took deep breaths of air filled with the fragrance coming from the huge spruce and cedar trees surrounding the walkways. We discovered beds of tiny lavender-and-white wildflowers. In fact, everywhere I looked I saw evidence of God's handiwork, and that caused me to praise the Creator and to thank Him for His awesome creation. I wondered how anyone enjoying such beautiful surroundings could fail to see the work of the Creator and to thank Him.

However, that does happen. The Apostle Paul said that godless people push the truth about God away, although they instinctively know the truth about Him. In fact, God puts that knowledge in their hearts. "From the time the world was created, people have seen the earth and the sky and all that God made. They can clearly see his invisible qualities—his eternal power and divine nature. So they have no excuse whatsoever for not knowing God.

"Yes, they knew God, but wouldn't worship him as God or even give him thanks…Instead of believing what they knew was the truth about God, they deliberately chose to believe lies. So they worshipped the things God made but not the Creator himself, who is to be praised forever" (Romans 1:20-25).

Thankfully, there are people who do not fail to see the beauty all around and to thank God for it. For example, in 1864 Folliott Pierpoint wrote these words: For the beauty of the earth,/For the glory of the skies,/For the love which from our birth/Over and around us lies;/Lord of all, to Thee we raise/This our hymn of grateful praise."

The second verse included more things for which Pierpoint praised the Lord: "For the wonder of each hour/Of the day and of the night,/Hill and vale, and tree and flower,/Sun and moon and stars of light." Years and years later, people still sing those words and use them to praise the Lord.

The writer of Psalm 104 says, "O LORD, what a variety of things you have made…The earth is full of your creatures…May the glory of the LORD last forever… I will sing to the LORD as long as I live. I will praise my God to my last breath!"

Anytime I look at the handiwork of God, I echo the sentiments of the aforementioned writers and my spirit joyfully sings: "When morning gilds the skies/My heart awaking cries/May Jesus Christ be praised!"

Reflections

A Time to Build Sand Castles?

The air blowing in off of the Gulf of Mexico heightened my awareness of the surroundings. I wondered, *Is the sky a brighter blue here than at home?* I laughed as the playful wind gave me a new hairstyle. Though the sun beamed down upon my untanned skin, the cool breeze made me oblivious to the sunburn that was in progress.

As Jena and I walked along the wet sand at the edge of the water, I noticed that there were only a few sand castles. Since I had seen many families enjoying the sand and the surf, the scarcity of sand castles puzzled me.

When I commented on that, Jena responded, "Why bother to build sand castles? They're going to get washed away."

At first, I accepted the logic in her conclusion. Indeed, why waste time constructing something that won't last 24 hours? Why not spend time doing something significant? Why invest our time and creativity in building sand castles when our energies are needed to solve the serious problems facing this world?

A voice inside me challenged those thoughts: "Lighten up. Not everything has to be 'serious and stuffy.' It's perfectly okay to do something just for the sheer enjoyment of it."

I pursued that line of thought. Those who build sandcastles do enjoy the sights and sounds of nature, but their pleasure is not the only benefit. For example, when builders are surrounded by noisy seagulls, brilliant sunshine, azure sky, gentle breezes, and wet sand, it's easy to praise and thank the Creator.

Building sand castles builds relationships also. As sandy walls go up, emotional walls come down. Parent and child bond as they delight in working together on a simple project that allows each of them to use their creativity and skills. Even though the sand castle itself may be worthless and quickly washed away, the memories associated with it are priceless and last for a lifetime.

As the Old Testament writer says in Ecclesiastes 3:1-8:

> There is a time for everything,
> a season for every activity under heaven.
> A time to be born and a time to die.
> A time to plant and a time to harvest…
> A time to cry and a time to laugh.
> A time to grieve and a time to dance…
> A time to tear and a time to mend.
> A time to be quiet and a time to speak up.

Perhaps he would also agree that there is a time to work and a time to play, a time to face responsibilities and a time to build sandcastles.

Reflections

No Shuttle Bus for Me!

As we neared the top of the mountain, we met folks who were returning from there. They said, "You're almost there. You can make it!"

A short distance from the top, I stopped to catch my breath. One lady who was descending smiled at me. Thinking she knew something about the struggle I was having on my way to the pinnacle, I inquired, "Is the view worth this climb?"

"Oh," she said, "I don't know about that. I rode the shuttle bus to the top."

With what little breath I had left, I mumbled, "I wish I'd known about the shuttle bus!"

With heart pounding and sweat dripping, I reached the paved area at the top of the mountain. I stood still and let the wind revive me. Though the journey up the steep, well-worn path had been strenuous, I was glad I had not ridden the shuttle bus. Had I taken the easy way, I would not have experienced the same degree of exhilaration I felt at that very moment.

Even though I had struggled to make it to the top, the spectacular view was worth the climb. As I looked around, I understood why the steep path had required so much time and energy. It led to the top of the world, or so it seemed! From where I stood, main roads looked like gashes in the green landscape; huge parking lots looked like postage stamps; large buildings resembled scale models.

A few weeks later, as I was reading the biblical account of the conversation between the prophet Nathan and king David, the memory of the mountaintop experience came to mind.

Nathan said, "This is what the LORD Almighty says: I chose you to lead my people Israel when you were just a shepherd boy, tending your sheep out in the pasture. I have been with you wherever you have gone, and I have destroyed all your enemies. Now I will make your name famous throughout the earth!…Your dynasty and your kingdom will continue for all time before me, and your throne will be secure forever" (2 Samuel 7:8-16).

After receiving the message Nathan delivered for God, David "…went in and sat before the LORD and prayed, 'Who am I, O Sovereign LORD, and what is my family that you have brought me this far?" (2 Samuel 7:18).

As David pondered that question, he began to understand that such a wonderful blessing had not come to him because he deserved it or because he worked hard to earn it. David realized that the idea for his move from the pasture to the palace originated in the heart of God; it was God's plan for David to rule over His people.

As I thought about David's experiences as he journeyed along the path God had marked out for him, I said to myself, *From the pasture to the palace is quite a long way*. Yet, God brought him that far. Like my climb up the mountain, David's path from shepherd boy to king had not been an easy one. God had not provided a "shuttle bus" for David to ride to the pinnacle of success. Instead, God allowed David to struggle in order to reach the goal God had set for him, but the view from the "mountaintop" had definitely been worth the climb.

Reflecting on the change God brought about in the life of David caused me to ask, *"What mountain does God have for me to climb? How far has He already brought me?"*

Wherever it is God is taking me, I'm not expecting Him to send a shuttle bus to take me there. But that's okay. I'm willing to climb, for I know the destination will be worth every struggle!

Reflections

Please Remain in Your Seats

After settling into our seats and listening to the flight attendant explain what to do in case of an emergency, we felt the plane move as the pilot backed away from the terminal and prepared to take his position on the runway. My excitement increased as we waited to take off.

Several minutes later, I wondered what was causing the delay. At last, the pilot began speaking over the intercom. When he spoke, everyone listened attentively. "We apologize for the delay," he said. "We expect to be cleared for takeoff in a few minutes. Please remain in your seats."

Having been reassured by the pilot's words, the passengers resumed making small talk with one another. As the minutes passed, the conversation slowed, and we became more aware of how uncomfortable we were. In response to the high heat and humidity, adults fanned, children squirmed, and babies cried. As we sat in that crowded, muggy plane I wondered, *Why don't they turn on the air?*

As if reading my mind, the pilot announced, "The air will be flowing again as soon as the engines get going. We apologize for any discomfort you are experiencing. Please remain in your seats."

After more than an hour of waiting, passengers became angry and restless. Someone said, "I'm going to miss my connecting flight from Denver to Seattle." Another said, "My family is waiting for me at the airport and wondering what's happened to this flight." Parents of small children ran out of "quiet" games to play. The noise level increased, adding to our discomfort. The irritability level rose rapidly like the mercury in a thermometer under the tongue of a feverish patient.

When we had had about all the discomfort and frustration we could take, we once again heard the pilot's calm voice. "We have been cleared for takeoff. Please remain in your seats."

Upon hearing those welcomed words, we started to relax, especially as the cool air began to flow. By the time we reached our cruising altitude and the flight attendants had served our snacks, peace prevailed. People talked softly to one another and the babies slept soundly. Previous discomfort and irritability had been forgotten.

The pilot, speaking in that soft, well-modulated voice that was now familiar to all of us, explained the reason for our delay at the airport in Houston, Texas. "Severe thunderstorms to the north made it necessary to reroute or reschedule flights. Everything seems to be okay now, though we may experience some turbulence. Please remain in your seats."

As we flew through the night sky, we could see large bolts of lightning on either side of the plane. Though they appeared to be quite near, I hoped they were miles and miles away! Despite having a slightly uneasy feeling, we enjoyed nature's magnificent show. Never before had my family and I been in the sky during an electrical storm. Though we knew the storm was potentially deadly, we agreed it was beautiful to watch.

Periodically, the pilot provided information. Each time he did so, his voice calmed me for I realized he was in control. He knew about the location of the storms and how to avoid them. Our safety did not depend on us, but on him. Although keeping us safe kept him busy in the cockpit, he took time to let us know he was aware of our need for information and for assurance that all was well.

Many times since that flight from Houston to Denver, I've thought about how much I appreciated that pilot. Even though I never saw him face-to-face, I knew he was there. That awareness enabled me to wait patiently during the long delay and to remain calm during the flight.

My relationship to God is much like that. I have not seen Him, but I am aware of His presence with me. His voice often reassures me as He lets me know that He is aware of my situation and that He is making wise decisions and taking actions that will benefit me, even when long delays occur. When the waiting becomes intolerable and I become restless, He may or may not explain what's going on. But His advice is similar to that given by the pilot, though, of course, God doesn't say, "Remain in your seat." However, the Bible does express that thought with words such as those spoken by Moses to God's people as they were being pursued by their Egyptian Army: "Don't be afraid! Just *stand where you* are and watch the LORD rescue you…The LORD himself will fight for you. You won't have to lift a finger in your defense" (Exodus 14:13, emphasis added).

Reflections

A Short Delay

The "short delay" lasted more than an hour. None of us on board the plane liked having to sit idly by. The heat, combined with the high humidity that is so typical in Houston, Texas, on a Summer evening, made everyone feel uncomfortable. People murmured, "How much longer do we have to wait?"

Every now and then the pilot updated us. "We regret the delay and apologize for any discomfort you may be experiencing. However, there's nothing to do but wait. There are severe thunderstorms in the area, and air traffic is being rerouted around the storms. We hope to be on our way to Denver in another ten minutes or so."

While we waited our turn to taxi down the runway, we wished the flight attendants could serve cold beverages, but they had to remain seated, just as we did. We longed for some cool air, but since the pilot had shut off the engines in order to conserve fuel, no air-conditioning was available. We used magazines to fan ourselves and tried to ignore the fussy babies and whining children. Those of us who normally weren't claustrophobic began to be as the minutes dragged by.

Finally, the pilot announced that he had received clearance from the control tower and that he would be starting the engines. Within moments, the cool air poured out the vents, and we began to relax.

As we flew West, the pilot instructed us to look at the lightning flashing to our North. As I watched nature's incredibly beautiful, but potentially dangerous display, I felt so thankful for the folks in the control tower who knew about the storms and diverted us around them. Had they not done so, we would have flown head on into what we later learned were not just heavy thunderstorms but tornadoes that injured several people on the ground.

Upon learning that, the delay and the discomfort seemed a small price to pay in return for our safety. However, at the time we were waiting and unaware of the extent of the danger around us, we just wanted to get airborne! We were tired and uncomfortable. Some of us had connecting flights. Some had worried family and friends waiting to greet them at Stapleton International Airport in Denver. Naturally, we resented the "short delay."

Since that night in June 1989, I've thought quite a bit about that experience and I've seen how it relates to other times in my life as well, times when I've been in a holding pattern. Wanting to "get on with it," yet not being able to do so has caused frustration and despair. During those times, I've become impatient, not realizing that God had good reasons for making me wait.

As I look back over those times of waiting, I'm thankful for several things. First, that God was in the "control tower" looking ahead and seeing those things that I could not. Second, that He mercifully selected a better route, albeit sometimes a longer one, for me to travel. Third, that He did not allow me to go my own foolish way, thus, sparing me from suffering and/or heartache. Fourth, that He forgave me for being impatient with Him and for failing to trust Him when He did not explain His reasons to me. Fifth, that He helps me recall the lessons He has taught me during some of life's seemingly ordinary happenings.

Perhaps, next time I have a "short delay," I won't ask, "How much longer must I wait?" Instead, I hope I'll be wise enough to say, "Thank You, God, for being in the 'control tower.'"

Reflections About Holidays

Johnnie Ann Burgess Gaskill

Reflections

As Unto the Lord

Strikingly similar events occurred on Thanksgiving Eve of 1986 and 1987. On both days I worked at the office later than usual. On both days I encountered needy people just as I prepared to rush home to complete last minute preparations for my family's Thanksgiving celebration.

On each of the two years, help was available for the needy families I encountered, thanks to the generosity of people in our community. All I had to do to find food and shelter for them was to call some of the dedicated volunteers who managed the Community Action Mission Program (CAMP) in our area and they took care of everything from that point forward.

With a grateful heart, I drove home. However, two questions troubled me: (1) What would I have done if I'd been unable to find the help the families needed? (2) Would I have invited the strangers to share my warm home and to enjoy the delicious Thanksgiving meal?

I'd like to think that I would have taken the needy ones home with me, but I probably would not have. I would not have left them alone, however. I probably would have secured shelter and food for them in a local motel and restaurant, even if I'd ended up with the bill. Then, though it is painful for me to admit, I would have gone home, relieved to have the unpleasant task behind me.

As I reflect on those two episodes on Thanksgiving Eve 1986 and 1987, the words of Christ come into my mind and shame me. "I assure you, when you [ministered to] one of the least of these my brothers and sisters, you were doing it to me" (Matthew 25:40).

Then, with a contrite heart I pray, "Lord, change my attitude about ministry. Help me to rejoice rather than to complain when needy people come my way. Help me to see each one as You do. Remind me that in each ministry situation I have an opportunity to be loving, kind, and generous—as if to You. By ministering as You would have me to, I'll show my thanks to You for meeting my needs."

Johnnie Ann Burgess Gaskill

A Grateful Heart—Always

My family and I rang the doorbell and waited quietly on the front porch. After several minutes, our elderly friend opened the door and invited us to come in. As he hugged us, tears slid down his kind face. "It's mighty good to see you," he said.

We chatted briefly with him, then he said, "Come on back. She's in the bedroom."

I followed him to the room where his wife lay. With trembling lips she gave me a smile. I saw how weak and frail she was.

I said, "Is there anything I can do for you?"

With a quavering voice, she asked, "Would you trim my toenails?"

"Certainly," I responded. As I began her pedicure, she started to cry. "Everybody's so good to me."

Then she began to name those who had been especially kind to her. Her husband Paul headed the list. "Paul takes such wonderful care of me, but I wish he didn't have to. He's not well, and I don't like being a burden to him. I wish I could do for him like I used to."

As I continued to file her toenails, she talked about her children and what a help they were. She mentioned the deacon from our church who brought cassette tapes of the worship service each week. She spoke of neighbors and other friends from the church who regularly brought food. She showed me the basket of cards she kept within arm's length so that she could read them again and again. She concluded her long list of blessings by saying, "Even my doctor is a wonderful Christian man."

She amazed me. She always had. Although she had been homebound all the years I'd known her, she always managed to focus on the positive aspects of her situation. Certainly she experienced the negatives: discomfort, loneliness, weakness, dependence, confinement…However, she kept those in the background of her mind.

She constantly expressed her gratitude, as she had that night I trimmed her toenails. She always had a good word to say about everybody. Not once did I ever hear her say an unkind word about anybody. Such an attitude made her a joy to be with, even in the midst of a difficult situation.

She died not long after we visited her that night. I think of her often, especially during the Thanksgiving season. She proved to me that gratitude is possible even when circumstances are not ideal. In fact, that's precisely when it is most meaningful to the one giving thanks and to the one who observes the expression of gratitude.

Though my friend never quoted Psalm 103:1-2 to me, I know she did just what Psalmist said. "Praise the LORD, I tell myself; with my whole heart, I will praise his holy name. Praise the LORD, I tell myself, and never forget the good things he does for me."

As a result, her heart overflowed with gratitude that touched my life. A thankful heart like hers is a joy to have and to share. It is one of the blessings the Lord gives to those who truly love Him.

Johnnie Ann Burgess Gaskill

The Things We Have and Have Not

A group of seventeen persons met for an annual banquet a few days before Thanksgiving. As we talked while enjoying the delicious food, the conversation shifted rapidly from person to person and from topic to topic.

We tried not to "talk shop" even though we were all involved in the same kind of ministry. Instead, we discovered other areas of common interest. As the convener of the group, I felt pleased that the conversation flowed easily, even between people who had not met each other prior to the meeting.

The time passed quickly as we enjoyed the food and the fellowship. To conclude the meeting, I stood to thank the group for attending. I also expressed my appreciation to them for the excellent work they were doing in their respective churches. Then I asked the group to share some things for which they were thankful. The way they responded reminded me of kernels of popcorn being popped, as first one and then another named their blessings.

Since I had asked them to refrain from naming the blessings that normally head the list, such as their relationship to Christ, their families, their health and etc., they looked beyond the obvious and came up with a variety of significant things for which they were thankful. One director expressed her gratitude for the fine staff that assisted her in the work. Another person mentioned the memories of special people and places. After a while, one lady quipped, "I'm thankful for Kroger!"

We exploded with laughter. Those of us who had sat near her knew exactly why she mentioned that particular blessings. Earlier we had talked about all the things our parents used to have to do to get a chicken ready to cook. (Yuk! Yuk!) Consequently, this lady was thankful for the opportunity to go to the store and buy a ready-to-cook turkey or chicken.

"Yes," I said when I managed to stop laughing, "we should be thankful for those things from which we are spared."

The minute those words came out of my mouth I remembered a similar though much more serious statement I'd heard on the news.

The night before a series of tornados had touched down in several states as well as in the surrounding areas of the town in which we were meeting. The early morning news had provided the sad details of the destruction and death caused by the severe storms. One man recalled how his vehicle was totally destroyed moments after he'd jumped from it to a place of safety. Overcome with emotion, the man stated simply and from the depth of his soul, "I thank God that He spared me."

Anytime we count our blessings, perhaps we do well to remember the good things we have and also the bad things we have not.

Johnnie Ann Burgess Gaskill

The Stable Must Go

Several years ago as we unpacked the Christmas decorations, I looked ruefully at the stable that sheltered our manger scene. It was in pitiful shape. In fact, it had never been a lovely thing, but I cherished it because Jennifer, our older daughter, had made it in Vacation Bible School when she was eight years old. It was made out of unpainted Popsicle sticks and glue. Over the years we added more glue and pieces of tape in an attempt to hold it together for one more Christmas.

So, putting sentiment aside, I said, "This shabby old thing has to be replaced—this year! We'll buy a new crèche."

However, my resolve to discard it weakened as I recalled all the years our two daughters had knelt around the coffee table and lovingly rearranged the tiny figures of Mary, Joseph, Jesus, the Wise Men and the animals that were sheltered inside the Popsicle stick stable. And I thought about how their pudgy little fingers had so carefully placed the three kneeling angels on the roof of the stable. (Because the manager scene was so inexpensive, it was never off limits for them.)

Since the children had been drawn to the simple stable, I began to reconsider my decision to replace it. While thinking about what to do, I re-read Luke 2: 1-20. I reflected on the utter simplicity of everything surrounding the birth of Jesus. The King of Kings and the Lord of Lords was born in a stable rather than a palace. The news of His birth was first announced to a group of lowly shepherds rather than to the distinguished men of that time.

Since God selected such a simple setting for the birth of His son, perhaps *He* might want our Popsicle stable to remain on the table, to stand in stark contrast to the commercial items in the rest of the room. "Yes," I said, "we'll definitely keep that stable to remind all of us of this wonderful truth: "…Though he was very rich, yet for your sakes he became poor, so that by his poverty he could make you rich" (2 Corinthians 8:9).

Reflections

He's More Than a Babe In Bethlehem!

Our daughters always wanted to rush the growing up process. For example, when they were preteens, they longed to be able to date and to drive. But they weren't ready for that and neither were their father and I.

I often reminded them, "When you're ninety-nine you'll still be my babies, my little girls." Then they'd roll their eyes at me as if saying, "Oh, Mama, get real. See us as we are! We aren't your babies any longer!"

And they were right. They were growing…maturing…become capable, responsible persons. My eyes saw the tell-a-tale signs of growth, but every now and then something they did or said or a certain mannerism caused me to see them as they used to be. For that brief moment, they'd become my little girls again and I'd feel a lump in my throat and tears in my eyes. Letting go of them has been difficult, awfully difficult.

I'm sure other mothers find it so. Even Mary, the mother of Jesus, must have found it hard to charge her perception of Jesus and let Him become all He was intended to be. Even before He was conceived in her body, she knew something of His identity and His special destiny. An angel had appeared to her and said, "Don't be frightened, Mary,…for God has decided to bless you! You will become pregnant and have a son, and you are to name him Jesus. He will be very great and will be called the Son of the Most High. And the LORD will give him the throne of his ancestor David. And he will reign over Israel forever; his Kingdom will never end!" (Luke 1:30-33).

Though given this prior knowledge, Mary and Joseph were amazed at the things people said about Jesus. But, like the loving mother she must have been, Mary treasured all these memories of Him in her heart. As He grew, she may have recalled those days when He was a Babe in Bethlehem.

I wonder how she viewed Jesus as He became a mature man, one who taught, preached, healed—all with great authority? How did she see Him as He hung on the cross? Did she see Him as the obedient Son of God who was giving His life for others? Did she see Him as her baby?

I don't know how she felt or what her perceptions of Him were. The Bible does not say. I do know that you and I have great reason to rejoice as we celebrate His birth. But if we only think of Him as the baby born in a stable, we must extend our perceptions of Him. He is more, so much more, than just the Babe in Bethlehem. He is our Redeemer. He is our Savior. He is the King of Kings and the Lord of Lords. We must learn to see Him as He *is*, in all His fullness, in all His glory.

Johnnie Ann Burgess Gaskill

Good News for Lonely, Fragmented People

Even before we tried to put up our Christmas tree that year, I knew things were different. What had always been a one-evening, family project stretched out for days. First, my husband got the artificial tree out of storage. The following night, while my husband took our younger daughter to a school-sponsored skating party, I assembled the tree. After they returned, he placed the lights on the tree while I did some Christmas baking. Several days later, Jennifer and Jena decorated the tree and we placed a few hastily wrapped gifts underneath it. When we finally finished, the tree looked pretty. But I felt an emptiness inside. I longed for the Christmases of the past when we'd worked together as a family to decorate our house.

Later, as I went shopping by myself and wrapped presents alone, my feelings of loneliness intensified. Oh, I knew that my family had not abandoned me. It was just that I had to do these kinds of things by myself because our evenings and weekends were so filled with activities that we could not schedule "Christmasy" family togetherness. I missed that. I felt our lives had become so fragmented.

Feeling weary, lonely, and fragmented caused me to long for the peace and joy that accompanied the birth of Jesus. As I read Luke 2, I experienced a surge of hope. Jesus had affected the lives of people of His day who were trying to cope with life. I believed He would do the same for me.

With new insight, I saw Mary the expectant mother traveling with Joseph some seventy miles from Nazareth to Bethlehem. How weary she must have been from riding that distance on the back of a donkey!

Next, I envisioned the shepherds as they kept their lonely vigil out on the hillside. I thought about these men who were pretty much at the bottom of the social scale. How much hope did they have for any change in their bleak lives? Yet, it was to *them* that the angel of the Lord first announced the birth of Jesus. "Do not be afraid!…I bring you good news of great joy for everyone! The Savior—yes, the Messiah, the Lord—has been born tonight in Bethlehem, the city of David!" (Luke 2:10-11).

As I reflected on their reaction, I recalled numerous accounts of people—sick, crippled, fearful, rejected, sad, greedy, lonely, busy, rich, poor—who met Jesus and were changed by Him. I asked myself, *Can Jesus affect my life today? Can He meet me at my point of need?*

Yes! Yes! To each of us Jesus says, "My purpose is to give life in all its fullness" (John 10:10). He came to give each of us an abundant life! No more loneliness. No more fragmentation. Instead, He offers to you and me the opportunity to experience His presence, and He always imparts a sense of joy, peace, and wholeness in the midst of every situation. The question is: Will I accept His gracious gift?

Johnnie Ann Burgess Gaskill

Room for Him?

I always enjoy the re-enactments of the birth of Christ. In them Mary is portrayed as gentle, pensive, and frail as she tenderly holds the Baby. Joseph is a quiet onlooker who stands by Mary's side, showing his support of and concern for his family. The Wise Men represent the "upper crust" of society as they make a grand entrance while wearing their elegant robes and crowns and carrying expensive gifts. In contrast, the shepherds come in wearing simple robes and bearing no gifts. All the visitors kneel in adoration of the Baby.

In every re-enactment, the main characters are familiar and predictable. However, I'm always curious to see how the innkeeper will be portrayed. Sometimes he appears angry when Mary and Joseph knock on the door and ask for a room. Often, he seems curt, almost rude, implying that he has a successful business to run and resents being interrupted by people with a problem. Sometimes the innkeeper sounds almost gentle when he says, "I'm sorry. I have no more rooms."

While we don't *know* exactly what attitudes and actions characterized Mary, Joseph, the Wise Men and the shepherds, we can infer them from Scripture. However, since we know nothing about the innkeeper, his reactions are anybody's guess. That's one reason I wonder about his role during the actual birth of Christ.

I also wish I knew the reactions of the guests in the inn. Did they know about the young couple who needed shelter? If so, why didn't they offer to give up, or at least share, their room? Surely the female guests could identify with Mary's obvious need for a comfortable place to rest.

My questions about the innkeeper and his guests will have to go unanswered—for now. Though I'd very much like to know about their attitudes and actions, I shouldn't focus too much of my attention on them. Instead, I need to ask myself, *Do I have room in my life for Jesus. If not, am I willing to make room?*

Those questions are of utmost importance. If I answer negatively, I will miss out on the most significant opportunity ever given me, as did the innkeeper and his guests. Like them, I deprive myself of experiencing a life-changing event if I refuse to make room for the Son of God.

If I answer affirmatively, I can feel the wonder and the joy of being in the very presence of God. Like the Wise Men and the shepherds, I can kneel before Him, knowing that it matters not what gifts I bring to Him so long as I offer myself to Him.

Whether or not I will make room for Him remains my decision. Just as God did not force the innkeeper and the guests to make room for His

Reflections

Son, neither will He force me to make a place in my life for Jesus. However, God will offer me the privilege of sharing myself and my possessions with the Christchild who is now the Savior of the world.

Johnnie Ann Burgess Gaskill

Rest Beside the Weary Road

"Weary" best described the way I felt that Sunday night. And because I was tired to the bone, I sang the familiar Christmas carols without much energy or enthusiasm, for, as my mother used to say, "I was fresh out of" both of them.

My weariness increased as I began thinking about the things I had to do within the remaining few weeks before Christmas. My "Must Do" list included: shopping, baking, cleaning, addressing cards, wrapping gifts, attending school and church functions, working at my regular job, and writing a weekly column.

The more I thought about that list, the worse I felt. I asked myself, *How will I ever get it all done?*

As depression settled over me like a heavy fog, I suddenly became aware of the words I was singing. Oh, how I needed to hear them!

The words invited me to "...rest beside the weary road, and hear the angels sing." As I sang them, my inner voice said, "Write down that sentence. You need to reflect on it."

I scribbled it down, then concentrated on singing the other carols. Their words and beautiful melodies refreshed me—from the inside out.

During the week, I continued to think about the invitation to "...rest beside the weary road, and hear the angels sing." As I re-read the Christmas story in Luke 2. I noticed how the shepherds responded in terror when the angel of the Lord appeared to them and the glory of the Lord illuminated the night sky. However, the angel hastened to say, "Don't be afraid!...I bring you good news of great joy for everyone! The Savior—yes, the Messiah, the Lord—has been born tonight in Bethlehem, the city of David!" (Luke 2:10-11).

I imagined how the shepherds thrilled to the good news that the long-awaited Savior had come. Not only would He be a Savior to them, but also to *all* people everywhere. Even before they understood the impact of the angel's words, that angel was joined by a throng of the heavenly hosts. Together they praised God with these words: "Glory to God in the highest heaven, and peace on earth to all whom God favors" (v.14).

If the shepherds had been weary as they kept their night watch over the sheep, their fatigue left them when they heard the angels sing! After the shepherds discussed the Good News the angels shared with them, they decided to go to Bethlehem to verify the "angel-gram.' They hurried off and found the Christchild about whom the angel had spoken. Believing He was indeed the Savior, they spread the Good News about Him.

Reflections

From the account of the shepherds, I understand more fully the meaning of "...rest beside the weary road and hear the angels sing." It is not an invitation to walk away from all responsibilities. Instead, it is an encouragement *to pause* and *to absorb* the message given by the angel. A Savior, a Deliverer has come! He came not only for the shepherds but also for you and me.

Knowing that we have a personal Savior enables us to rejoice and to give thanks to God. It makes us eager to share the Good News. It gives us energy and enthusiasm for the tasks at hand. As we carry out our daily responsibilities, we do so with joy in our hearts.

We can experience this renewal, this relief from fatigue and discouragement, as often as we take time to "...rest beside the weary road and hear the angels sing."

(The words used in this chapter were taken from "It Came Upon a Midnight Clear" by Edward Sears, 1849.)

Johnnie Ann Burgess Gaskill

The Best Gift of All

During final preparations for the holidays, I often imagine what I'd like to give to the people whose names are on my list.

How about a monitoring device that allows only nutritious food to be taken into the mouth? Or an alarm clock that motivates one to get up on time—without being grumpy. For the lady of the house, a sure-to-please gift is a truly automatic washer and dryer—one that gathers, sorts, washes, dries, folds, and puts away the laundry. For ultimate convenience, how about an automatic dishwasher, one that unloads and reloads itself?

Consider also a friendly robot that gently pulls a lazy person out of the recliner and sets him or her outside the door for some much-needed exercise. To pack rats like me, I wish I could give a simplified, foolproof filing system that maintains itself. The absentminded among us would enjoy having library materials equipped with built-in alarms that alert the borrower to return media on the date due.

(As far as I know, these gifts are not yet available. However, if you should find a supplier of any one of them, please let me know!)

Seriously, I wish I could give cancer-free bodies to everyone, correct an insulin imbalance, restore life to a beloved one, and provide freedom from fear. To the one who struggles with academics, I'd give the ability to earn "a straight A" report card. To the childless, I'd give a baby. To the person haunted by past mistakes, I'd give a clear conscience and a fresh start. I'd give health and mobility to those confined to a nursing home. To the emotionally disturbed, I'd give serenity and stability.

My list is long, but still incomplete. Each person who comes to mind has an assortment of needs, all of which I long to meet. Since I cannot give them the gifts I'd really like to, I'll settle for the usual clothes, gadgets, and the like.

As I wrap each gift, I'll mention the name of each recipient and say, "I wish You to know Jesus. Not just about Him, but to know Him personally and intimately and to have daily communication with Him. Jesus is the One Who can supply all your needs. He is the One Who will give you the deepest desires of your heart."

What better gift could I wish for someone than the experience of understanding the absolute adequacy of Jesus Christ?

Reflections

Let There Be Peace

I stood on the upper level of the mall and looked down at the crowds below. For several minutes I listened intently to the Christmas music being performed by students from a local high school. Then my attention shifted to the lady who was standing beside me.

As we chatted with one another, we discovered that each of us had a daughter in the group below. As we talked a bit more, we realized that our daughters were friends and that my daughter knew the lady's son who had graduated the previous June.

That information prompted her to tell me that her son was in basic training in North Carolina and that he wouldn't be coming home (to Georgia) for Christmas.

"This will be his first Christmas away from home," she said softly.

Struggling to keep her emotions under control, she added, "We can't even send him anything for Christmas because he has no place to store anything. His small locker holds personal items only."

She continued, "This will definitely not be a good Christmas for us."

Since I didn't know what to say to her, I felt glad she didn't expect an answer. A compassionate silence settled over us, although my emotions churned within as I realized that many others would be in similar situations.

I thought about folks who would be separated from family members—for a variety of reasons. Some would be on the mission field. Others would have to deal with the loss of a loved one due to death, divorce, abandonment, or imprisonment. I blinked back tears as I thought of those who, for the first time, would have a vacant chair at the table, a too-quiet house, a silent doorbell, an empty bed, and a void in their hearts bigger than the State of Texas.

Suddenly, I became aware of the music being performed by the students. These words, "Let there be peace on earth and let it begin with me," challenged me. I asked myself, *Am I at peace. Can peace really begin with me?*

If the definition of peace is not just the absence of conflict but rather a *settledness* even in the midst of a difficult situation, then perhaps that is what Jesus meant as He talked with His disciples just prior to His arrest and subsequent crucifixion. Knowing that their stress level reading was "off the charts," Jesus comforted them with these words: "I am leaving you with a gift—peace of mind and heart. And the peace I give isn't like the peace the world gives. So don't be troubled or afraid" (John 14:27).

Surely His words sounded strange to them. Peace? When the One in whom they trusted was going to be arrested and killed? Peace? When they had no idea what would happen to them? Peace? When they had no idea what to do with the rest of their lives, assuming that they did not meet the same fate as their Master? Peace? When the establishment hated them?

Even though His words sounded strange, He was indeed offering them a solution. Peace is possible for anyone who has entered into a right relationship with God the Father by believing in and accepting His Son, Jesus Christ. He gives the peace, which the Apostle Paul describes as being beyond any human ability to comprehend, to the believer. That peace isn't something persons have to create for themselves. **Jesus gives peace**, His peculiar peace. When we are at peace with God and receive His gift of peace, we experience a tranquility that neither internal nor external forces can disturb.

Jesus makes that kind of peace available to us as we deal with separation from loved ones, the threat of war, and all other uncertainties of life as well. Such peace is a gift to all who will receive the Prince of Peace into their hearts.

Reflections

Christmas Will Come!

As I hurried down the hallway at church, I paused to speak to a friend. "Johnnie," she said, "have you finished your shopping yet?"

I shook my head. "I still have a few more things to get," I replied. "How about you?"

"I haven't finished either," she said.

"Every year I promise myself that I will not wait until the last minute, but I never finish early," I said remorsefully.

"Well, you know," she said cheerily, "Christmas always comes, doesn't it?"

We laughed, and I walked on. My friend had not told me anything new, but she had helped me gain a new perspective on the holiday season.

So what if I don't have time to make Christmas goodies? Christmas will still come. So what if I don't decorate as much as I planned? Christmas will still come. So what if I don't find the perfect gift for everyone on my list? Christmas will still come.

I sighed with relief and decided that we would make adjustments for whatever was lacking. Life would go on!

With twelve days remaining until Christmas, I listed all the things I wanted to accomplish, and then I highlighted the most important ones. I decided that I would either do those myself or have someone in the family do them. I simply would not worry about the "nice-to-do-but-not-essential" things on my list.

With a great sense of relief, I began my activities for the day, knowing that the day set aside to celebrate the birth of Christ would come—whether or not I was ready—just as He had come to a world unprepared for Him.

Even His parents weren't ready for Him. They were away from home and family. There was no doctor or midwife to assist in His birth. In fact, there was no suitable place for His mother to deliver Him. There was no comfortable crib or white-skirted bassinet in which to place the newborn, only the animals' feeding trough. Yet, Christ came despite the fact that people were not prepared for His arrival.

Even so, His birth was so glorious that I doubt His parents ever regretted their lack of preparedness. Instead, they rejoiced that a Savior for the world had been born—and to them! Rather than berating herself for not having everything perfect for His arrival, Mary watched and listened carefully to all that went on after His birth. The Bible says that she "quietly treasured these things in her heart and thought about them often" (Luke 2:19). I'm sure she felt glad that God's selection of her as the mother of Jesus had not depended upon her ability to make all sorts of dazzling preparations in order to receive Him.

Therefore, I will not fret over all that remains to be done between now and Christmas. Instead, I will focus on the Christ whose birth I am celebrating. If I make room in my life for Him, my heart will be so full of joy that, like Mary, I won't grieve over any lack of other preparations.

Reflections

The Struggle to Understand

After reading the Christmas story, I did as Dr. Howard Hendricks suggested in **Living By the Book**. I tried to "crawl inside the skin" of the characters, especially Mary.

In previous readings, somehow my familiarity with the story prevented me from contemplating Mary and Joseph's struggle to understand what God was doing in their lives.

Initially, they were just one of many engaged couples living in Nazareth. Yet, without any apparent warning, their lives were forever changed when they learned that Mary would conceive and bear Jesus, the Son of God.

I wondered how they and their families dealt with Mary's pregnancy. Did they move the wedding date up in order to make it appear that Jesus was conceived after they married? How did the townspeople react? Did they ostracize Mary, Joseph, and their families?

Even if they discreetly "handled" their situation, other difficulties faced the young couple. At the end of her pregnancy Joseph and Mary made the 70-mile trip from Nazareth to Bethlehem—an arduous journey for anyone, especially a woman "great with child." Did she ask, "Why me, Lord?" Did she hope that all she was experiencing was just a bad dream and that she would wake up and find everything "normal" again?

Having endured the discomfort of the long trip, Mary surely wanted to find a nice room in which to rest. Although one was not available, the innkeeper allowed them to rest in a place where the animals were kept. It was there in those unsanitary, primitive conditions that the young Mary gave birth to her firstborn son. Was she frightened? Did she wish for her mother or one of the women from Nazareth to be with her? Had she remembered to bring the tiny blankets and clothes for her baby?

When the Child was about a month old, Mary and Joseph traveled to the Temple in Jerusalem to present Him to the Lord. There they encountered an elderly man named Simeon who said to Mary, "This child will be rejected by many in Israel, and it will be their undoing. But He will be the greatest joy to many others. Thus, the deepest thoughts of many hearts will be revealed. And a sword will pierce your very soul" (Luke 2:34-35).

During all these alternating high and low moments did Mary feel as if she were on a roller coaster ride? Did she wonder if the God who had singled her out for such a special blessing had lost control of the situation?

Regardless of Mary's feelings, God was very much in control, for as the Bible repeatedly says, "All of this happened to fulfill the Lord's message through his prophet." (For example, Matthew 2:22).

After reflecting on this great truth, I prayed, "Father, help me to understand that even though You are at work in my life, that doesn't guarantee me a problem-free life. However, what matters most is not how comfortable I am, but that Your will is done."

Reflections

Because He Loved Us First

The Christmas cards we received were signed in a variety of ways. A few were imprinted with names of the sender, while others bore handwritten signatures preceded by "Merry Christmas" or "Love." A few of our friends had taken time to write a personal message.

As I opened each card, I thought of the sender and felt grateful that he or she had remembered us at Christmastime. One friend, whom I hadn't talked with in a long while, signed his card, "Because He loved us first," followed by his initials. Even if he hadn't initialed his card, I would have known who had sent the card, for he signs *all* his correspondence to me with "Because He loved us first." However, he doesn't use the phrase casually. He uses it to remind himself and the recipient that Christian love is possible "Because He loved us first."

The Bible verifies the truth of my friend's closing phrase. John the Apostle wrote these words to other Christians: "Dear friends, let us continue to love one another, for love comes from God. Anyone who loves is born of God and knows God. But anyone who does not love does not know God—for God is love. God showed how much he loved us by sending his only Son into the world so that we might have eternal life through him. This is real love. It is not that we loved God, but that he loved us and sent his Son as a sacrifice to take away our sins. Dear friends, since God loved us that much, we surely ought to love each other" (1 John 4:7-11).

The Apostle John went on to say, "We love each other as a result of his loving us first" (1 John 4:19). And the Apostle Paul explained how God expressed that love for us. "When we were utterly helpless, Christ came at just the right time and died for us sinners. Now, no one is likely to die for a good person, though someone might be willing to die for a person who is especially good. But God showed his great love for us by sending Christ to die for us while we were still sinners" (Romans 5:6-8).

Thus, we are able to love God (and each other!) only "Because He first loved us." Since we have received God's love, we have love to share. That love, which is certainly much more than an emotion, expresses itself in many ways. Love may prompt us to give gifts—simple or extravagant—this Christmas. Love may inspire us to write notes of appreciation and encouragement. Love may cause us to lend a helping hand. Love may impress us to support missionaries with our prayers and our money. Love may sensitize us to the needs of the poor and motivate us to provide for them. Love may urge us to hold someone close. Love may remind us to spend time with our families. Love may require us to put the needs of others before our own. Love may lead us to be kind to ourselves as well as to others. Love may demand that we speak the truth. Love may ask us to come to the defense of another. Love may motivate us to apologize and to seek forgiveness.

Genuine love always expresses itself through some action, for real love cannot be passive and apathetic. Instead, it seeks ways to help others. As we demonstrate the love we have for others, some may ask, "Why are you doing this for me?" Our response should be the same as the one my friend always uses: "Because He loved us first."

Reflections

Big Goals

Two days before Christmas, our twelve-year-old daughter marched into our bedroom and announced, "I am going on a diet. I will lose 25 pounds by next June."

I smiled for I knew what was motivating her: the Miss American Pre-teen Pageant. While I admired her for wanting to look her best for the competition, I knew that if she lost even fifteen pounds she'd look anorexic! Even though I encouraged Jena to set a more reasonable goal, she remained adamant. "I am going to lose 25 pounds," she repeated as she left the room.

Minutes later, she returned with a hastily scribbled note. "No more cookies, potato chips, ice cream, fattening cereals. Less starches!"

Apparently she considered the note to be a contract she'd made with herself. Using a magnet, she posted it on the refrigerator door where it could constantly remind her to avoid the forbidden items she loved so much. Not wanting to be the only one to wrestle with such temptations, Jena enlisted the support of her sister. Jennifer did sign a contract, but chose a rather non-specific goal: "lose as much weight as possible." I declined to sign—because of my previous lack of success with weight management.

Jena's contract caused me to think about goals. They are often unrealistic or so vague that we never know whether or not we ever met them. On the other hand, some worthy goals are never set—for various reasons, perhaps because we feel that if we can't attain at least a small measure of success we shouldn't try at all.

As I thought about goals and resolutions for the New Year, I recalled an old saying: "Yard by yard, life is hard. Inch by inch, life's a cinch." I didn't completely agree with that. Life is seldom a cinch, but it is definitely more manageable when we tackle small portions of it. It is possible to move toward the things that we feel are beyond our grasp if we keep the desired goals in view and make diligent, concerted efforts to attain them.

While thinking about some personal goals for the New Year, I read some verses in the first chapter of 1 Peter. I gulped as I read, "But now you must be holy in everything you do, just as God—who chose you to be his children—is holy" (v.15).

Holiness is a *big* goal. I instinctively shrink from even contemplating what it means. I realize it not only involves having morally and ethically pure actions, but it also requires pure thoughts and motives which, in turn, produce pure/holy words and behavior.

It didn't take me but an instant to figure out that, if left on my own to achieve such holiness, I'd never succeed! However, the Good News is that assistance has been provided. God, who is my heavenly Father, is completely righteous and pure. As I live in close relationship with Him, I begin to absorb His nature and His character, and, in the process, I become more and more like Him. As His holiness affects my innermost person, it begins to influence every area of my life.

Even so, when I think about agreeing to pursue the goal of holiness, I'm still tempted not to sign the contract. Why bother with what seems such an unrealistic goal, a goal that I cannot fully meet even if I spend a lifetime working on it? But then I remember the old adage and decide to strive for purity "inch by inch." Attempting to be holy for one day at a time, even one thought or one action at a time, is better than making no effort to become pure.

Like my daughter who signed the "No more..." contract, I'll face many days filled with temptations. Knowing my human nature, there'll be times when I will "blow it." However, as I make a concerted effort to be pure in every area of my life, it will help me to remember that it is out of reverence for God and through His strength that I move toward His likeness—"inch by inch."

As I move toward that goal, as well as toward any others I might choose to pursue, I need to remember what else Peter had to say. "So think clearly and exercise self-control. Look forward to the special blessings that will come to you at the return of Jesus Christ. Obey God because you are his children. Don't slip back into the old ways of doing evil; you didn't know any better then, [but now you do!]" (1 Peter 1:13-14).

The Cross-stitched Prayer

A piece of cross-stitch I did when I was pregnant with our first child hung in a highly visible place in our home. I passed that framed 16x20 prayer many times each day during the years that it remained there. Regrettably, after I grew accustomed to its being there, I ignored its message.

Give Me Time

Time for patience, for understanding, too.
Time to remember thoughtful deeds to do.
Time to believe in all fellowmen.
Time to perceive the value of a friend.

I wanted to do all of those things, but often by the end of a busy day, I'd realize I had left them out. "Oh, if only I had more time," I'd moan. Then God would gently remind me that He gives to each of us exactly the same amount of time each day—twenty-four hours, no more and no less. Along with the gift of the hours themselves, He gives us the freedom to choose how we will use those precious moments.

Instead of asking for more time, I think I should ask for wisdom in using the time allotted to me. Of first priority is the command found in Colossians 4:5: "…make the most of every opportunity." As I interact with others, I should take time to do the things mentioned in the cross-stitched prayer. Most of them can be done in just minutes, yet they mean so much to others.

As each new year approaches, I need to read the cross-stitched prayer once again and let its message motivate me. However, I think I should change the title from "Give Me Time" to "Lord, Help Me Use the Time."

Johnnie Ann Burgess Gaskill

Facing the Future Fearlessly

Beginning a new year is somewhat like turning the pages of a suspense novel or watching the next scene in a thriller movie. We want to know what's going to happen, but we're not altogether sure we have the courage to face the unfolding events that may include: war, natural disasters, illness, financial reversals, career changes, aging, divorce, death, parental challenges, and the like. With such ominous clouds looming threateningly on the horizon, we long to find bright rays of hope. Calm will follow every storm. Good things will happen. Healthy babies will be born. Medical breakthroughs will be made. Marriages will be restored. Many children will make their parents proud. Peace will prevail.

Even so, this question remains uppermost in our minds: "What does the New Year hold for me and for my loved ones?" While that is a valid question, no human knows the answer.

How, then, are we supposed to cope with the uncertainties? Should we bury our heads in the sand and pretend that all is well? Should we be so aware of the goings-on that fear holds us in its suffocating grip? Should we allow "what if" thinking to prevail and to paralyze us?

God's Word contains the best instructions for coping with the uncertainties of the future. Read the writings of David, the prophets, Paul, and many others. They told it like it was. They were not blind to their circumstances; neither did they quote pious phrases to cheer themselves up. Having no pat answers, they grappled with their uncertainty about the future, as well as with their own lack of understanding about the present, just as you and I do. Yet, each of the writers reached essentially the same conclusion: "Trust the Lord."

For example, the book of Lamentations consists of five poems of mourning written by the prophet who was grieving the destruction of the city of Jerusalem and the Temple that was located there. The unidentified writer (probably Jeremiah) describes not only the desolation around him, but he also tells of his personal anguish.

"The thought of my suffering and homelessness is bitter beyond words. I will never forget this awful time, as I grieve over my loss. Yet I still dare to hope when I remember this: The unfailing love of the LORD never ends! By his mercies we have been kept from complete destruction. Great is his faithfulness; his mercies begin afresh each day. I say to myself, 'The LORD is my inheritance; therefore, I will hope in him!' The LORD is wonderfully good to those who wait for him and seek him…For the LORD does not abandon anyone forever. Though he brings grief, he also shows compassion according to the greatness of his unfailing love. For he does not enjoy hurting people or causing them sorrow" (Lamentations 3:19-33).

That conclusion reminds of a quote my mother shared with me a long time ago: "Whether He spare or share, He will be there." That sentence didn't originate with Mother; she came across it in some of her readings. However, she believes it and has received much comfort from it, as I have.

Since we do not know what the future holds, we must believe that whether God spares us from the disasters that lurk uncomfortably near or whether He allows them to enter our lives, God will be with us. Even if we can't understand His ways, we can learn to trust His heart, for He is loving, compassionate, merciful, and faithful.

Great men and women learned to trust God even when they did not understand His ways. That's how they achieved victory over circumstances that normally would have defeated them. That's how they found comfort in the midst of their mourning. That's how they gained freedom from the fear of the unknown. That's how they confidently faced an uncertain future.

As we begin not only each New Year but also each new day, may we hear God whisper, "Fear not. I am with you. Whether I spare you from pain or share it with you, I will be there."

Johnnie Ann Burgess Gaskill

Their Contribution to Freedom

My husband and I, along with our two daughters and my niece, hurried up the hill to the Tomb of the Unknowns at Arlington National Cemetery in Washington, D.C. in order to be on time for the changing of the guard at 4 p.m. Once there, I was surprised at how quietly the hundreds of people watched the lone soldier pace back and forth with such precision.

The guard followed an exact path. He took twenty-one steps to the right. Then he faced the tomb for twenty-one steps. With perfect posture and timing, he marched back and forth in front of the large white tomb that contained the body of the Unknown soldier from World War I. (Unknown soldiers from World War II, the Korean conflict and the Vietnam Conflict are buried in an adjacent tomb.) The reverential silence was broken only by the guard as he clicked his heels together.

At the appointed time for the changing of the guard, a second soldier commanded the crowd to stand and to remain silent. As the impressive ceremony continued, the replacement guard approached from the right and the three soldiers moved with predetermined precision.

I sensed they considered it a high honor to have been chosen to guard the Tomb of the Unknowns.

As the ceremony continued, I thought about how the four soldiers who were "known but to God" represented all the men and women who served our country so valiantly and sacrificially. Gratitude swept over me as I reflected on their contributions to freedom.

I also felt thankful for the young men from the Army's 3rd Infantry who guard the Tomb of the Unknowns. Those volunteers train for months to carry out that responsibility. And, despite the weather, they keep their lonely vigil 24 hours a day. Even during the night watches when no crowds are present, they continue to guard the tomb, changing shifts every two hours, in order to prevent any interruption in the tribute paid to the dead who served in our country's armed forces.

Such constant tribute doesn't lessen our personal responsibility to honor those who helped provide the freedoms we enjoy. We ought to pause often to remember them. We need to offer frequent prayers of gratitude for the sacrifices they made. Just as the guards at the Tomb of the Unknowns maintain the highest standards of military bearing and conduct at all times, so also should we conduct ourselves in such a way that we do not devalue the sacrifices made on our behalf.

Reflections

Freedom Isn't Free!

On the Sunday preceding the Fourth of July, my emotions were stirred as the church choir presented patriotic music. When the ensemble sang "The Statue of Liberty," I worshiped the God who had enabled Americans to achieve and to maintain freedom, not only for the native-born but also for all who choose to become citizens of the United States.

Following the congregational singing of "God of Our Fathers," the invocation, and the presentation of colors, we recited pledges to the American flag and the Christian flag as well. I listened reflectively as the pianist and the organist played "The Battle Hymn of the Republic."

One thought became crystal clear: Freedom isn't free. Someone paid a high price for the freedoms we enjoy today. As I thought about that, scenes stored in my mind flashed into my conscious awareness: battlefields, family members waving tearful goodbyes, flag-draped coffins, twenty-one gun salutes, weeping children who didn't understand why Daddy wouldn't be coming home again…

During those moments of quiet reflection, I recalled the reverence I felt while visiting the Tomb of the Unknown Soldier(s). Sitting in the church sanctuary, I again felt an awesome awareness of the toll exacted by the fight for freedom, the same awareness I experienced as I looked at row upon row of tombstones at Arlington National Cemetery.

I also recalled the reverential silence at the Vietnam Memorial. I remembered seeing people run their hands lovingly over the name of a loved one. I remembered seeing one woman make an etching of the name of someone dear to her. I recollected seeing people stand for long periods of time and read the names engraved on each section of the wall. I do not know why they read so intently. Perhaps they were searching for certain names or simply offering prayers of gratitude for the deceased's contribution to freedom.

Indeed, freedom is not free. People throughout the centuries have paid a high price. Some have given their lives in order to secure and/or preserve freedom for others. Whatever the nature and the cost of their investment, they sacrificed not only for themselves and their loved ones, but also for strangers and for generations yet unborn.

To all who have paid or are paying a high price for freedom, we owe a debt of gratitude and should be ever thankful for each effort made in behalf of freedom.

Because we do not often reflect on the high cost of freedom, we tend to take our freedoms for granted, to treat them casually rather than accept them as precious gifts. Because freedom—in the various forms it takes—

is infinitely valuable, we must cherish it, guard it, avoid losing it, and do all we can to preserve it and pass it on.

A Mother's Love

My friend blinked back tears as she told me about the difficult time she was going through. "I just need my mother to hug me and tell me everything's going to be okay," she said, "but my mother died nearly twenty years ago." She shook her head. "I should be over needing her so much, but I'm not!"

My heart ached for my friend. Her present circumstances were almost unbearable, yet she was dealing with them without the benefit of the comfort a mother brings.

After our conversation ended, I continued to reflect on our need for the comfort mothers bring. From our earliest moments, mothers comfort us by meeting our physical needs. They change our diapers, feed us, keep us warm, and make sure we are protected from harm. As they cuddle us and we snuggle close to their bodies, our emotional needs are also met. From our mothers we learn about love, security, and trust. As we grow, we learn more and more about the sacrificial love mothers give us.

I recall that my own mother put her nursing career on hold so that she could stay home with my sister and me. Knowing that Mother would be home each afternoon and that she would have prepared a good meal for us to enjoy whenever we returned from school comforted us. When we made a trip to the fabric store, Mother bought material for dresses for my sister and me. She "made do" with her old ones.

I remember also how Mother cared for us when we were sick. I especially liked the feel of her cool, soft hand on my feverish brow. She made frequent trips to our bedside, always checking to see if we needed anything. Sometimes she sat on the edge of the bed and visited with us. If we needed her, day or night, she was always there, always ready to do everything she could for us.

When the weather was cold or rainy, Mother assigned jobs inside the warm house to my sister and me while she carried the water from the spring, toted in the stove wood, and fed the animals. On cold nights, she got up frequently to be sure we had enough quilts and blankets to keep us warm. She and Daddy got up first every morning, made a fire, and cooked a hot breakfast before they called Kathie and me to get out of our warm beds.

Times have changed since the good old days, but loving mothers haven't. They still comfort their children, make sacrifices for them, and express love in many ways. Because they are a tremendous blessing to us, we never stop needing our mothers nor do we stop missing them when they are absent from us.

Our all-wise God sends other people into our lives to supplement the love of a mother, but they can never replace it. A faithful spouse, devoted children, special friends, caring teachers, wise counselors, and loving ministers are but a few of the people God sends to love us and comfort us as we walk through life.

Thus, we know that God, whom the Apostle Paul describes as "the God of all comfort," doesn't forget about us whenever we go through difficult circumstances. Instead, He continues to be completely aware of even the smallest details of our lives, and He makes the same promise to us as He did to His children of long ago. When we, like they, feel that we have no one to turn to, God reminds us, "Can a mother forget her nursing child? Can she feel no love for a child she has borne? But even if that were possible, I would not forget you! See, I have written your name on my hand" (Isaiah 49:15-16b).

Our needs are ever before Him. He knows when we need to be comforted. He knows when we long for a mother to hug us and tell us everything will be okay. If Mother can't do it, then God promises something even better: "I will comfort you…as a child is comforted by its mother" (Isaiah 66:13).

Reflections

Honors Day Program

When I attended the Honors Day Program at a local high school, I noticed the variety of awards that were given. School administrators and faculty members presented certificates, plaques, or medals to those who had excelled in academics, fine arts, vocational education, physical education, ROTC, leadership, community service, and so forth. Several seniors were presented partial scholarships to colleges of their choice, and a few seniors received full scholarships. One student was recognized for having had twelve years of perfect attendance.

The students did not know which awards they were going to receive, or so I surmised from the surprised expressions on their faces. So, I concluded that they must have been consistently doing their best in particular areas, not to receive recognition, but simply because they possessed the inner motivation to reach their full potential. The long hours they had spent studying, rehearsing, practicing, serving, working out, revising, refining, and polishing had paid off. Teachers had kept careful record of the students' achievement records and had made them available to colleges and community agencies that wanted to reward and commend those who had worked hard to excel.

The Honors Day Program reminded me that what we do on a day-by-day basis is very important. Excellence is not achieved overnight, but is the result of much time, energy, and talents used wisely and diligently over a long period. Even during those days when the struggle seems useless, when the price seems too high, when failure seems more certain than success, those who persevere are making an investment in excellence.

The students know that a special time of recognition will take place at the end of each year. However, the Honors Day Program is not the only significant time for evaluating and recognizing quality work. One day the work of all Christians will be judged. For those of us who received the free gift of salvation, our Lord will evaluate the motivation of our hearts and the quality of our service in order to determine the rewards we will receive.

The Apostle Paul explained it this way: "Because of God's special favor to me, I have laid the foundation like an expert builder. Now others are building on it. But whoever is building on this foundation must be very careful. For no one can lay any other foundation than the one we already have—Jesus Christ. Now anyone who builds on that foundation may use gold, silver, jewels, wood, hay, or straw. But there is going to come a time of testing at the judgment day to see what kind of work each builder has done. Everyone's work will be put through the fire to see whether or not it keeps its value. If the work survives the fire, that builder will receive a reward. But if the work is burned up, the builder will suffer great loss. The builders themselves will be saved, but like someone escaping through a wall of flames" (1 Corinthians 3:10-15).

Whether as students or as Christians, evaluation of our work is certain. Therefore, let us strive always for quality in all we do, knowing that rewards and honor await those who use the finest building materials and who persevere despite all odds.

Graduation

Graduation is that bittersweet time when students say farewell to the familiar and hello to the unknown. It is also a time for evaluation, a time for serious contemplation of both the past and the future. Part of the assessment involves an accounting of all that has been given in order to enable him/her to gain an education. Funding to support the education system, whether from taxes or private sources, should come to mind immediately, for schools cannot exist without financial resources. Neither should seemingly less significant contributions be overlooked.

What about the tons of clothes mothers have purchased, washed, ironed, mended, and handed down? How about all those lunch containers busy moms filled with yummies? Don't forget all the car pools, parent-teacher conferences, PTA meetings, fund raisers, class trips and parties, as well as homework supervision at the kitchen table.

While moms were busy rounding up all the stuff for school projects, the teachers spent long hours at school and at home planning additional learning activities and plowing through the ever-growing stack of to-be-graded papers and projects. Some teachers sacrificed time, energy, and talents in order to provide extracurricular and/or enrichment activities for students.

Therefore, at graduation each student, though justifiably proud of personal accomplishments, should pause and reflect on just how much has been given in order that he/she might be standing at a major intersection on the road of life. Considering all that has gone into the making of that moment causes one to think more seriously about which path to follow into the future.

Hopefully, after careful evaluation of the past, the student will glimpse a least a little bit of what they have been given. Having considered that, the graduate should ask, "Lord, how do You want me to share my gifts? How can I make an investment in the lives of others so that they, too, can reach important milestones? From among all the roads before me, which one should I take so that not one of the gifts I've been given shall be wasted?"

Congratulations, graduates! As you experience your bittersweet moment, be thankful for the gifts you've been given and the successes you've enjoyed. As you bid a tearful farewell to the past, may you rejoice over the opportunities ahead that will encourage you to become a grateful giver.

Johnnie Ann Burgess Gaskill

The Father Who Waits

Mother said that as soon as Daddy heard our car crunching the gravel on their long driveway, he headed for the carport. By the time we arrived, Daddy was there waiting to give bear hugs to my husband and me and our two little girls.

Since we weren't able to be together but once every four to six weeks, each visit was special. Our daughters loved to go there because Daddy, who was already in his seventies when the girls were born, always did or said silly things that made them shriek with laughter.

Since we always let Mother and Daddy know the date and time of our arrival, Daddy watched the clock and listened carefully for the first sound of our approach. As soon as he heard it, not even failing health kept him inside. He didn't want to waste even a few seconds with his "babies."

Because of the memories I have of a loving father who longed to have me return home, the Biblical account of the father and his prodigal son is extra special to me. In fact, I can't read Luke 15:20 without feeling deep emotion. That verse describes the response of a loving father to his son who had been the cause of much grief and disappointment. Yet, when the wayward son came to his senses and decided to return to his father, he didn't have to search for his father and plead for forgiveness. No, the Bible says, "And while [the son] was still a long distance away, his father saw him coming. Filled with loved and compassion, he **ran** to his son, embraced him, and kissed him" (Luke 15:20, emphasis added).

That father, like my daddy, waited, watched, hoped, and longed for the day when he would see his child once more. Because of his abiding love and that intense longing to see his adult child, the father did not stay inside the house to wait for his son to knock on the door and beg for forgiveness, feeling that he was entitled to be angry with the son who had broken his heart. Rather, the father was ever watchful, ever waiting for his son's return, and when the wayward young man arrived, the father gladly welcomed him home.

Likewise, our Heavenly Father sees us when we are a long way off and He feels great compassion for us. When we begin our return to Him, He meets us on the road and stretches wide His arms to receive us, regardless of the past, regardless of how long we've been away, regardless that we do not deserve His love and His forgiveness.

About the Author

In February of 1984, Johnnie Ann Burgess Gaskill sensed God calling her to be a writer. In August of that year, a newspaper in Austell, Georgia, accepted her "Reflections" for publication, and she has written weekly inspirational/devotional columns since then. Currently, she writes for three newspapers in Georgia: the *Douglas County Sentinel*, the *Paulding County Sentinel*, and the *Upson Citizen*. Her work appears in various other print publications, as well as on the Internet.

Johnnie earned a B.S. degree in Elementary Education from Tift College and a Master's Degree in Early Childhood Education from West Georgia College. She taught third grade in Cobb County, GA, for six years, then served for thirteen years as the Media Library/Education Director for the West Metro Baptist Association in Austell, GA.

She and her husband are the proud parents of two daughters and two "sons-by-marriage" (Jennifer and Shane; Jena and Richard) and the doting grandparents of Ryan, Bailey, and Peyton. As an empty nester and retiree, Johnnie enjoys having more time for writing, taking daily walks, journaling, volunteering, participating in the local writers' group, traveling with her husband, taking lots and lots of photos, and—of course—spoiling the grandchildren!